Phantom Britain

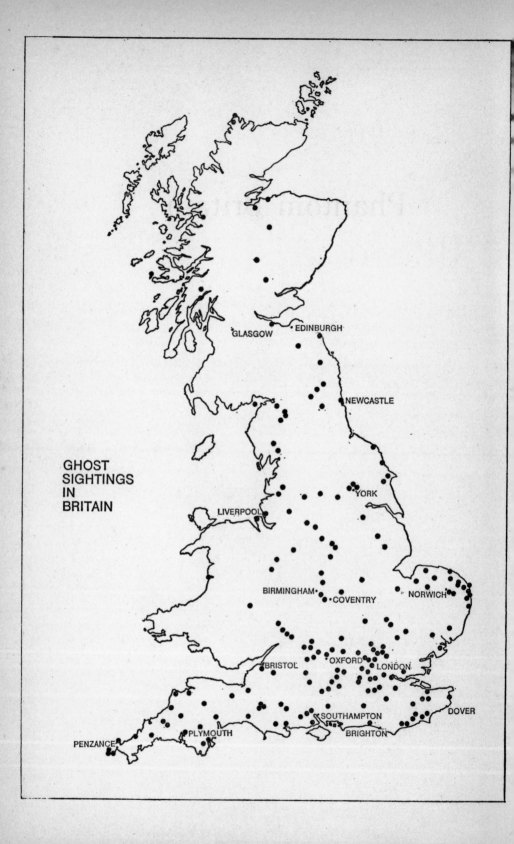

GHOST
SIGHTINGS
IN
BRITAIN

GLASGOW •EDINBURGH

•NEWCASTLE

YORK

LIVERPOOL

BIRMINGHAM• •COVENTRY •NORWICH

BRISTOL OXFORD •LONDON

SOUTHAMPTON DOVER

PENZANCE PLYMOUTH BRIGHTON

MARC ALEXANDER

Phantom Britain

This spectre'd isle

Is all *that we see or seem*
But a dream within a dream?
—Edgar Allan Poe

FREDERICK MULLER LIMITED

*First published in Great Britain 1975
by Frederick Muller Limited,
London NW2 6LE*

ISBN 0 584 10210 0

Made and printed in Great Britain by
The Garden City Press Limited
Letchworth, Hertfordshire SG6 1JS

For my charming and spirited grandmother
Louisa Poole

Contents

Contents

List of Illustrations

(appearing between pages 128–129)

1. Newstead Abbey
2. 50 Berkeley Square
3. Croglin Low Hall
4. Calgarth Hall
5. Skull of Theophilus Broome
6. Sedgemoor Battlefield
7. Burgh Castle, Norfolk
8. The Culloden Monument
9. Wallington Hall, Northumberland
10. The Pass of Killiecrankie
11. Blisworth Tunnel
12. The Black Horse, Pluckley
13. Caister Castle
14. Hatfield House
15. Langley Castle, Northumberland
16. 20 Dean's Yard by Westminster Abbey
17. Fountains Abbey, Yorkshire
18. Michelham Priory, Sussex
19. Effigy of Lady Elizabeth Hoby, Bisham Church, Berkshire
20. Houghton Castle, on the banks of the North Tyne.
21. All Saints Church, Renwick
22. Lapford churchyard

Acknowledgements

The author wishes to express his sincere gratitude to the many people who gave up valuable time to provide information necessary for this book – owners and tenants of haunted houses, those who have had first-hand experience of the supernatural and busy clergymen who have supplied information on their churches. He also wishes to thank The British Travel Association, the staffs of the British Museum Reading Room and the Colindale Newspaper Library for helpful co-operation; Anne Williams for skilful editing, Carole Samuels for assistance with research, Mrs Barbara Cheeseman for the transcription of tapes, Mrs L. M. Alexander for help with proof-reading, the Roy Reemer Organisation for processing photographs, and Simon Alexander for map-reading. Special thanks are due to Derrick H. Baker, Colonel Francis Claridge, Mrs Doreen Montgomery, the Reverend Dr Donald Omand, Clara Silvolli, Ken Slocombe and Gianna Thorne.

Photographs are by the author, unless otherwise stated.

Introduction

In Italy a frequent introduction to a ghost story or tale of Gothic horror is "*C'era una volta un castello in Cornovaglia . . .*" ("There was once a castle in Cornwall . . .") This suggests that whatever else may have happened to Britain's prestige abroad, her reputation for the supernatural remains as macabre as ever. No other country can boast such a fine population of phantoms—believed to be in the region of ten thousand, nor such a variety of them, and this book—the final of a trilogy on aspects of British hauntings—is an attempt to show the scope of the spectral world superimposed upon us.

It has been both intriguing and frustrating to write. Unlike the first two books, which dealt with haunted inns and haunted castles, a strict theme has not been followed. Without this discipline I have been able to select material with only two criteria in mind, that it is entertaining and that it runs the gamut of our ghostlore. The frustration came with the amount of material I had to omit. But, although this book is not intended as a compendium, I have listed some haunted sites I have not had space to describe fully for the benefit of those who have an interest in visiting such places. I have also omitted some material which, though it would fit into some of the following chapters, has appeared in my previous books. I do not want anyone who has bought them—bless you, Gentle Reader, if this applies to you—to feel they are being told the same tale twice.

I have often been asked if I believe in ghosts. The answer is that of course I do, though I cannot say what I believe they are.

One theory that I have heard repeated a lot lately is that phantoms come about through electric emanations given off by people at the point of death, especially if accompanied by dramatic or harrowing circumstances.

These "waveforms" remain in some way and are "replayed" when they come in contact with the minds of psychic persons. I think this explanation is too easy. If what we regard as the supernatural can be explained by a scientific theory the rules of science must apply. Therefore, just as two atoms of hydrogen and one of oxygen inevitably make up a molecule of water, then certain conditions must always be productive of ghosts. If this was the case the battlefields of the First World War, for example, would have more ghosts than living people about them. Yet many ghostly manifestations happen without rhyme or reason; others are linked to some trivial action the phantom performed when alive and have nothing to do with his dying. And what about a ghost reputed to appear in different locales?

Another theory is that ghosts are the result of time slips, that we do not see a spirit but merely have a glimpse of some past event. If true it would mean patterns of haunting could not possibly alter. Many phantoms do seem to be "echoes", repeating their performances over and over without variation, but as this book will show there are also ghosts who alter their behaviour in order to try and influence the living. Some have even foretold the future. Yet, on the other hand, if ghosts are conscious spirits of the dead as was once generally accepted, they surely would not be content with repetitious and trivial roles.

As one gathers accounts of ghosts and compares them, the more one realises that the only rule about them is that there is no rule. What does a poltergeist have in common with a phantom army; can there be a link between aural hauntings and the appearance of an animal, vegetable and mineral thing such as a spectral coach? The questions are endless, the answers so far are only speculative. It may not always be so; one would be hard put to explain the workings of a colour television set to someone of a century ago.

As more and more becomes known about our physical world, it seems that we are becoming less inclined to dismiss the invisible and so far mysterious world about us. Over a hundred years ago an almost forgotten German philosopher named Albert Kremnitz wrote: "The Age of Materialism will almost certainly drive people back to mysticism rather than away from it. In the beginning, of course, popular taste will seem to move in quite the opposite direction, towards the mundane and the banal, towards the frenetic pursuit of possessions, towards a contempt for all that is lyrical in man. The first stage will see no attempt to justify this distaste for the mystic and the unexplained. Although this stage will be prolonged for many years, it will gradually give way to another stage in which the course of mankind will find itself troubled by what it has cast aside. During this stage there will be many explanations as to why the mystic nature of man no longer has any value in an ever changing world, yet none of these 'explanations' will remove . . . the painful awareness that man, for all his material progress, remains bound to all that is barbaric in his past. The fourth stage will see a great reversal of the first stage . . . If compelled to predict the time when this fourth stage would come about I would set the date at midpoint in the twentieth century, at which time the Industrial Revolution will itself be undergoing the transition to which all revolutions, indeed all things, are subject."

If we do not recognise ghosts as easily as our ancestors it is because our minds are focused on more material things than theirs, though in fact we may see more ghosts than we realise. Certainly ghosts are not just figments from our superstitious past. There is plenty of evidence to suggest that the ghost world keeps apace with the world we like to think of as reality—Britain's roads are gradually building up their own particular brand of modern ghostlore, the phantom of a German officer is seen at the Bovington Tank Museum gazing at the Tiger tank in which he served, while a spectral plane has been reported as re-enacting its crash into a lake at Llanrwst in Denbighshire. I wonder if we will ever hear of a ghostly spacecraft, or are flying saucers really phantoms from a forgotten past or a far off future?

Whatever phantoms are—and may we long speculate—they have inspired one of the oldest aspects of story telling, and if only for this reason their legends should be preserved as a precious heritage and as an endorsement to something that we should never forget, namely that nothing is ever what it seems.

Crooks Cottage   Marc Alexander
Gilsland
Cumbria
January 26, 1975

I

HOUSES OF DREAD

Few people I have met who have seen ghosts have expressed any fear of them once they have got over the initial surprise. Their reasoning usually runs: "Why should anyone harm me just because they have passed over; I'm not afraid of living people so why should I fear them when they are dead?" But as a few living people *are* evil and frightening, it must be expected that some members of the ghost world are filled with hatred or the desire to exercise power over others. So let us sit closer to the fire and examine some of the sinister aspects of phantom Britain . . .

The sound of footsteps on the stairs came closer and closer, and the hearts of the two trespassing sailors raced with a fear they had never known when at sea in their frigate *Penelope*. The door creaked open and *something* entered the room. One of the sailors, Robert Martin, was aware of a whitish shape and two outstretched arms—but arms without hands, talons rather. It seemed to glide towards his friend, Edward Blunden, but he did not wait to see what happened. He darted out of the room and down the echoing stairs of the deserted house. The next thing he knew he was racing along the foggy pavement until he saw the light of a policeman's bulls-eye lantern.

"Come quickly," he gasped. "My mate and me were dossing in that house. Now he's up there alone . . . with . . ."

"Good God! You ain't been there?" the constable muttered.

Together they ran to where the halo of a gaslamp dimly illuminated the "To Let" sign by the open door of No 50 Berkeley Square. Suddenly there was a crash of glass, a wild cry and the body of Edward Blunden struck the spiked railings. No one ever knew exactly what it was that sent him hurtling to his death that Christmas Eve in 1887, but it came as no great surprise. The Victorians had long regarded No 50 as a haunted house of particular evil. Its ghost was no traditional phantom, no gliding monk, no grey lady in a crinoline . . . Whatever it was, it was a killer. Such was the reputation of the dilapidated house that when people visited London they frequently made a pilgrimage to Berkeley Square just to stand and stare at its grimy brick exterior with the neglected paintwork.

On April 26, 1879, under the heading of "The Mystery of Berkeley Square", the magazine *Mayfair* wrote: "It appears that the house had an evil reputation for being badly haunted so long ago as when it was last lived in—that is to say, once upon a time. One day, a maidservant, newly arrived was put to sleep in one of the upper rooms. An hour or two after the household was at rest, it was awakened by fearful screams from the new servant's room and she was found staring in the middle of the floor, as rigid as a corpse, with hideously glaring eyes—she had suddenly become a hopeless and raving madwoman, who never found a lucid interval wherein to say what made her so. However, this, I would say, would not mean much, even when taken in connection with the character of the house and of the room—women may go mad now and then, without any ghostly dealings. The room was given up, but the house still remained occupied, and that seemed to be the end. But some little time afterwards, a guest arrived when the house had many visitors; and he, not unnaturally, laughing at such a skeleton in the cupboard . . . perhaps, like many sceptics, inclined for a little experience in such ventures, eagerly volunteered for the room which all others were so shy of entering. It was arranged that if, after a certain time, he rang the bell for the room once, it was a sign that he felt himself as comfortable as could be expected; but that if he rung it twice, someone should come up and see what was the matter. At the end of the given time the bell only rang once, but presently the same bell gave a frantic peal; and those who ran to his aid found the ghost-defier a corpse where the girl had gone mad before. And dead men tell no tales.

"What had he or she seen, or felt, or heard, to kill the man on the spot, and send the woman out of her mind?"

The house's sinister reputation began at the end of the eighteenth century when a certain Mr Dupre was said to have confined his insane brother in one of the upstairs rooms. His violence was such that no one could handle him and he had to be fed through a special opening in the door. According to one legend it was the ghost of the maniac which became the Horror of Berkeley Square.

Other reports about the house suggested one of its ghosts was a child in a Scottish dress, who had been frightened to death by a sadistic servant in the nursery; another that there was the phantom of a girl who had thrown herself out of an upper floor window to escape being raped by her uncle. Her ghost sometimes hovered outside the window, tapping on the panes of glass.

Apart from the well authenticated case of the two sailors who passed a night in the house when it was deserted, there is the story of Sir Robert Worboys. He was a handsome young man-about-town whose country home was at Bracknell in Berkshire. When he visited London he stayed at the best clubs, and the tragic event began one day in White's when the talk turned to London's haunted houses and to No 50 Berkeley Square in particular. During the conversation, in which Sir Robert took on the role of a sceptic, Lord Cholmondeley introduced him to a man called Benson who was actually the owner of the Berkeley Square house. He seemed reluctant to discuss the matter and Sir Robert suggested that it was perhaps because Mr Benson didn't believe in ghosts either. He replied that the hauntings at No 50 were so well known that he did not doubt the existence of a supernatural agent.

As a result of the discussion which followed, Sir Robert's friends challenged him to spend a night in the haunted room which Mr Benson had closed up. Benson agreed providing that Sir Robert would be armed, would ring for assistance should he find himself in trouble and that his friends would stay the night on the floor below—very much in the manner of the case reported in *Mayfair* magazine. Soon afterwards Sir Robert Worboys and his friends went to the house where he wished them goodnight and went up a flight of stairs from the drawing room on the first floor to the fateful haunted bedroom. There he lay down on the bed, one hand close to his pistol, the other near the bell-pull. Below in the drawing room, Lord Cholmondeley and several others dozed off.

At midnight the bell close to the drawing room door began to ring. The waiting men aroused themselves when a second peal jangled through the house. Mr Benson was the first up the stairs and was approaching the door of the bedroom when a shot rang out. Moments later he opened the door of the bedroom to see Sir Robert Worboys lying across the bed, his head almost touching the floor. Seeing his face in the lamplight someone cried: "Cover him up!" His features were drawn back in a rictus of terror. At first it was thought that he might have shot himself, but when his body was examined there was no wound on it.

Another well-known person to spend a night in the haunted room was Lord Lyttleton. He armed himself with two guns loaded with silver coins. He survived the night though he fired at "something" which came at him out of the darkness and which fell "like a rocket" before disappearing.

During the 1870's neighbours of the deserted house were alarmed by the sound of cries and the noise of heavy objects being dragged across bare boards, bells ringing and windows being slammed in true poltergeist fashion.

Towards the end of the last century another mystery was added to the story of No 50 Berkeley Square. A journalist wrote: "The house . . . is uninhabited, save by an elderly man and woman who act as caretakers; but even these have no access to the room. That is kept locked, and the key being in the hands of a mysterious and seemingly nameless person, he comes to the house once every six months, locks up the elderly couple in the basement, then unlocks the room and occupies himself in it for hours."

Nearly a century has passed since No 50 Berkeley Square enjoyed its ghastly reputation. Today it looks as respectable as its neighbours and is the office of a well-known firm of booksellers.

An apparition frightening enough to cause a man to faint— though not evil enough to kill him—used to materialise at the notorious mill at Willington, which lies between Wallsend and North Shields. When the haunting of Willington Mill was at the height of its fame William Howitt wrote a description of it : "The mill is a large steam flour mill, like a factory, and the house stands near it but not adjoining it. None of the cottages which lie between these premises and the railway either, are in contact with them. The house stands on a sort of little promontory, round which runs the channel of a watercourse, which appears to fill and empty with the tide . . . The house is not an old house, as will appear; it was built about the year 1800. It has no particularly spectral look about it. Seeing it in passing, or within, ignorant of its real character, one should by no means say that it is a place likely to have the reputation of being haunted . . . There is not any passage, however, known of under the house, by which subterranean noise could be heard. Nor are they merely noises that are heard; distinct apparitions are declared to have been seen."

When the haunting was at its most extraordinary stage, the occupiers of the house were the family of Joseph Proctor who was a stalwart member of the Society of Friends. During the years between 1835 and 1837 he kept a diary which listed the various mysterious happenings which finally caused the family to quit its home. Phenomena thus described included sounds of heavy footfalls heard at any time of the day or night, the sound of tapping as though a hammer was hitting wood, chattering and jingling sounds and a noise like the mechanism of a clock being wound up.

A translucent female figure was seen by neighbours as well as a figure of a bald man said to resemble a priest. It was these two apparitions which gave rise to the legend that a woman, who had once lived in the house, wished to confess to some horrendous crime she had committed at the mill but was refused by a priest. After death their ghosts were doomed to remain at the site of their mutual crimes.

Eric Maple, in his book *Realm of Ghosts*, described the female apparition as being "seen to have no eyes only empty sockets". The so-called priest "wandered from room to room via the walls, emitting a mysterious light as he did so . . ."

A graphic description of the priest was given by Thomas

Mann, the foreman of the nearby mill who, with his wife and daughter and Mrs Proctor's sister, saw "a bald-headed old man in a flowing robe like a surplice gliding backwards and forwards about three feet from the floor, level with the bottom of the second storey window".

"He then stood still in the middle of the window and the part of his body which appeared quite luminous, showed through the blind," Mr Mann recorded. "In that position the framework of the window was invisible, while the body was as bright as a star, and diffused a radiance all round; then it turned a bluish tinge and gradually faded away from the head downwards."

On June 2, 1835, Mr Proctor made a statement to a Mr Parker of Halifax by letter, declaring : "the disturbances came to our knowledge in the beginning of the first month, but existed some time previously. There are several credible witnesses to the apparition of a woman in her grave clothes at four separate times outside the house."

The next month a young Sunderland doctor by the name of Edward Drury, who was fascinated by the Willington case, obtained permission from Mr Proctor to spend a night in the haunted house. With him came a friend, a medical man by the name of Thomas Hudson. On arriving at the house, Drury and Hudson made sure it was locked up and then examined every corner. They found that the third storey rooms were unfurnished and that the closet from where an apparition later issued was too small to contain a human being.

Later Drury admitted that he was sceptical as to whether the haunting was genuine when he arrived at the house. In a letter to Mr Proctor he described his experiences: "Having received your sanction to visit your mysterious dwelling, I went on the 3rd of July, accompanied by a friend of mine, named T. Hudson. This was not according to promise, nor in accordance with my first intent, as I wrote you I would come alone, but I felt gratified at your kindness in not alluding to the liberty I'd taken, as it ultimately proved for the best. I must here mention that not expecting you at home, I had in my pocket a brace of pistols, determining in my mind to let one of them drop, as if by accident, before the miller, for fear he should presume to play tricks upon me, but after my interview with you I felt there was no occasion for the weapons, and did not load them after you had allowed us to inspect as minutely as we pleased every portion of the house.

"I sat down on the third storey landing, fully expecting to account for any noises I might hear in a most philosophical manner; this was about eleven o'clock p.m. About ten minutes to twelve we both heard a noise, as if a number of people were pattering with their bare feet upon the floor; and yet so singular was the noise that I could not minutely determine from whence it proceeded. A few minutes afterwards we heard a noise as if someone was knocking with his knuckles among our feet; this was immediately followed by a hollow cough from the very room from which the apparition proceeded. The only noise after this was as if a person was brushing against the wall in coming up the stairs.

"At a quarter to one I told my friend that, feeling a little cold, I would go to bed, as we might hear the noises equally well there. He replied that he would not go to bed till daylight. I took a note, which I had accidentally dropped, and began to read it; after which I took out my watch to ascertain the time, and found it wanted ten minutes to one. In taking my eyes from the watch, they became rivetted upon a closet door, which I distinctly saw open, and also saw the figure of a female, attired in greyish garments, with the head inclined downwards, and one hand pressed upon the chest as if in pain, and the other, that is the right hand extended towards the floor, the index pointing downwards. It advanced with an apparently cautious step across the floor towards me; immediately as it approached my friend, who was slumbering, its right hand was extended towards him. I then rushed at it, giving at the time, as Mr Proctor states, a most awful yell, but instead of grasping it I fell upon my friend and recollected nothing distinctly for nearly three hours afterwards . . . I hereby certify that the above account is strictly true and correct in every respect . . ."

His story was corroborated by this statement written by Thomas Hudson : "His (Dr Drury's) hair was standing on end, the picture of horror. He fainted, and fell into my arms, like a lifeless piece of humanity. His horrible shouts made me shout in sympathy and I instantly laid him down and went into the room from whence the last sound was heard but nothing was there and the window had not been opened. Mr Proctor and the housekeeper came quickly to our assistance and found the young doctor trembling in acute mental agony. Indeed, he was so much excited that he wanted to jump out of the window."

In his journal the author William Howitt described a different haunting which affected two young ladies on a visit to the house, and which suggests that poltergeist activity was mixed up with the appearance of the phantoms.

He wrote: "The first night, as they were sleeping in the same bed, they felt the bed lifted beneath them. Of course, they were very much alarmed. They feared lest someone had concealed himself there for the purpose of robbery. They gave an alarm, search was made, but nothing was found. On another night, their bed was violently shaken and curtains suddenly hoisted up all round the tester, as if pulled up by cords, and as rapidly let down again, several times. Search again produced no evidence of the cause. The next day, they had the curtains totally removed from the bed, resolving to sleep without them, as they felt as though evil eyes were lurking behind them. The consequence of this, however, was still more striking and horrific. The following night, as they happened to awake, and the chamber was light enough—for it was summer—to see everything in it, they saw a female figure, of a misty substance, and a bluish-grey hue, come out of the wall, at the bed's head and through the headboard, in a horizontal position, and lean over them. They saw it most distinctly. They saw it as a female figure come out of, and again pass into the wall. Their terror became intense and one of the sisters from that night, refused to sleep any more in the house but took refuge in the quarters of the foreman during her stay; the other shifting her quarters to another part of the house."

There are many other, though less dramatic, accounts of the Willington haunting but when the Quaker family left in 1847 the house was divided into separate apartments for the mill workers. From then on the supernatural activity seemed to die away though there were reports of strange sounds and apparitions which were seen at least twice.

It was some years ago, under the pale blue dome of the Reading Room of the British Museum, that I came across what is probably Britain's most unpleasant haunting. I was glancing through a book by Augustus Hare when I read his account of the vampire of Croglin Low Hall. He claimed that he had obtained the details from Captain Fisher whose family owned the Cumberland property. The story, which was supposed to have taken place twenty-three years before the publication of Bram Stoker's book *Dracula*, was so neat that I concluded Mr Hare had been taken in by a piece of ingenious fiction, for it is my experience that real life stories tend to be inconclusive and incomplete. Yet this "melodrama" intrigued me to the extent that I bought an Ordnance Survey map of the Penrith area of Cumberland to see if Croglin Low Hall actually existed. I found that it did, although it added little to the story. No doubt the ingenious Captain Fisher could have made up a tale as easily about a real place as a fictitious one. But the germ was planted in my mind, and in 1970 I found myself driving along the road which ran south from Croglin village in the direction of Kirkoswald. After a mile or so the low shape of the farmhouse came into view, standing at the end of a long avenue of trees—the avenue down which the vampire was supposed to have fled if one was to believe Augustus Hare.

I now had a problem as I do not believe in barging in when it is a question of the supernatural. Most likely the owners of the house knew nothing of what Augustus Hare had written about their home in the last century, and if I started discussing it there was the danger that it might alarm a nervous person. So when I met Mrs Mary Watson, who had lived at the farm with her husband for twenty-five years, I merely discussed the historical aspect of the interesting old place.

She told me it had once been fortified and how a secret room had been discovered where mass had been celebrated in the days of Catholic persecution. I was led through an archway into a farmyard alive with hens, ducks and peacocks while she discussed the history and architecture of her home. After half an hour I came to the sad conclusion that the story was a hoax after all.

I was just about to leave when I pointed to a window on the

ground floor which had been bricked up and asked Mrs Watson why it had been done.

"Oh, that was done soon after the vampire attacked Miss Cranswell," she answered, and then to my delight told me the story which had been handed down locally and which tallied exactly with the account given by Augustus Hare.

"It happened nearly a century ago to three Australians by the name of Cranswell, two brothers and their sister," she said. "For a long time Croglin Low Hall and its farm had belonged to a family named Fisher and in 1874 they moved to Thorncombe in Surrey and were very pleased when the Cranswells, who were over in this country for a long stay from Australia, took a seven-year lease."

The new tenants seemed to settle happily in the peace of Cumberland and, as Captain Fisher had noted, they "shared in all the social pleasures of the district and made themselves very popular".

One early summer night in 1875 the three young people sat out on the grass watching a brilliant moon rise. The nearby brook gurgled pleasantly and a gentle breeze sighed in the ancient trees of the farm. There was no hint of the horror that was to come. At eleven o'clock they went to bed. In her room Amelia Cranswell closed the window but did not fasten her shutters. Not feeling sleepy, she sat up in bed and looked out at the farmyard bathed in silver light.

Suddenly she was aware of two points of yellow light in the dark shadow of the old barn on the right of the courtyard. As she watched they seemed to float nearer to her window. She thought they were like the eyes of an animal except they were too high above the ground to belong to a cat or dog. For a moment they vanished from her line of sight, then reappeared close to the window. Amelia sat paralysed in bed as the burning eyes peered in. Around them she could make out the dark outline of the creature's head. Then came a noise of fingernails scratching at the glass pane. This scrabbling sound released Amelia from her spell. Fearing a burglar or worse—an escaped lunatic perhaps—she ran to the door. It was locked. She tried to turn the key but in her panic her fingers fumbled and it fell to the floor. As she bent down to try to find it in the dark a new sound reached her ears ... Whatever it was outside was starting to unpick the lead which held the glass panes.

Looking over her shoulder she was aware of a brown wrinkled face staring at her. She tried to scream but the cry froze in her throat. Then, in the words of Captain Fisher, as recorded by Augustus Hare, "a long bony finger of the creature came in and turned the handle of the window. The creature came in ... and twisted its long bony fingers into her hair, dragged her head over the side of the bed and bit her violently in the throat."

At this point the girl did manage to scream. Her cries echoed through the hall and Edward Cranswell and his younger brother Michael came running. Unable to open the door, they broke the lock with a poker. As they burst into the room they saw their sister lying unconscious with blood trickling from wounds on her face, throat and shoulders. One of the brothers ran to the broken window and saw a tall figure vanishing through the arch in the farmyard wall.

Luckily the wounds were not deep and when they healed the three Cranswells went to Switzerland where the girl soon began to forget her ordeal. The brothers concluded that it had been the work of a madman. A neighbouring farmer had told them how one of his children had been attacked by an intruder a little earlier.

In September of the same year the Australians returned to Croglin. Amelia said she liked the farm so much it would be silly not to live there when they had taken such a long lease on it, but from then on she closed her shutters at night and did not lock her door. Edward had bought a gun in Switzerland and slept with it by his bed.

One night in March, 1876, Amelia was awakened by the terrifyingly familiar sound of fingernails on glass. Her shrieks brought Michael running into her room while Edward ran outside. There, at his sister's window, he saw what he described as "a tall spindly fellow in a curious cloak". The figure turned and ran through the arch, round the curving avenue towards the Croglin road. As it raced between the trees Edward raised his gun and fired. For a moment the shape seemed to stumble then continue. It crossed the narrow road and ran across the open country in the direction of Croglin village.

Edward laboured over the rough ground in pursuit until he reached the outskirts of the village where he had a final glimpse of the figure as it disappeared into the old churchyard. Realising that here was something supernatural Edward returned to Croglin Low Hall for Michael, then summoned several neighbours and the local gamekeeper.

At first light the small party stepped grimly through the wet grass of the graveyard looking for the creature's lair in the mossy tombstones. One of the searchers discovered a stone slab out of place, below was a coffin with its lid partly off. A member of the party plucked up enough courage to pull it to one side. In the cold dawn the party saw a tall mummified body. As they lifted it out they noticed with horror that there was a bullet wound in its leg. A fire was hastily lit and as the sun rose the vampire of Croglin was reduced to ashes . . .

Luckily Britain has escaped the vampire epidemics which at intervals through history have swept the Continent like a plague; in fact outbreaks of plague were often attributed to these ghastly creatures. In parts of Europe today the belief in the "undead" still exists, and an odd and tragic echo of this was reported in the press in January, 1973.

At an inquest in Stoke it was revealed how a Polish exile, Demetrious Myiciura, was so afraid of vampires that it led to his death. At night he slept with a clove of garlic in his mouth to guard himself from them but this ancient safeguard proved fatal when he choked to death while asleep.

A police constable, John Pye, broke into his room and found various other talismans which the retired pottery worker had used to protect himself. There was salt sprinkled on his bed, bags of it were between his legs and on his face, and garlic cloves placed at the keyhole and windows. The coroner was told that such charms were used in Bulgaria.

The city coroner recorded a verdict of Accidental Death and added: "This is a strange case. This man took precautions against vampires he thought were in the neighbourhood."

2

SKULLDUGGERY!

One of the stranger aspects of our supernatural scene is skull haunting. It is something which would be more in keeping with remote parts of South America or the Pacific where skulls are trophies of war ostentatiously displayed in the huts of successful warriors; yet perhaps there is a vague link between this practice and the spirited skulls of Old England. It was an ancient and almost universal belief that the soul dwelt in the skull, and that in some exceptional cases it remained there after physical death. Certainly, if one is to believe the records, something remained which through the centuries has caused these relics to be regarded with deep but cautious respect.

To see one of these skulls for myself, I drove to a little Somerset village prettily named Chilton Cantelo. It stands at the western tip of an uncanny triangle with Sandford Orcas and its heavily haunted manor house, and Cadbury Castle, believed by many to be the original Camelot, where cavalcades of spectral knights have been seen riding on King Arthur's Hunting Causeway which links North Barrow and South Barrow. When I reached the village I had no difficulty in finding Higher Chilton Farm which is opposite the church where the mortal remains of Theophilus Brome (minus his head) are buried in the north transept. His skull remains in the lovely old stone farmhouse which he owned just over three hundred years ago.

The present owners of the farm are Mr and Mrs Kerton, and the latter kindly invited me into her house where, in the hall, she opened the door of a special cabinet built close to the ceiling, and I saw the eyeless sockets of the skull gazing down at me.

"Does it worry you at all having such a thing in your home?"
I asked.

"Not at all," she replied. "People expect me to be frightened
but I know that, provided he is not taken outside the house, he
would never do me any harm."

Carefully—almost affectionately—she lifted down the highly
polished cranium and placed it on a leather chair for me to
photograph.

"He'll be all right there," she said, "but he doesn't like being
handled too much. If he objects he'd soon let us know, but as
long as he is treated with respect he never causes trouble."

When the pictures had been taken and the skull was safely
back in his familiar resting place, Mrs Kerton showed me a
visitors' book going back to before the Second World War in
which were signatures of people from all over the world whose
curiosity had taken them to Chilton Cantelo to see the relic. As
I leafed through the pages she explained that Theophilus Brome
had come from Woodlowes, near Warwick, and settled at Higher
Chilton Farm where he died at the age of sixty-nine on August
18, 1670. His dying request was that his head should be cut from
his body and kept at the farmhouse in perpetuity.

The reason for this is not clear, though there is one theory
that Brome had been active in the Civil War, and had left
Warwickshire for Somerset to escape retribution for some part
he had played in those troubled times. After the Restoration
there were cases of dead enemies of the monarchy being disinterred and decapitated. (This happened with Oliver Cromwell
whose body was gibbeted at Tyburn, and whose head was spiked
at Westminster.) Perhaps Theophilus Brome hoped to escape
such an indignity by having his head removed and placed in
safety before the public executioner could lay his hands on it.

Brome's epitaph declares that he was a man "just in his
actions in this life, true to his friends, forgave those that wronged
him, and died in peace". The fact that he had been "wronged"
suggests that he may have felt himself victimised and lends
weight to the idea that he might have feared some posthumous
punishment. But we do not know for certain, any more than we
know if Brome actually laid a curse on anyone who should
interfere with his skull or remove it from the farmhouse. Whether

there was an actual curse or not, it seems that the ghost of Brome made its presence felt when this happened. An example of his wrath—in the 1860's—was described thus in Collinson's *History of Somerset* : "There is a tradition in this parish that the person here interred requested that his head might be taken off before his burial and be preserved at the farmhouse near the church where a head—chop-fallen enough—is still shown, which the tenants of the house have often endeavoured to commit to the bowels of the earth, but have as often been deterred by horrid noises portentive of sad displeasure; and about twenty years since (which was perhaps the last attempt) the sexton, in digging a place for the skull's repository, broke the spade in two pieces, and uttered a solemn asserveration never more to attempt an act so evidently repugnant to the quiet of Brome's Head."

Mrs Kerton told me of an earlier desecration in 1826 when some workmen were employed to make renovations at Higher Chilton Farm. They celebrated the completion of their work by drinking beer from the skull—a macabre act of bravado which resulted in the usual noises "portentive of sad displeasure". Over the years the ghost of Theophilus Brome has made his point, and now his skull is allowed to rest peacefully within his old home.

The Chilton Cantelo skull is well documented. We know the name of its owner, when he died and where he was buried. The screaming skull of Bettiscombe House—which stands close to the B3165 which runs between Lyme Regis and Crewkerne—has far more mysterious origins, and there are several versions of the legend behind it. It first gained prominence in 1872 when a letter from J. S. Udal, a judge and folklore expert, appeared in *Notes and Queries* : "At a farmhouse in Dorsetshire at the present time is carefully preserved a human skull, which has been there for a period long antecedent to the present tenancy. The peculiar superstition attaching to it is that if it be brought out of the house the house itself would rock to its foundations, whilst the person by whom such an act of desecration was committed would certainly die within the year. It is strangely suggestive of the power of this superstition that through many changes of tenancy and furniture the skull still holds its accustomed place 'unmoved and unremoved'."

31

This gave rise to some correspondence in the journal, and Mr Udal gave further details: "The farm-house (formerly, I believe, an old manor-house), now called Bettiscombe House, in which the skull remained, or still remains for ought I know to the contrary, lies in the parish of Bettiscombe, about six miles from Bridport, in Dorsetshire. I cannot ascertain the time when the 'ghostly tenant' first took up its abode in the place, but it is tolerably certain that it was some considerable time ago. It has, I understand, been pronounced to be that of negro; and the legend runs that it belonged to a faithful black servant of an early possessor of the property, a Pinney, who, having resided abroad some years, brought home this memento of a faithful follower. It is reported that a member of the above family, in recent years, has visited the house, but was unable to give any clue that might assist in clearing up the identity of the skull."

This version is the most popular, and it goes back to the seventeenth century when the house was owned by the Reverend John Pinney (an ancestor of the present owner). A Puritan minister, he had been forced to live for some years in Ireland after the Restoration, but finally he was able to return to his home where he lived until 1705. The politics of the time had cast a tragic shadow over his life. In 1685 his two sons had been involved in the Monmouth Rebellion and were taken before Judge Jeffreys in its bloody aftermath. One was hanged, but the other, by the name of Azariah, was transported as a slave to Leeward Island in the West Indies. After some years he obtained his freedom and prospered, finally returning to Bettiscombe House and bringing with him a black servant. When he was on his deathbed the Negro declared that his spirit would never rest until his body was taken back to the West Indies for burial.

Instead he was buried in the Bettiscombe churchyard, but soon the displeasure of his troubled ghost was felt. In Bettiscombe House there was poltergeist-type activity with doors banging and wild cries echoing through rooms and corridors. Screams were even heard issuing from the servant's tomb. In order to try and stop these disturbances the body was disinterred, and in the process of this its skull became separated.

We do not know if the body was shipped back to the West Indies, but the story goes that the skull was kept in the house, and the terrifying screams were heard again whenever anyone tried to remove it. On one occasion a tenant of the house tried to dispose of the grisly relic by throwing it into a pond, but the disturbances were so bad that he was forced to wade through the water with a rake until he located it in the mud and returned it to its accustomed place. There is also a legend that the skull was once buried to a depth of nearly ten feet, but somehow it managed to work its way up through the earth until it was found and fearfully replaced. The last time the skull was heard to scream was at the beginning of this century. Then the cries were so loud that, apart from the occupants of the house, they were heard by farmworkers in the fields outside.

There are other explanations for the Screaming Skull of Bettiscombe. One is that it belonged to a Negro servant as in the first version, but who then was murdered; another says that the skull only was brought back to England by Azariah Pinney as a *memento mori* of a faithful servant. A completely different story suggests that the skull never belonged to a Negro at all but to a young woman who was murdered at Bettiscombe. Weight was given to the latter version in 1963 when the skull was examined by a professor of anatomy who pronounced it to be the skull of a female in her twenties. But whatever the truth behind the Bettiscombe skull, its power of screaming has kept it where it wishes to be.

Another case of skull haunting with differing legends relates to Tudor-beamed Wardley Hall which stands at Worsley, just north of Salford. The best known legend is that the skull, which has become such a part of the house that it has been protected by a special clause in the lease, belonged to Roger Downe who was a young rakehell during the reign of Charles II. In 1676 he was killed in an affray on London Bridge where his head was severed from his body. The head was then packed in a box and sent home to Wardley Hall where his sister Penelope only once attempted to have it buried—such were the terrifying manifestations which accompanied the interment that it was taken back to the house.

The flaw with this story is that while Roger Downe did die as the result of a wound received in a scuffle with watchmen, his

33

body was taken to Wigan for burial and when the grave was opened in 1779 it was found that only the top of his skull was missing.

The real owner of the Wardley Hall skull is more likely to have been Alexander Barlow, a Roman Catholic priest, whose family were close friends of the Downes of Wardley Hall. As a young man he went to Doui where he studied at the Roman Catholic college there. He was duly ordained and as Father Ambrose returned to England to minister to persecuted Catholic families.

On April 25, 1641, he was celebrating mass at Morely Hall when he was captured by a mob of several hundred fanatical Protestants and taken to Lancaster Castle. On September 10 he was executed and his head exhibited on a spike at a Manchester church. Later it was taken secretly to Wardley Hall where it has remained. It is thought that the first version was deliberately spread about in order to divert suspicion from the real origin of the relic.

Thomas Barritt, a once famous Manchester antiquary, visited Wardley Hall towards the end of the eighteenth century.

"There is a human skull", he wrote, "which, time out of mind, hath had a superstitious veneration paid to it, by [the occupiers of the hall] not permitting it to be removed from its situation, which is on the topmost step of a staircase. There is a tradition that, if removed, or ill-used, some uncommon noise and disturbance always follows, to the terror of the whole house; yet I cannot persuade myself this is always the case. But some few years ago, I and three of my acquaintances went to view this surprising piece of household furniture, and found it as above mentioned, and bleached white with the weather, that beats in upon it from a four-square window in the hall, which the tenants never permit to be glazed or filled up, thus to oblige the skull, which, they say, is unruly and disturbed at the hole not being always open. However, one of us, who was last in company with the skull, removed it from its place into a dark part of the room, and there left it and returned home—but the night but one following, such a storm arose about the house, of wind and lightning, as tore down some trees, and unthatched outhousing. We hearing of this, my father went over in a few days after to see his mother, who lived near the Hall, and was witness to the wreck the storm had made."

In John Roby's *Traditions* there is this description of the skull : "It hath been riven to pieces, burnt, and otherwise destroyed; but on the subsequent day it was seen filling its wonted place. This wilful piece of mortality will not allow the little aperture in which it rests to be walled up—it remains there—whitened and bleached by the weather, looking forth from those rayless sockets upon the scenes which, when living, they had once beheld."

At one stage of its history Wardley Hall suffered from lean times and was divided into miners' tenements. Despite a clause in the lease protecting the skull from removal, the tenants were determined to get rid of it, but their attempt failed because "there was no peace in the house until it was restored". On another occasion it was tossed into the moat—and then the moat had to be drained to recover it. The last spectacular manifestations occurred in 1897 when the skull was temporarily removed while the house was restored to its former glory. Peace returned along with Father Ambrose's skull.

Probably the most bizarre incident in the history of skull haunting came when the lid was lifted from the coffin of Anne Griffith. The sexton and gentry gathered about the tomb saw that the shrouded body was in a state of perfect preservation but the head ... the head, which had somehow become detached from the body, had become a gleaming skull. For a minute there was silence, then one of the onlookers conquered his revulsion, bent forward and picked up the skull, taking it back to Burton Agnes Hall where it can be found today.

The story goes back to the reign of Elizabeth I when Sir Henry Griffith began building Burton Agnes Hall near Driffield in Yorkshire. He lavished such loving care on the project—it is still a stately home and open to the public—that his three daughters were infected with his enthusiasm and after his death they devoted themselves to extending and improving the property. Of the three the most dedicated was Anne.

The design of the hall was by Inigo Jones and Rubens was responsible for much of the decor. By 1620 the work was completed, but tragically Anne had little time to relax and enjoy her beautiful home. When visiting friends at nearby Harpham, she was—to use a chilling modern word—mugged. She was still alive when she was found and carried to Burton Agnes Hall where for several days she lay dying from her injuries.

During this distressing period Anne's sisters kept watch by her bed, listening to what they considered was her delirious talk. Sometimes she spoke quite rationally, saying that her regret in dying was that it meant quitting the hall which they had all worked so hard to make beautiful. At other times she wildly implored her sisters to keep her head safely in the house so that part of her would remain there for ever.

At first the two women were horrified at the thought, but as Anne raved on and made wild threats about what would happen if her head was taken out of the hall, they gave her their word that they would fulfil her wishes just to calm her. When Anne died her sisters had her buried in the family vault of the Griffiths, not giving a thought to the bizarre promise they had made to hush the unhappy patient's morbid ramblings.

Soon they had reason to remember as a terrible poltergeist force swept through the hall. It reverberated with inexplicable crashes, and in the intervals between them low groans were heard in the corridors, doors opened and then slammed of their own accord until sleep was impossible for the ladies or their terrified servants. They consulted their vicar, explaining their promise to Anne and at the same time expressing their repugnance at the thought of having their sister's corpse exhumed and the ghastly memento placed in their home. The vicar said that if they wanted to have a quiet life at the hall they had better honour their promise.

So it came about that Anne's coffin was opened and her skull was taken to Burton Agnes Hall, whereupon the alarming manifestations ended.

Many years later a maid, new to Burton Agnes Hall and unaware of the story, came across the skull and, with a cry of revulsion, threw it out of a window on to a passing cart. At that moment the horse seemed to be struck by paralysis, and although the farmer belaboured the unfortunate beast, he might just as well have been beating a statue. In the hubbub the girl admitted throwing the relic into the cart. It was found and brought indoors

36

again, whereupon the horse seemed to return to life as though a spell had been lifted from him.

On a later occasion, new and sceptical owners of the hall buried the skull in the garden, but the resulting commotion was so alarming that they hastily retrieved it and returned it to its usual place for safe-keeping.

Such manifestations are not the only haunting connected with Anne Griffiths. Occasionally over the years the phantom of a small slender woman in a fawn gown is glimpsed, and is believed to be the ghost of Anne. The last documented account of her appearance was in 1915 and was published in Lord Halifax's *Ghost Book*. He received the account from Mrs. Wickham Boynton who was then the owner of Burton Agnes.

"We were having tea in the hall, when I looked up and saw a small thin woman dressed in *fawn* colour come out of the garden, walk very quickly up the steps, and disappear through the front door, which I thought was open, into the house," wrote Mrs Wickham Boynton. "I imagined it must be the parson's wife and remarked to my husband, who had seen nothing : 'There is Mrs Coutts. Go and bring her in.' He went out at once, but presently came back to say that there was no one there and that the front door was shut."

She then remembered an old story of a fawn lady who had been seen at the hall and who, when she had appeared the last time, had been hurrying up the same steps.

"My father saw her and followed her inside but she had vanished," Mrs Wickham Boynton continued. "She is probably the Griffith ancestress, A.D. 1620, whose skull is still in the house, though no one knows exactly where it is walled up."

Today if you should visit Burton Agnes Hall you will see a portrait of Anne Griffiths with her two sisters hanging above a staircase. Her skull is now thought to be placed behind an ancient screen.

A skull which has actually been beneficial to the various occupants of the house where it elected to stay, has been an object of curiosity in the Peak District of Derbyshire for over three centuries. At one time it was even pictured on local postcards, grinning on a window ledge which was its favourite resting place.

Known as Dickie, it has acted as the guardian of the rather grim and remote Tunstead Farm which looks over Coomb's Reservoir between Chapel-en-le-Frith and Whaley Bridge.

Early last century John Hutchinson wrote in his *Tour through the High Peak* : "Having heard a singular account of a human skull being preserved in a house at Tunstead . . . and which was said to be haunted, curiosity induced me to deviate a little, for the purpose of making some enquiries respecting these *natural* or *super*natural appearances. That there are three parts of a human skull in the house is certain, and which I traced to have remained on the premises for near two centuries past, during all the revolutions of owners and tenants in that time. As to the truth of the supernatural appearance, it is not my design either to affirm or contradict : Though I have been informed by a credible person, a Mr Adam Fox, who was brought up in the house, that he has not only repeatedly heard singular noises, and observed very extraordinary circumstances, but can produce fifty persons, within the parish, who have seen an apparition at this place. He has often found the doors opening to his hand—the servants have been repeatedly called up in the morning—many good offices have been done by the apparition, at different times—and, in fact, it is looked upon more as a guardian spirit, than a terror to the family—never disturbing them but in case of an approaching death of a relation or neighbour, and shewing its resentment only when spoken of with disrespect, or when its own awful memorial of mortality is removed. For twice within the memory of man, the skull has been taken from the premises, once on building the present house on the site of the old one, and another time when it was buried in Chapel church yard—but there was no peace—no rest—it must be replaced! Venerable time carries a report, that one of two coheiresses residing here was murdered, and declared, in her last moments, that her bones should remain on the place for ever."

There are two conflicting explanations of the skull and the reason for its desire to reside at Tunstead Farm. The theory that Dickie was really the skull of a murdered girl is given weight by the fact that the farmhouse has also been haunted by a female spectre. About a hundred years ago a certain Mr Lomas, then the tenant of the farm, was sitting in the kitchen with his ailing baby daughter in a cradle close to the fire. He heard the sound of someone coming down the stairs and a moment later saw a figure cross the room, moving between him and the fireplace, and bend down over the cradle. He thought it was a servant girl and asked her not to disturb the sleeping infant. At his words the wraith vanished, and soon afterwards the child was dead.

The other claimant to Dickie's skull is Ned Dickson who left Tunstead to become a soldier during the Huguenot Wars. After distinguishing himself and being wounded near to death at the Battle of Ivry, he quit the army and returned to Derbyshire to take over his farm. When he reached it he found that his cousin and his wife, having eagerly believed a rumour that he had died of his wounds, had taken over the farm for themselves. The welcome they gave the ex-soldier was far from cordial, though they did invite him to stay the night. After that Ned Dickson was never seen again, and the suspicion was that he had been murdered in his bed—a suspicion which was confirmed a few months later when the cousin's wife saw the skull of their victim which had returned to its rightful inheritance to haunt them.

Whatever the sex of Dickie, the skull has built up an extraordinary reputation for its activity, and has even got its name immortalised on the Ordnance Survey map. As with the other skulls mentioned in this chapter, Dickie resented being removed from what he or she regarded as home, and J. Castle Hall wrote some time ago: "According to the evidence of many local inhabitants, the house is peaceful and quiet while the skull remains there, but if it be removed . . . a voice is heard in the wind as the latter, with strange moanings, comes through the keyholes of every door in the house, saying, 'Fetch poor Dickie back . . . Fetch poor Dickie back . . .', and to this day the weird skull rests in the quiet corner of the window, and in the room a peculiar silence reigns."

This aspect of the skull was dramatically outweighed by the good deeds it performed for its hosts. When an animal was ill on the farm—and especially during the lambing season—the farmer could rely on Dickie to call him out if he was needed. The summons was always three light taps on the window pane. It even acted as an alarm clock for sleepy servants and on one occasion roused a tenant farmer in time to save the life of a cow which was being accidentally strangled by a length of chain. Once a thief came to Tunstead in the night, but he was speedily caught after Dickie set the house vibrating with thumps and bangs. In 1938 the folklore writer Christina Hole was told by the Dixon family at Tunstead that the skull still continued to warn them if there was anything amiss on the farm.

Dickie's greatest triumph was in getting the course of a railway altered. It happened during the construction of the London and North Western line which was to run between Buxton and Stockport. The railway engineers wanted to push it across part of Tunstead Farm, and when the owner objected compulsory powers were obtained and work began on making a track over the disputed land. At one point it was necessary to make a bridge and an embankment, but every time work began the earth slipped and the disgruntled labourers would have to start digging all over again. Finally the engineers realised that they were never going to complete the link through Tunstead Farm and diverted the line, giving as an excuse "the unstable nature of the ground".

The local people knew that it was really the work of Dickie, once again protecting the interests of the farm, and the skull's part was finally recognised (perhaps with the idea of placating it) when a bridge on the railway line was officially named Dickie's Bridge—a name still to be seen on large-scale maps of the area. Dickie's victory was celebrated in a dialect poem written by Samuel Laycock, the first verse of which went :

> "Neaw, Dickie, be quiet wi' thee, lad,
>   An' let navvies an' railways a' be;
> Mon tha shouldn't so soa, its too bad,
>   What harm are they doin' to thee?
> Deed folk shouldn't meddle at o',
>   But leov o' these matters to th' wick;
> They'll see they're done gradely, aw know—
>   Dos' t'yer what aw say to thee, Dick?"

Dickie of Tunstead Farm is not the only skull to gain recognition for supernatural powers in Derbyshire. At Flagg Hall a skull was preserved in a glass case, and any attempt to move it met with the manifestations which characterise the displeasure

of these temperamental relics. On one occasion the owners of the
hall made a determined effort to give the skull a Christian burial
in the Chelmorton churchyard. Before the hearse reached the
church the horses halted as though held back by an invisible wall,
and nothing would persuade them to move until the undertaker
pulled their heads round and headed back to Flagg Hall. It is
thought that this skull was once the property of a doctor who
rented the hall, and that he had obtained it for his medical
studies through the offices of a body-snatcher.

Today Calgarth Hall, a sixteenth century manor house standing close to the shore of Lake Windermere, is one of the most
pleasant guest houses you could find, and has no hint of the
two vengeful skulls which once haunted it. The story goes back a
long time to when the land surrounding the hall was farmed by
Kraster Cook and his wife Dorothy. Their holding was bordered
by the estate of a wealthy magistrate named Myles Phillipson.
He and his wife coveted the Cooks' few acres, wishing to site a
new manor house there. Kraster Cook resolutely held out against
Phillipson's tempting offers, and this angered the magistrate so
much that a feeling of hostility developed between the neighbours.
Then, just before Christmas, Phillipson rode over to the Cooks'
humble farmhouse and with a jovial smile said that as it was
the season of good will they should let bygones be bygones, and
to show that he meant it he invited the couple to his house for
Christmas dinner.

Kraster and Dorothy were somewhat awed by the invitation
but were also greatly relieved, for Myles Phillipson had the
reputation of being a dangerous enemy. They gladly accepted
and on Christmas morning arrived at the Phillipsons' house
where, conscious of their rustic clothing, they mingled uncom-
fortably with the fashionable guests. At dinner the farmer could
think of little to say to those seated about him, and in his
embarrassment he concentrated his gaze on a silver bowl on the
table opposite him.

"I see that you greatly admire that bowl," declared Phillipson's
young wife in a voice loud enough to carry through the room.
"Well, it is worth any man's admiration."

When the long meal was over and the Cooks were about to

gratefully depart there was a sudden commotion. Glowering with anger, Myles Phillipson shouted that his precious silver bowl had been stolen. No doubt to allay any unpleasant suspicions, the guests consented to be searched. Kraster and Dorothy had just buttoned themselves into their outer garments, which had been left hanging by the entrance, and when their turn came to be searched the silver vessel was found concealed in one of their pockets.

In the uproar which followed the guests reminded each other how the uncouth farmer had eyed the bowl during the banquet. The couple were arrested. So astonished were they that the bowl should have found its way into their possession that their muttered protestations of innocence were ignored by the jeering guests as they were led away.

They were tried before Magistrate Phillipson and, as theft could carry the death penalty in those days, he lost little time in sentencing them to hang. As soon as he had finished his dread pronouncement, Dorothy Kraster shouted at him: "Guard thyself, Myles Phillipson! Thou thinkest thou hast managed grandly, but that tiny lump of land is the dearest a Phillipson has ever bought or stolen, for you will never prosper, neither will your breed. Whatever scheme you undertake will wither in your hand; the side you take will always lose; the time shall come when no Phillipson shall own an inch of land; and while Calgarth walls shall stand we'll haunt you night and day. Never will ye be rid of us."

The bodies of Kraster and Dorothy were still dangling in irons when the Phillipsons took over their farm, demolished the old farmhouse and ordered work to commence on Calgarth Hall. By next Christmas it was ready for occupation, and a grand banquet was planned to celebrate its completion. During the feast Phillipson's wife had cause to go upstairs to her bedroom. As she went up the staircase, the light from her candle casting strange leaping shadows before her, she suddenly shrieked and ran back to the dining hall, babbling that she had seen two leering skulls perched on the balustrade—one still had hair, hair like the hanged Dorothy Cook.

In consternation the guests came to the stairs, and there, as she had described, were the two skulls. A guest drew his sword, nervously approached and tapped one with the point. It was solid enough, and with sudden relief it was decided that the whole thing was a joke in very bad taste. The skulls were hurled into the night and a page, who had reason to have a grudge against his master, was accused and locked in a cellar where he was to remain until he confessed. His innocence was soon to be dramatically proved.

Not long after the guests had retired Calgarth Hall echoed with ghastly screams, and when a frightened crowd gathered before the staircase it was seen that the skulls had mysteriously returned to their original position.

The curse of Dorothy Cook was recalled in whispers, and when the sun rose the guests were glad to make an early departure. As the sound of their horses and the creak of heavy carriages receded Myles Phillipson threw the skulls into the duck pond. But he probably knew that this was no answer, that the skulls would return to the staircase, and indeed they did night after night.

From then on Myles Phillipson suffered misfortune after misfortune, and it seemed to him that each setback was accompanied by wilder laughter and screams from the skulls. His position and lands were lost, and when he died he only had Calgarth Hall to leave to his son.

The skulls eased their persecution of the heir, appearing only at Christmas time and on the anniversary of their execution. But the power of the curse continued to plague the Phillipson family until it sank into poverty and oblivion, and the hall passed into other hands. All that remained of the man who had built the hall was his coat of arms on one of the fireplaces. With the curse fulfilled the skulls quit the scene of their haunting for ever.

Another establishment to have had the attentions of two skulls was a farmhouse known as Warbleton Priory—now Priory Farm —which was built on the site of an old Augustinian monastery close to Rushlake Green in Sussex. The skulls were found by workmen engaged on demolishing a massive wall. No one knows who they belonged to, though there was a vague legend that they belonged to a murderer and his victim. Like other such skulls

43

they were notable for the disturbances they caused when taken
from their resting place. There were the usual screams and
crashes when a tenant farmer, leaving the farm, tried to take
one of the skulls with him. When an attempt was made to bury
the other skull the man who was digging the hole was struck by
a whirlwind. Yet the power of the two relics did not prevent
them being stolen at the beginning of this century.

There was a connection between a skull and the extraordinary
haunting of the Manor House at Hinton Ampner, in Hampshire,
which reached such a frightening climax that it had to be
abandoned and then demolished in 1793. The house was built in
the sixteenth century, and in 1719 Edward Stawell—who was to
become Lord Stawell—took up residence there with his wife
Mary, who had inherited the property. Her sister Honoria also
lived at Hinton Ampner. Mary died in 1740, after which an
attachment grew between Edward Stawell and Honoria, a
relationship which set the district seething with gossip. The
couple were not permitted by law to marry, and if they had an
intimate relationship they were technically guilty of incest.
Scandalous gossip spoke of a child being born to Honoria which
was secretly done away with.

Honoria died in 1754 and a year later, on April 2, Lord
Stawell followed her, dying from a stroke. Soon afterwards a
groom at the house declared that he had seen the ghost of his
late master "drably dressed", but this was nothing compared with
what was to come some years later.

The property remained empty until 1765 when it was let
to the Ricketts family, and it is mainly thanks to Mrs Mary
Ricketts that we have such a clear picture of the Hinton Ampner
hauntings. This lady came from a distinguished family, her
brother later being created Baron Jervis of Meaford and Earl
St Vincent for his success at the naval battle of that name. She
was highly educated, and had a fine reputation for her logic and
straightforwardness. While Mr Ricketts, a well-to-do merchant,
was on a long business visit to the West Indies, Mary Ricketts
described, in letters to her husband, her brother and the rector
of Hinton Ampner, the phenomena which she and others
experienced. She also chronicled them in a "Narration" which

she wrote for posterity. This Narration was kept by the family until a version appeared in the *Life of the Rev. Richard Barham*, after which a fuller account was published by *The Gentleman's Magazine* in 1872.

Almost immediately the Ricketts family moved into their new home they were plagued by continually slamming doors despite the fitting of new locks throughout. A nursemaid saw the phantom of a "gentleman in drab clothes"; servants saw a female ghost and heard the rustle of a silk dress, and sounds which were described as "dismal groans".

The hauntings increased in intensity when Mr Ricketts was away in Jamaica and Mary Ricketts wrote: "Some time after Mr Ricketts left me, I, then sleeping in the bedroom over the kitchen, frequently heard the noise of someone walking in the room within ... Although we often made instant search, we never could discover any appearance of human or brute being ..." And from then on it is possible to see from her Narration how the paranormal phenomena in the house was increasing while new forms of hauntings began.

"I once or twice heard sounds of music and one night in particular three distinct and violent knocks as though someone was beating with a club or other heavy weapon against the door downstairs," Mary Ricketts recorded. "I thought that housebreakers must be forcing their way in and immediately rang my bell. No one answered it, but as the noise ceased I thought no further of it at the time. After this, and in the beginning of the year 1771, I was frequently conscious of a hollow murmuring which seemed to fill the whole house. It was like no other sound that I have heard and could not have been caused by the wind, as it occurred on the calmest nights."

This strange and sinister murmuring continued through the months along with other disturbances which reached a new peak by the middle of the year, including the sounds of people—two men and a woman—talking. Mary Ricketts was unable to distinguish the words actually used in these ghostly conversations which inevitably ended with a scream that slowly died away.

Captain Jervis, Mary's celebrated brother, now visited Hinton Ampner and was soon experiencing the disturbances which she had described to him, as did a neighbouring friend named

Captain Luttrell who agreed to help investigate them. To do so he stayed at the manor house and after a thorough search of the house, which yielded nothing abnormal, sat up through the night in a tense vigil.

The next morning Captain Luttrell declared that he had heard the footsteps of a person walking across the lobby. He immediately threw open the door and cried, "Who goes there?"

"Something flitted past him and my brother cried, 'Look against the door'," wrote Mary Ricketts. "My brother was awake and had heard Captain Luttrell's challenge, as well as the noise. He rose and joined the other. To their astonishment they continued to hear various noises, but, although they examined everything everywhere, they could see nothing and found the staircase door fast secured as I had left it . . . My brother sat up every night during the week he spent at Hinton. In the middle of one of them I was alarmed by the sound of a gun or pistol, discharged quite close to me, and immediately followed by groans as of a person in agony or on the point of death . . . My brother now earnestly begged me to leave the house."

She took his advice, leaving Hinton Ampner with her family in August, 1771, to settle in a house in Curzon Street, London. The manor house—now the talk of the neighbourhood—remained empty for a year after which it was rented briefly by a family called Lawrence. Disturbances continued though the Lawrences tried to hush them up, then they departed abruptly in 1773. After that Lady Hillsborough, the owner of Hinton Ampner manor, was unable to get anyone to stay there. The house became shunned, derelict, and finally she ordered its demolition and the building of a new house on a site in the grounds.

And now we come to the skull theme again. As workmen were tearing up the floorboards in one of the rooms they found "a small skull said to be that of a monkey". The skull was not submitted to any proper medical examination, and it is quite likely that it was the skull of a baby. Was it the remains of the infant that was rumoured to have been born to Honoria and her brother-in-law and then disposed of, and were the phantom figures and the frightening sounds echoes of the agony experienced by the guilty parents?

3

ENGLAND'S MARTIAL SPIRITS

The most widely witnessed—and best attested—clash of phantom armies in England was the re-enactment of the Battle of Edgehill two months after it had actually taken place. Regularly on Saturday and Sunday nights ghostly Cavaliers and spectral Parliamentarians took the field against each other and, as the news spread, people journeyed to the spot from miles around to see the display almost as we would go to the cinema. I can almost imagine them looking forward to Prince Rupert's spectacular cavalry charge as the highlight of the evening. When word of the wonder reached Charles I he sent a group of investigators to report on the recurrent phenomenon.

The actual Battle of Edgehill took place on October 24, 1642, and was the first real fighting in the Civil War. There were thirteen thousand five hundred combatants on each side, and both sides claimed the victory. In fact the advantage went slightly to the Royalists, but total victory was thrown away by the King's nephew Prince Rupert—Dashing Rupert of the Rhine—who led his horsemen in a devastating charge. He got so carried away in pursuing fleeing Roundheads that when he finally led his Cavaliers back to the field, the advantage that the continuous presence of a cavalry force would have given the King had been lost.

At the end of the day Charles did at least have the opportunity of marching on the capital which, had he done so, might have altered the course of history. But it was the gentle monarch's first battle, and he was so horrified by the carnage that he could not concentrate on military strategy, while his commanders would

47

not agree on the best course of action. Thus the chance of winning London was lost forever and the King finally decided to retire to Oxford to establish his headquarters there.

So much for the real battle. Details of the phantasmal one were published about a month after it had been witnessed in the form of a pamphlet which rejoiced in the following title :

"A Great Wonder in Heaven, showing the late Apparitions and Prodigious Noyses of War and Battels, seen on Edge-Hill, neere Keinton in Northamptonshire.—Certified under the Hands of WILLIAM WOOD, Esquire, and Justice for the Peace in the said Countie, SAMUEL MARSHALL, Preacher of GODS Word in Keinton, and other Persons of Qualitie."

After a long introduction on the reality of the supernatural which began :

"THAT there hath beene, and ever will be, Laruae, Spectra, and such like apparitions, namely, Ghosts and Goblins, hath beene the opinion of all the famousest Divines of the Primitive Church, and is (though oppugned by some) the received Doctrine of divers learned men at this day; their opinion being, indeed, ratified and confirmed by divers Texts of Scripture . . ."

the account told how some travellers, shepherds and "other countrymen", who were in the vicinity of Edgehill just after midnight on the morning of the last Saturday before Christmas, were startled by a distant rataplan of drums which, as it seemed to come nearer, was joined by "the noise of soldiers, as it were, giving out their last groans".

"They sought to withdraw as fast as they possibly could," wrote the seventeenth-century journalist in a style so lively I would not presume better, "but then, on the sudden, whilest they were in these cogitations, appeared in the ayre the same incorporeall souldiers that made those clamours, and immediately, with Ensignes display'd, Drummes beating, Musquets going off, Cannons discharged, Horses neyghing, which also to these men were visible, the alarum or entrance to this game of death was strucke up, one Army, which gave the first charge, having the Kings colours, and the other the Parliaments in their head or

front of the battells, and so pell mell to it they went; the battell
that appeared to the Kings forces seeming at first to have the
best, but afterwards to be put into apparent rout; but till two
or three in the morning in equall scale continued this dreadful
fight, the clattering of Armes, noyse of Cannons, cries of souldiers,
so amazing and terrifying the poore men, that they could not
believe they were mortall, or give credit to their eares and eyes;
runne away they durst not, for feare of being made a prey to
these infernall souldiers, and so they, with much fear and affright,
stayed to behold the successe of the business, which at last suited
to this effect : after some three houres fight, that Army which
carryed the Kings colours withdrew, or rather appeared to flie;
the other remaining, as it were, masters of the field, stayed a good
space triumphing, and expressing all the signes of joy and conquest, and then, with all their Drummes, Trumpets, Ordnance,
and Souldiers, vanished . . ."

When the last sounds of the conflict's aftermath had died
away, the terrified spectators hurried to Keinton where they
hammered at the door of William Wood, a Justice of the Peace,
who in turn roused his neighbour the Reverend Samuel Marshall.
Before these two worthies they described their extraordinary
group experience and affirmed it with their oaths.

The pamphlet continued : "At which affirmation of theirs,
being much amazed, they should hardly have given credit to it,
but would have conjectured the men to have been either mad or
drunk, had they not knowne some of them to have been of
approved integritie : and so, suspending their judgments till the
next night about the same houre, they, with the same men, and
all the substantial Inhabitants of that and the neighbouring
parishes, drew thither; where, about halfe an houre after their
arrivall, on Sunday, being Christmas night, appeared in the same
tumultuous warlike manner, the same two adverse Armies,
fighting with as much spite and spleen as formerly : and so departed the gentlemen and all the spectators, much terrified with
these visions of horrour, withdrew themselves to their houses,
beseeching God to defend them from those hellish and prodigious
enemies."

The eldritch armies failed to appear on the Monday night, and
it was not until the following Saturday that the stutter of drums

heralded yet another engagement which this time lasted for four hours before the troops vanished "appearing againe on Sunday night, and performing the same actions of hostilitie and bloudshed; so that both Mr Wood and others, whose faith, it should seeme, was not strong enough to carrie them out against these delusions, for sook their habitations thereabout, and retired themselves to other more secure dwellings; but Mr Marshall stayed, and some other; and so successively the next Saturday and Sunday the same tumults and prodigious sights and actions were put in the state and condition they were formerly. The rumour whereof coming to his Majestie at Oxford, he immediately dispatched thither Colonell Lewis Kirke, Captaine Dudley, Captaine Wainman, and three other Gentlemen of credit, to take the full view and notice of the said business, who, first hearing the true attestation and relation of Mr Marshall and others, staid there till Saturday night following, wherein they heard and saw the fore-mentioned prodigies, and so on Sunday, distinctly knowing divers of the apparitions or incorporeall substances by their faces, as that of Sir Edmund Varney, and others that were there slaine; of which upon oath they made testimony to his Majestie."

In 1831 Lord Nugent published *Memorials of John Hampden*, the biography of one of the most celebrated leaders of the Long Parliament who exhibited great personal bravery at Edgehill before being fatally wounded the next year at Chalgrove Field by a marauding force under Prince Rupert. Referring to the Edgehill phenomenon in his book, Lord Nugent commented: "A well supported imposture, or a stormy night on the hill-side might have acted on the weakness of a peasantry in whose remembrance the terrors of the Edge Hill fight were still fresh; but it is difficult to imagine how the minds of officers, sent there to correct the illusions, could have been so imposed upon. It will, also, be observed, that no inference is attempted by the witnesses to assist any notion of a judgment or warning favourable to the interests or passions of their own party."

The Civil War has left behind it several other echoes, though none have been as spectacular as Edgehill. In the churchyard of Poynington Church in Somerset is the grave of a young supporter of Charles I named Baldwin Malet. With ill-considered enthusiasm he raised a band of locals to attack a troop of Parliamentarian cavalry which had arrived in the area in June, 1646. The untrained farmers were no match for the battle-trained veterans and they were all killed. From time to time there have been reports of the brief reappearance of this phantom band, together with the spectre of a young girl who was shot in the skirmish.

The first really decisive battle of the Civil War was fought at Marston Moor, seven miles west of York, on July 2, 1644. Here eighteen thousand Royalists, under the command of Prince Rupert, fought twenty-seven thousand Roundheads, but it was not so much the superiority of numbers that won the day for the Parliamentarians as the discipline of Oliver Cromwell's new Ironsides. It was the first time that infantry had been able to stand up to Rupert's cavalry charges which in the past had been so effective, and as a result the North of England was lost to the King.

Over the centuries phantom soldiers have been glimpsed at the site of this battle, including several eye-witness accounts in our own. One day in November, 1932, a motorist named Arthur Wright was driving with a friend over the moor on the road which leads from Filey to Harrogate when they saw in front of their car a group of long-haired men wearing cloaks and Cavalier-style hats. For a moment the attention of the two men was distracted by a passing coach, and when they looked again the road was clear.

As there was nowhere on the roadside where anyone could have hidden, and thinking it unlikely that normal pedestrians would have been in seventeenth-century dress, the two concluded that they had seen ghostly stragglers from the defeated Royalist army.

A similar sighting was reported in 1968.

A phantom army was witnessed several times in Cumberland but, unlike the Edgehill re-enactment, no explanation can be given for its appearance nor is there any suggestion as to who the soldiers actually were. Although it was later seen by a group of people simultaneously, it was first noticed by a farm labourer who worked on William Lancaster's farm at Blakehills near Penrith in Cumberland.

On June 23 (Midsummer Eve), 1735, he chanced to look up at the impressive bulk of Souter Fell about half a mile away and beheld a column of troops marching from the north across the east side of its summit to disappear in a great cleft.

At first there was nothing to suggest that the army he was watching was other than flesh-and-blood, except that it was almost impossible for a march to be made in such precipitous terrain. As he watched fascinated for an hour as the column moved like an endless, colourful snake across the fell top, it dawned on him that a normal army would have taken an easy route round the desolate hill.

Next day he related his experience to his employer and his fellow workers, but his story was greeted with incredulous laughter. Firstly, he was told, if such a large body of troops had been in the neighbourhood everyone would have known about it, and, secondly, what army would march across Souter Fell whose north and west faces were sheer drops of nine hundred feet? No doubt the poor man felt like Galileo Galilei when he stamped his foot and cried, "*E pur si muove*," but exactly two years later, again on Midsummer Eve, the strange army was seen again.

On this occasion it was William Lancaster himself who looked up to the fell where he saw some horses with men walking behind them. He thought that it was probably a hunting party, but when he looked up again he saw that the men were now mounted and were being followed by an army marching five abreast, and taking the same route that his man had described. He noted that the column was divided into companies, each under the command of a mounted officer who rode up and down the ranks. By now Lancaster had called his family and they watched the sight spellbound.

As twilight gathered about the fell the spectators saw that the discipline of the soldiers seemed to relax, they fell out of step and broke ranks, and the mounted men milled about in some confusion.

When Lancaster told his story he was treated to the same ridicule as the labourer had been, and eight years were to pass before he and his family saw the phantoms again and on this occasion the story was justified.

In her book *The English Lakes*, the nineteenth-century radical writer Harriet Martineau, who had made a study of the Souter Fell Phenomenon, described the scene thus :

"On the Midsummer-eve of the fearful 1745, twenty-six persons, expressly summoned by the [Lancaster] family, saw all that had been seen before, and more. Carriages were now interspersed with the troops; and everybody knew that no carriages had been, or could be, on the summit of Souter Fell. The multitude was beyond imagination; for the troops filled a space of half a mile, and marched quickly till night hid them—still marching. There was nothing vaporous or indistinct about the appearance of these spectres. So real did they seem, that some of the people went up, the next morning, to look for the hoof-marks of the horses; and awful it was to them to find not one foot-print on heather or grass. The witnesses attested the whole story on oath before a magistrate; and fearful were the expectations held by the whole country-side about the coming events of the Scotch rebellion."

The only explanation put forward for the Souter Fell vision was made by the editor of the *Lonsdale Magazine* who suggested that through the agency of what he vaguely described as a "transparent vapour" the Lancasters and their neighbours had seen a mirage of the Jacobite army on the march in Scotland, but this theory in no way explained the sightings of 1735 and 1737.

A bizarre haunting of Burgh Castle is reputed to go back to a battle which was fought in the chaotic times which followed the departure of the Roman legions in 406, to defend Rome herself against Alaric's Goths, leaving the Britons at the mercy of Picts, Saxons, Angles and Jutes. Little wonder the following centuries were known as the Dark Ages, for all that we can be historically certain of is a pattern of invasions and the names of a few leaders so remarkable that somehow their reputations survived the smoky anarchy which replaced Roman civilisation.

From across the Channel in their long, mastless "waveriders" came the Saxons, demon-haunted forest men in green cloaks, carrying long spears and a cult of blood-letting. To them the universe was a terrifying chaos in which no man could escape his pre-ordained destiny—his "wyrd"—and his only hope of dignity, the only justification for his existence, lay in the manner with which he faced his wyrd.

Having subdued the English and torn down the fine Roman towns (abominations to forest dwellers who worshipped trees), the Saxons in turn found themselves harassed by invaders from Scandinavia, the dreaded "white strangers" whose moeurs were similar to their own in that conflict was their creed. To die gloriously in battle was the peak of their ambition because it assured a man of his place in Valhalla where he could fight every day and, with his wounds magically healed, carouse every night in the halls of the gods.

According to legend it was a clash between Saxons and Danes which led to the haunting of the great Roman fort which stands at the confluence of the Bure and Waveney rivers, three miles south-west of Yarmouth.

It was a fine summer day when I visited the site. Leaving my car by a small church, I followed a sign along a blackberry-bordered track beyond which were corn fields rippling like a yellow sea as winds played across them. And suddenly I saw the ramparts of Burgh Castle—and what dramatic ramparts they were. The fifteen foot high wall parallel to my path stretched two hundred and fourteen yards. From each end of it other walls, equally massive, ran down towards the river. In places they were angled, not because of any fault in their construction of cemented rubble faced with flint but because the ground itself had shrunk beneath their incredible weight.

In the third century, when the fortress was built as one of the great bastions of the Saxon Shore, it was known as Gariannonum, and housed a company of Roman cavalry ever on the alert to gallop out and confront any Saxon raiders who dared to land on the Suffolk coast. When the Romans departed and the Saxon Shore was unguarded, the Saxons themselves took it over and although they pulled down villas and temples, the eleven-foot wide walls withstood them, as did the straight Roman roads.

As I wandered in the huge area enclosed by this mighty masonry, I tried to picture the battle which had once been fought here and which has somehow left a recurring echo. It was strange to think—if the tale was to be believed—that where I stood in the gentle sunlight hundreds of mutilated corpses had once been impaled on stakes as a hideous show of strength.

The legend of Burgh Castle haunting goes that a large band of Saxons landed in the region of what was then known as the Isle of Horsa (Horsey today) and, under the command of their leader Siberg, moved south-west across the Halvergate Marshes with the idea of colonising an area now known as Reedham. They found that their biggest obstacle was not the treacherous marshes or the almost impenetrable forest which then covered England, nor the demoralised Romanised Celts, but a tribe of Danes which had settled in the old Roman fort under a cruel war chief named Gonard.

When Siberg's scouts told him of this potential enemy so firmly in command of the territory surrounding Gariannonum, he knew that here was a threat to his plans for settlement which he could not ignore, for once Gonard realised that the Saxons were migrating close to him he would delight in providing a feast for "the black and horn-beaked raven and dun-feathered eagle, greedy hawk of battle". Siberg, therefore, sent a messenger north to his half-brother Cerdag, who had already settled with his tribe north of the Humber, asking him to come and help him deal with this nest of Danes.

Because of the wild nature of the forest and the complete lack of roads, it took the messenger a long time to find his way to Cerdag. Meanwhile Gonard learned that a number of Siberg's Saxons had arrived at Reedham and, with gratitude to his terrible war god in his heart, he led his warriors to what became a wholesale massacre. He then sent an arrogant message to Siberg inviting him and the remainder of his followers to come to Gariannonum where, no doubt, he would enrol them as his serfs. Hoping to gain time, Siberg decided to go alone with the messenger, telling his men that if he did not return from the old Roman fort within three days they were to fetch him with their spears.

Gonard received him arrogantly and demanded why the Saxon had not brought his people with him. Siberg replied that his people would come soon enough if he did not return within a certain time, but added that he expected Gonard to respect the fact that he had come in peace and without weapons.

"Then they had better come," one can imagine the grim Dane saying. He had Siberg bound and cast into a foul pit close to the foundations of one of the great walls.

On the fourth day the starving Saxon was aroused from delirium by the familiar war shout of his warriors who were surging against the walls of Gariannonum like waves washing against a cliff. Used to skirmishing in forest glades, the nearest they had ever come to besieging a castle was vaulting over the wooden fences of enemy stockades—the stonework of the Romans was something that was beyond their military ingenuity.

When they had exhausted themselves against the sheer walls, and many were wounded by missiles which Gonard's men had hurled down at them, two different gates of the castle opened and the Danes attacked the weary Saxons from opposite directions. The pagan gods of war must have been well satisfied with the following slaughter, and by the end of the day the area round the fort was heaped with dead Saxons. Gonard ordered that the wounded as well as the dead should be dragged up to Gariannonum's ramparts where all were spitted on sharp stakes and set up like rows of scarecrows as a warning to any who might challenge the might of the Danes. Then, as was the custom—one that William the Conqueror followed at the blood-soaked field of Senlac—Gonard feasted surrounded by his dead and dying victims.

A couple of days later he was seated on the highest part of the wall, no doubt gloating over the lines of Saxon corpses with savage satisfaction, when he had a vision. High in the summer sky he saw a fight between a black angel and a white angel. Like warring eagles they soared and dived, their pinions flaying the air as they sought to destroy each other. At last the white angel appeared to get the better of the aerial combat, its fingers locked on its enemy's black throat and in this grotesque embrace both plummeted down and vanished beneath the sparkling waters of the Waveney.

Gonard was bewildered by the vision. He doubted that any of his own people could explain its meaning to him, but his Saxon prisoner might have some understanding of it. After all, the Saxons had been approached by missionaries with the mad doctrine of the White Christ who had taught about such ridiculous things as brotherhood and love. So Siberg was released and brought reeling to the rampart where Gonard sat behind a table with his war axe before him. The Dane laughed as he saw the Saxon look around at the grotesque corpses of his followers.

Not wishing to talk about his experience in front of his men, Gonard waved them away and then told Siberg of his vision and demanded an explanation. Siberg said nothing for a while then, with a ghastly smile on his emaciated features, he pointed to the river. Gonard's eyes followed the direction of the shaking finger and to his horror he saw an armada of ships sailing up the river towards Gariannonum.

"Those are the ships of my kinsman Cerdag," said Siberg. "His spears will avenge my people, but I shall have my own vengeance." With a supreme effort he seized Gonard's axe and struck him while he gazed at the approaching fleet, inflicting a ghastly wound on his head.

Gonard's scream went unheeded as the Danes sounded their war horns and rushed to defend themselves against the great host of Saxons which was now disembarking and running towards the fort. When it was completely surrounded Cerdag sent a messenger with a flag of truce to the Danes demanding their surrender. The gate opened to allow the emissary to enter. He was next seen by his friends when his body, wrapped up in the flag of truce with which it had been strangled, came flying in a wide arc over the castle parapet.

It was the signal for Cerdag's Saxons to begin their attack with warriors climbing on each other's shoulders to gain the top of the wall. Soon they were leaping down into the enclosed space where I stood pondering on that peaceful summer's day. Such was their rage at the staked corpses of their fellow Saxons and the treatment of their messenger that they fought berserk until the very last of Gonard's men fell beneath the wet points of their spears.

Then Cerdag climbed to a high point of the castle to look over the carnage with grim satisfaction. Hearing a groan he turned and saw his half-brother Siberg lying beside the body of the dead Gonard. An arrow protruded from his side and it was obvious that he would only take a few more gulping breaths. With tears running from his eyes, Cerdag withdrew the shaft and tried to staunch the blood, but Siberg died in his arms without speaking.

Such is the story of Burgh Castle. The haunting is said to take place on July 3, and it takes the form of a body wrapped in a white cloth falling from the castle wall to disappear as soon as it touches the earth. There is no explanation as to why this particular aspect of the bloody drama should be replayed; it could equally be the staked bodies of Siberg's Saxons, the massacre of the Danes by Cerdag's warriors or the death of Siberg after he had been accidentally shot by one of his own side. Yet it is the comparatively trivial incident of the messenger which transcends time and space to mark this anniversary of this long-ago battle. But then, who can understand the supernatural?

Another fort of the Saxon Shore which retains an eerie hint of ancient conflict is the impressive ruin of Pevensey Castle in Sussex. When the Romans built it in the fourth century they named it Anderita. It stood on an island of dry ground surrounded by treacherous swamps which added to its impregnability. Following the Roman withdrawal it became deserted until 491 when a large number of Britons banded together within its walls only to be massacred by invading Saxons. After 1066 its strategic importance was recognised again and Norman fortifications rose within the old Roman ramparts.

In 1088 Odo, the Bishop of Bayeux who supported the claim to the throne of Robert, brother of William the Conqueror, held the fort against William II—the hated Red King—until the garrison was starved into surrender. It is from that time that the main haunting of the castle dates. There have been reports of a phantom band of Norman soldiers being seen silently approaching the old moat before vanishing.

In 1399 the castle was besieged by Richard II's forces because the constable of the castle, Sir Richard Pelham, was loyal to Henry Bolingbroke who was to become the first King of the House of Lancaster. At the time the attack took place Sir Richard was away in Yorkshire with his master, and the organisation of the castle's defence fell to Lady Jane Pelham. This she did so successfully that when Bolingbroke was finally crowned he presented the castle to her husband, and since then her watchful spectre has been occasionally glimpsed as it walks the crumbling ramparts which once she defended so well.

It would be surprising if the Wars of the Roses, which divided England and decimated its nobility from 1455 to the Battle of Bosworth in 1485, did not leave some phantoms in their wake. One of these is said to be a messenger who was on his way to the Battle of Tewkesbury, which was fought on May 4, 1471, and where Edward IV defeated Margaret, the Queen of Henry VI, who was trying to secure the crown for her son Edward. As he was galloping through Shaw Green Lane to the scene of the battle the courier was brought down by an archer. Up until recent times the ghostly hoofbeats of his horse have been heard and the dim outline of a rider on a white steed has been seen.

A touch of authenticity was added to the legend earlier this century when some road repairs were being carried out at Shaw Green Lane and part of a skeleton was unearthed with an iron arrowhead stuck firmly between its ribs.

St Albans was the scene of two battles in the Wars of the Roses, in 1455 which ended in a victory for the White Rose of York, and in 1461 when the Lancastrians won. I do not know from which battle the sound of hoofbeats and the martial clash of steel on armour came, but such sounds were frequently heard in a house appropriately called Battlefield House which was built on the site of the fighting in Chequers Street, an aural haunting which continued after the house had been demolished and a row of shops had replaced it.

One of the most evocative battlefields I have visited is Sedgemoor where, on July 6, 1685, James, Duke of Monmouth, the natural son of Charles II and Lucy Walter, attempted to surprise a royal army of two thousand seven hundred encamped there. At Taunton he had been proclaimed James II and now he had an army of two thousand six hundred foot and six hundred horse—mostly made up of miners and peasants. When these unfortunate men were scythed down by expert artillery fire, the Duke fled (outdistancing his companions it was said),

59

though two days later he was captured hiding in a ditch near Ringwood. When he was taken before his uncle the King, he threw himself on the floor and even offered to turn Catholic in return for his life but James, after he had enjoyed the spectacle of his grovelling for an indecent time, had him taken to the Tower where he was beheaded on July 15.

Perhaps it was the thought of the simple rebels forfeiting their lives for a remote ideal, armed with makeshift weapons and who were no match for the unemotional discipline of a well-drilled fighting machine, which seemed to impregnate the flat wet field with a sense of tragedy; perhaps it was just because the sun was almost touching the western horizon that the puddles on the track I followed seemed to turn to blood. Whatever the reason, it was not difficult to believe the stories that abound of the phantoms who return to the scene of the carnage. Some are said to be vapour-like figures which move in the direction of the River Cary while—according to some accounts—disembodied voices call: "Come over!" But the saddest Sedgemoor phantom —sadder even than that of the terrified Duke who has been glimpsed making his escape from the battlefield—is that of a girl who committed suicide on the spot.

The story goes that her rebel sweetheart was captured by the soldiers who, because of his reputation as an athlete, told him that if he could run as fast as a galloping horse his life would be spared. Wagers were laid and the frantic man, watched by his lover, did manage to keep pace with a cavalry rider. But the girl's joy turned to anguish when the panting runner was shot just the same—an anguish which did not end when she drowned herself close to the battlefield.

When her sad phantom has been seen there, it has been accompanied by the drumming of hooves and the terrible panting of the running rebel.

A similar aural phenomenon of hoofbeats and panting has been heard at Heddon Oak which is really a tree standing at a crossroads about fifty miles west of Sedgemoor. Here some Monmouth rebels were caught by mounted soldiers and hanged, which is borne out by the unpleasant fact that the ghostly panting is said to turn into the sounds of strangulation.

4

SCOTLAND'S SPECTRAL SOLDIERS

It would be more surprising if the Celtic twilight of Scotland did not have its armies of the dead than if it did, and this land of fairies, second sight and ancient memory does not disappoint when it comes to its warring wraiths. In examining this phenomena the most obvious place to start is at Culloden where Stuart hopes were dashed by Stuart indecision and a new and tragic page was added to Scottish folklore.

Charles Edward—known as the "Young Chevalier" or "Bonnie Prince Charlie"—landed with seven followers at Eriskay in the Hebrides on July 23, 1745, to attempt to win the kingdom his father, the Old Pretender, had failed to gain in the Jacobite Rebellion of 1715. By September 17 Edinburgh had surrendered to Charles Edward's Highland army and he symbolically held court at Holyrood Palace in the tradition of his ancestors. Four days later the rebels defeated a royal army under the command of Sir John Cope. The way south was now clear and on November 1 the Prince started out for London with a force of six thousand five hundred men. He managed to advance as far as Derby and alarm spread through London, especially as England's best regiments were fighting on the Continent. Plans were made for a royal evacuation to Hanover.

At Derby Charles Edward's bickering commanders persuaded him to withdraw to Scotland where, at Falkirk, they achieved their last victory over an army loyal to George II. They then moved to Inverness to await a force under the command of the Duke of Cumberland who was soon to earn his nickname of "Butcher".

61

The battle which ended the Rebellion of '45, and which was the last to be fought in Britain, took place on April 16, 1746, on Drummossie Moor, now known as Culloden. The site for the Jacobite stand against the English army was chosen by the Prince's Irish Quartermaster, John O'Sullivan, who was better at flattering the temperamental Stuart than at military strategy. The moor gave no advantage to the Highlanders whose method of fighting was the wild charge, but it was ideally suited for English cavalry and well-drilled troops who relied on the speed with which they could fire and reload Brown Bess, the British army musket which Kipling described as "an out-spoken, flinty-lipped, brazen-faced jade".

The night before the battle, which was to be the first commanded by the Prince, the rebels attempted a night attack against Cumberland's camp at Nairn but got lost in the fog and darkness. The result of this doomed manoeuvre was that the Highlanders were exhausted as they waited for the English to appear on the moor—some even slept through the battle.

At eleven o'clock the rebels caught the terrible rumble of drums as the English army advanced towards Culloden. In those days drums were the pulse-beat of the army, in battle the soldiers even went through reloading drill to their beat, and the drummers of Cumberland's army were to provide a cruel obbligato to the slaughter which lay ahead. There were about five thousand rebels watching from their thin lines which stretched from north to south as the English regiments swung smoothly into position opposite them. The Scots were hungry (their rations had not arrived from Inverness the previous day), soaked by sleet, weary and dispirited—not all burned with patriotism for the Stuart cause, many were there because their clan chiefs had threatened to fire their cottages unless they joined the rebellion.

The battle opened with a dreadful cannonade from the Royal Artillery, cannonballs smashing through the clansmen's ranks as they stood like impotent skittles while Bonnie Prince Charlie sat on his horse unable to decide upon a command. The decimated Highlanders begged for an order to charge the enemy which was now screened by the smoke pall from its remorseless guns. Finally the Prince yielded to a plea by his Lieutenant-General, Lord George Murray, and gave an order for a general advance but his courier was killed by a cannonball and the suicidal delay continued.

The clans could stand no more, they broke ranks and raced over the heather through fusilades of grapeshot until they were close enough for the English infantry to begin its controlled musket fire. As soon as the front rank fired its men stepped back to allow the second to fire. While the third prepared to fire the original rank reloaded and in turn knelt in the firing position.

Despite the terrible firepower, some rebels reached the English lines where their claymores were met with bayonets, but such was the despairing fury of the clansmen's attack that some ranks were broken and platoons driven back, costing Cumberland three hundred and nine killed. By the time Bonnie Prince Charlie quit the field and the survivors began to flee with the vengeful dragoons spurring after them, upwards of two thousand Jacobite dead were sprawled on Culloden's heather.

With the drums still rolling the English advanced to the lines recently held by the Scots and began to eat bread and cheese amidst the carnage. John Prebble, in his book *Culloden*, quoted an English officer who wrote: "The moor was covered with blood, and our men, what with killing the enemy, dabbling their feet in the blood, and splashing it about one another, looked like so many butchers rather than Christian soldiers."

After they had eaten, some of the soldiers roamed the battle-field to bayonet enemy bodies which still showed signs of life. Others slew innocent spectators along with the miserable wretches who were slinking about the perimeter of the battle to plunder the dead. Still the drums thudded their endless tattoo, and when the women camp-followers of the English army came searching for their menfolk they hoisted high their skirts to prevent them becoming blood-soaked.

"The Duke of Cumberland," wrote the Chevalier Johnstone in his *Memoirs of the Rebellion*, "had the cruelty to allow our wounded to remain amongst the dead on the field of battle, stript of their clothes, from Wednesday, the day of our unfortunate engagement, till three o'clock on Friday, when he sent detachments to kill all those who were still in life; and a great many, who had resisted the effects of the continual rains which fell all that time, were then dispatched. He ordered a barn, which contained many of the wounded Highlanders, to be set on fire; and having stationed soldiers round it, they with fixed bayonets drove back the unfortunate men who attempted to save themselves, into the flames; burning them alive in this horrid manner, as if they had not been fellow-creatures."

Culloden, and the savage repression which followed it, has cast a long shadow and I found that even today there is something indefinably gloomy about the moor which the brightest sunshine cannot allay. Several ghosts have been seen there including at least one re-enactment of the battle in the sky above it. A phantom which has been glimpsed quite frequently is that of a rebel in Highland dress, obviously weary or wounded after the conflict, standing close to the huge cairn which has been erected by the road which runs across the moor.

Nearby are the mounds of rebel graves, and it was on one of these that a visitor saw the recumbent figure of a warrior. When the lady realised that it was not a flesh-and-blood human who was lying there but the shade of a long-dead rebel whose bones lay beneath the mound she fled from the spot, later giving details of her experience to the Edinburgh Committee for the Recording of Abnormal Happenings.

To me more ghastly than any of the sad ghosts who wander the moor were the living ghouls who, for a long time after the battle, dug there in the hope of finding bones to take away as souvenirs—the forbears of those who race to the scenes of air crashes and motor accidents for a sight of blood or mutilated flesh. William Howitt, in his *Visits to Remarkable Places*, which was published in 1840, wrote: "As we sate on the greensward of one of these battle-graves, we observed that in many places the turf had been broken up by digging; and our young guide told us that scarcely a party came there but was desirous to carry away the fragment of a bone as a relic. 'What,' said we, 'are the bones soon come at?' 'Yes,' he replied, 'in some places they lie within a foot of the surface.' These graves have been dug into in hundreds of places, yet you can scarcely turn a turf but you come upon them. He dug out a sod with his knife, and throwing out a little earth, presently came to fragments of the crumbling bones of the skeleton of 1746. He told us that in one instance, a quantity of bones which had been carried off by a traveller, had been sent back at a great expense, and buried again; the person who conveyed them away being continually tormented by his conscience and his dreams, till that was done."

For a while Culloden was haunted by the phantasmagoria of a battle which did not reflect the one which had been fought in 1746—the local people believing they were seeing a battle which still had to take place. It was a belief still held strongly in William Howitt's time, and in his book he described how he discussed with the local people the battlefield and its traditions.

"They told us that the name Drummossie was not now used for that Moor—Culloden had superseded it," he wrote, "but it was retained on a wild track at its extremity in the direction of Badenoch. They assured us, with the utmost gravity, that a battle would some day be fought *there*. We inquired how they knew that. They replied, because it had been repeatedly seen. On a summer's evening, people going across that moor had suddenly on various occasions found themselves in the very midst of the smoke and noise of a battle. They could see the various clans engaged, and clearly recognise them by their proper tartans; and on all these occasions the Laird of Culdethel, a neighbouring gentleman, was conspicuous on his white horse. One woman was so frightened and bewildered by this strange spectacle that she fainted away, and on coming to herself, found all traces of the battle gone, and made the best of her way home again without proceeding on her original object. We told them that these must be strong impressions left on the imaginations of the people by the memory of the old battle, but they only shook their heads. They were perfectly satisfied that a battle was to be fought on Drummossie, and that the Laird of Culdethel would be in it— though with whom the clans would fight, and for what, they could not pretend to tell."

A similar preview, thought to be associated in some way with Culloden though seen a good distance away from it, was recorded on oath before the Aberdeen Town Council in August, 1748. Eleven people claimed that on August 5, in a valley some miles west of the city, they saw two armies facing each other in the sky—one in dark blue with St Andrew's Cross as its insignia while the other was in English scarlet. Twice the army in blue was attacked, and twice it beat back the redcoats. Then, following a third attack, the blue army scattered the red and the ghostly battle silently dissolved.

An account of a phantom army seen at Glen Aray, some miles north of Inveraray, appeared in the correspondence columns of *The Times* on August 2, 1926. It was introduced by a letter from Frances Balfour who explained : "This document is in the narrator's own handwriting, and is docketed by my father, the eighth Duke, as being written for his aunt, Lady Charlotte Bury. In passing along the road where the 'Vision' was seen I have heard my father tell the tale to visitors. A thorn tree existed till a few years ago . . . marking the spot where the head of the army was last seen. I read the paper to a Highland Society in London. At the finish I attempted some physical explanations. I was abruptly arrested by being told that there were still in our midst many who could see things hidden from the normal mortal. 'Vision' is not granted to the Saxon."

The lengthy piece which followed had been signed by Archibald Bell at Inveraray on November 8, 1808, and began by describing how the writer's father and his grandfather, who was then a farmer at nearby Glen Aray, were returning from some business at Glen Shira on a clear and sunny day "in the month of June or July between the years 1746 and 1753". When they reached the Garran Bridge they were surprised to see a vast number of soldiers coming towards them.

"This extraordinary sight, which was wholly unexpected, so much attracted their attention that they stood a considerable time to observe it," Mr Bell wrote. "They then walked slowly on, but stopped now and then, with their eyes constantly fixed on the objects before them. Meantime the army continuing regularly to advance, they counted that it had fifteen or sixteen pairs of colours, and they observed that the men nearest to them were marching upon the road six or seven abreast, or in each line, attended by a number of women and children, both above and below the road, some of whom were carrying tin cans and other implements of cookery, which I am told is customary upon a march. They were clothed in red, and the sun shone so bright that the gleam of their arms, consisting of muskets and bayonets, dazzled their sight : they also observed between Kilmalieu and the Salmon draught an animal resembling a deer or a horse in the middle of a crowd of soldiers who, as they conjectured, were stabbing it or spurring it on with their bayonets.

"My father, who had never seen an army before, naturally put a number of questions to my grandfather (who had served with the Argyllshire Highlanders in assisting to suppress the Rebellion in 1745) concerning the probable route and destination of the army which was now advancing towards them, and the number of which it seemed to consist. My grandfather replied that he supposed it had come from Ireland and had landed in Kintyre and that it was more numerous than the armies on both sides at the battle of Culloden.

"My father having particularly remarked that the rear ranks were continually running forward in order to overtake those who were before them, and inquiring into the reason of that circumstance, my grandfather told him that that was always the case with the rear—that the least obstacle stopped and threw them behind, which necessarily and in a still greater degree retarded the march of those who were behind them, and obliged them to run forward till they gained their own places again, and he therefore advised my father if ever he went into the army, to endeavour if possible to get into the front rank, which always marched with leisure and ease . . .

"My father and grandfather were now come to the thorn bush between the Garran bridge and the gate of the Deer Park, and at the same time the van of the army had advanced very near to that gate, and the front of the army being then directly opposite to them, they had of course a better opportunity of observing it minutely than they had at first done. The vanguard, they then observed, consisted of a party of forty or fifty men, preceded by an officer on foot; at a little distance behind them another officer appeared riding upon a gray dragoon horse; he was the only person they observed on horseback, and from his appearance and station in the march they considered him as the Commander-in-Chief. He had on a gold laced hat, and a blue hussar cloak, with wide open loose sleeves, all lined with red; he also wore boots and spurs; the rest of his dress they could not see . . .

"My father's curiosity being now sufficiently gratified, he thought it was high time to provide for his own security. He represented to my grandfather that it was very probable that these men who were advancing towards them would force them to go along with them, or use them otherwise ill, and he therefore proposed that they should both go out of their way, by climbing over the stone dyke which fences the deer park from the high road . . . To this my grandfather objected, saying that as he was a middle-aged man, and had seen some service, he did not believe they would give any trouble to him, but he told my father as he was a young man and that they might probably take him along with them, he might go out of their way or not as he thought fit.

"Upon this my father leapt instantly over the dyke; he then walked behind it for a little time in the direction of the Garran Bridge, and when he had got about halfway he turned up towards the clumps in the neighbourhood of the bridge . . . But when he arrived near the clumps, he looked back to observe the motions of the army, and whether any person attempted to follow him, but he found to his astonishment that they were all vanished, not a soul of them was to be seen! As soon as he recovered from the surprise which this extraordinary scene had occasioned him, he returned to my grandfather, and cried out, 'What has become of the men?' My grandfather, who seems not to have paid much attention to them after my father left him, then observing that they had all disappeared, answered with an equal degree of astonishment that he could not tell . . .

"They met one Stewart, an old man, who then resided in Glenshiray, going home and driving a horse before him. This, as they believed, was the same animal they had observed before, surrounded by a crowd. My father . . . asked Stewart 'What had become of the people who were travelling with him?' Stewart, not understanding the drift of the question, answered that nobody had been in company with him since he left Inveraray, but that he had never travelled on so very warm a day, that the air was so close and sultry he was hardly able to breathe, and that his horse had become so weak and feeble he was obliged to alight and drive him before him.

"The account I now send you of this vision was not only communicated by my father and grandfather to me, but was also communicated by them to many others in this place and neighbourhood soon after it happened, it being scarcely possible that so extraordinary an occurrence should be long concealed. It is, no doubt, extremely difficult to account for it upon the ordinary principles which regulate human events, but no person acquainted with my father and grandfather ever supposed that either of them was capable of inventing such a story, and accordingly, as far as I can understand, no person to whom they told it ever doubted that they told anything but the truth.

"My grandfather died several years ago; my father only died within these two years, but neither of them saw their vision realised, although, indeed, my father had strong expectations of seeing it a few years before his death, particularly at the time of the Irish Rebellion and of the last threatened invasion by the French. It may perhaps be not improper to add that upon the day on which the vision was seen neither my father nor grandfather had tasted anything stronger than milk, so that whatever was the cause of the impression made upon their imaginations, it could not be owing to any intemperance."

Nearby Inveraray Castle* was also the scene of a martial vision, when the famous doctor Sir William Hart was walking in its grounds with a friend and servant on July 10, 1758. Suddenly he and his companions saw the enactment of a battle in the sky. Men in the uniform of Highlanders appeared to be attacking a fort manned by French soldiers. After a while they were driven off by musket fire leaving a large number of dead behind them.

The vision was independently observed by two ladies on the road to Kilmalieu who rushed to Inveraray with their story. Weeks later news came from Canada that at that date a British force under General James Abercomby with an army of fifteen thousand, including six thousand regulars, had attacked the French fort of Ticonderoga on Lake George, held by the Marquis of Montcalm, and had been forced to withdraw leaving behind one thousand nine hundred and ninety-four killed. In the action the 42nd Regiment of the Black Watch lost half its men and twenty-five officers killed and wounded.

* A more detailed account appeared in *Haunted Castles,* published by Frederick Muller Ltd in 1974.

In October, 1941, *The Scotsman* quoted a strange account from *The Mountain Vision*, a book by the celebrated mountaineer Frank S. Smythe. In it the author described a journey he had made across the Highland hills from Morvich to Loch Duich. Although it was a bright, sun-dappled day, the climber experienced a sensation of something sinister as he entered the defile which led down to Glen Glomach; it was as though the place had once been the scene of some dreadful happening whose horror had returned through some psychic echo.

Mr Smythe was so intrigued by this feeling that he halted and began to have his lunch in the defile, hoping to analyse whatever it was that was oppressing him. Afterwards he lit his pipe, and it was then that he experienced a vision.

"A score or more of ragged people, men, women and children, were struggling through the defile," he wrote. "They appeared very weary, as though they had come a long way. The pitiful procession was in the midst of the defile when all of a sudden from either side concealed men leapt to their feet and, brandishing spears, axes and clubs, rushed down with wild yells on the unfortunates beneath. There was a short fierce struggle, then a horrible massacre. Not one man, woman or child was left alive; the defile was choked with corpses.

"I got out of the place as quickly as I could. Screams seemed to din my ears as I hastened down the broad heather slopes into Glen Glomach. I am not a superstitious person, but it seemed to me that I was vouchsafed a backward glimpse into a bloodstained page of Highland history. I know nothing about the history of that part of Scotland and should be grateful for any information throwing light on what I still believe was a genuine psychical experience."

The author did receive some intriguing but inconclusive information, and he wrote to *The Scotsman*: "In conection with my curious experience which you quoted from my book *The Mountain Vision* . . . it may be of interest that, as I have recently learned, a massacre did take place on the road between Morvich and Glen Glomach either in 1715, when General Wade laid an ambush and slaughtered a number of Highlanders, or in 1745–46 after Culloden. I doubt, however, whether my experience had anything to do with this, as the venue was on the ridge between

Morvich and Glen Glomach, not on the road; also the weapons I saw, or seemed to see, were those of an earlier date."

A supernatural glow is said to appear on the anniversary of the Battle of Killiecrankie where it was fought in Perthshire on July 27, 1689. Then General Mackay with three thousand four hundred troops loyal to William of Orange was defeated by two thousand five hundred Highland Jacobites under the command of Viscount John Graham of Claverhouse, better known as Bonnie Dundee. Prior to the battle a phantom with a bloodstained head had appeared in Dundee's tent, apparently warning him that death lay in wait for him at Killiecrankie.

Next day Dundee seemed reluctant to descend towards the plain of Killiecrankie, and it was only as sunset filled the pass through which the enemy were marching, that he gave the command to charge which ended in victory for the Jacobites. But as he waved on his victorious Highlanders he was struck fatally by a stray musket ball. Some think that the ghostly glow in some way relates to that vivid sunset in whose ruddy light the brief battle was fought.

5

WATER WRAITHS

As the sea is such an integral part of Britain's history, it follows that much of her ghostlore is connected with water. Unfortunately, since sail gave way to steam and steam to diesel many of the old seafaring legends have been forgotten. Where are the spectral ships of yesteryear, the phantom wreckers and the poor drowned sailors who returned from watery graves to unintentionally bring terror to their mates! Somehow super-tankers and atomic-powered submarines seem soulless compared with galleons and clippers. And ships without souls cannot become phantoms.

Only occasionally does one get a hint of modern salt-sea spectres, and such a hint came last year on the BBC Television programme Nationwide which carried a report on a phantom sailor. An old liberty ship was being broken up at a Newcastle breaker's yard when suddenly the workers walked off hurriedly and refused to return for some hours. As the welders had begun to cut the plates of the Second World War veteran, the phantom of an officer in an American uniform had materialised on the deck and caused them understandable consternation. It was surmised that he was the ghost of a man who had seen war service on the old vessel, and had returned to pay it his last respects.

For the best stories of waterborne wraiths we must look to the past—and to our inland waters.

One of the most famous phantom ships to sail the British coast was the *Lady Lovibond* which sank on February 13, 1748, off that ships' graveyard, the Goodwin Sands. Its captain, Simon Peel, had gone cruising with fifty guests, aboard the vessel that

was so dear to his heart, to celebrate his wedding breakfast. What
he did not realise was that the man at the helm, a seaman named
Rivers, was desperately in love with the bride. In a fit of jealousy
he steered the *Lady Lovibond* on to the treacherous sands with
the result that all aboard perished. Since then the wreck of the
Lady Lovibond has been repeated on the anniversary every fifty
years, the last reported sighting of it being towards the end of
the last century.

The Goodwin Sands are the scene of other ghostly happenings.
There is a tradition of a spectral Spanish galleon being driven
up the Channel by a supernatural wind until it hits the sandbank
and breaks up. Perhaps it was a straggler from the doomed
Armada.

On one occasion lifeboatmen set out to help a ship that was
ablaze on the Goodwins. As they drew closer to the wreck it
was clearly seen when the wind lifted the pall of smoke, but soon
afterwards the burning ship vanished before their eyes and,
although they conscientiously patrolled the area, not one scrap
of wreckage was found.

A story similar to that of the *Lady Lovibond* concerns a
phantom ship which used to appear in the Solway. It too had
been wrecked maliciously while a bridal party was abroad, but
its appearances were more sinister than those of the *Lady
Lovibond*. It always materialised close to a ship that was destined
to be wrecked soon afterwards, and one can imagine the horror
with which the old seafarers in that region must have viewed it.
Another Solway Firth apparition is that of a murdered woman
who appears over the water in a halo of flame.

A harbinger of doom was the *Rotterdam* which sank off a
Scottish coast and reappeared to warn ships of impending
disaster. Another phantom, though without any reputation for
being an evil omen, was a ghost lugger which was sometimes
seen off the Lizard.

A black square-rigged sailing ship used to appear off Porth
Curno in Cornwall, when the horizon became blurred with haze,
and was regarded as an omen of evil. There was also a legend of
ghostly vessels sailing into the bay and continuing their unearthly
voyages over the beach and across dry land like silent hovercraft.

A delightful little bay, known as Priest's Cove, is situated between Sennen Cove and Cape Cornwall. It is hard to associate it with the evil that was once committed there, for it was in Priest's Cove that a wrecker used to lure vessels to their doom with his false lights. If any sailors managed to struggle ashore through the surf he killed them in order to cut the rings from their fingers. Evidence of his fearful trade was washed away by the tide. But reckoning came with old age. He was lying on his deathbed; a storm blew up and through the spindrift a black square-rigger, fitted with black sails, was seen to come sailing around Cape Cornwall *against* the gale-force winds.

The ship continued until it was opposite Priest's Cove and then hove to, riding out the storm as though it was on the calmest sea. The wrecker and his family saw it through the windows and realised that it was a ship which had come to take his soul to Hell. Perhaps the terror of seeing the uncanny vessel lying there so calmly amidst the raging seas hastened his end. With a moan he fell back dead and at that instant the vessel turned and disappeared out to sea.

Stories of phantom wreckers used to be common along the coasts of Cornwall and Wales. One concerned a notorious woman wrecker named Madge Figg whose ghost has been seen on Cornish beaches together with the phantom of one of her victims, a lady who managed to swim ashore only to be robbed of her jewels and thrown back into the sea.

A curious legend of a ghost ship is associated with St Ives. One day the port was aroused by the sound of distress rockets and it was seen that a ship was in difficulty. Some fishermen launched their boat and rowed out to the vessel confident that they were approaching a perfectly normal craft. The man in the bows shouted for a line to be thrown down when they pulled alongside. A rope came snaking down but the instant he grasped it the ship vanished. The shaken men returned to port convinced that they had gone to the aid of a phantom but the story had a strange sequel.

Not long afterwards a storm blew up and above the howling of the wind the inhabitants of the port again heard the sound of maroons. This time it was a real ship, the *Neptune* out of London under the command of Captain Grant. To the amazement of the fishermen it was identical to the ship they had seen earlier, but on this occasion it was wrecked at the very spot where they had rowed out and asked for the rope. In some strange way they had glimpsed the future rather than witnessed a spectre from the past.

Another St Ives apparition, known as The Lady and The Lantern, has been seen wandering the beach in search for her child who slipped from her arms while she was being rescued from a sinking ship off the shore. It was believed that to see her pitiful wraith was a warning that a ship would soon be wrecked.

In summertime the Norfolk Broads are so jammed with pleasurecraft that one receives the impression that many people have changed city rush hours for rush hours on water. But when the autumn chill drives tourists away, and the big white cruisers are hauled into the boatyards, the Broads regain something of their wild and mysterious atmosphere. Until this century, and the advent of the internal combustion engine, they had always been a secret place where things happened that were rarely heard of in the outside world. Over ten centuries ago Viking ships, those terrible dragon-headed vessels of war, nosed quietly along the creeks until some hamlet or monastery worthy of plunder was sighted. Then with pagan yells the dreaded White Strangers would leap on to the reed-fringed banks to make a berserk raid. Such a long ship has been seen in phantom form at South Walsham, though in this case some believe it to be the funeral vessel of a Norse chief.

It is a ghost wherry named the *Mayfly* which haunts Oulton Broad, a wherry being a large type of shallow-bottomed barge with a single sail specially used for transporting cargo along these waterways. Once it was a common sight to see their great sails moving as serene as swans above the fringes of rushes. In the middle of the last century the *Mayfly* was regarded as one of the fastest wherries on the Broads. It was captained by a man named Stephenson who, in the past, had a reputation for violence.

One day he was called to the owner's office at Beccles and told that he had to take down to Yarmouth, on the *Mayfly*, a chest containing £4,000—it was considered a safer method of transport than by road. The owner, a Mr Dormey, added that his daughter Millicent would also go as a passenger so that the chest containing the money would look like part of her baggage. The trip began quite calmly with the *Mayfly* sailing sedately along the river Waveney towards Oulton and thence past Somerleyton towards Bredon Water. Aboard the wherry was Stephenson, his mate, a deckhand known as George and a seventeen-year-old youth who acted as cook and roustabout.

As dusk was falling the *Mayfly* approached Bredon Water and Stephenson made up his mind to abscond with the chest of money and his employer's daughter. When he put his plan to the mate the man declared his loyalty to Mr Dormey and declared he would do all in his power to thwart Stephenson's plans. Stephenson got rid of this opposition by knocking the mate overboard. Following this display of determination George seemed willing to throw his lot in with his captain. Millicent, who was asleep below, knew nothing of this drama. By moonrise the wherry had sailed down the Yare, passed Gorleston and headed out into the open sea under full sail.

The unusual motion of the vessel aroused Millicent. She got up to find that she had been abducted along with her father's money, and that Stephenson was endeavouring to sail the shallow-bottomed rivercraft across the North Sea to some foreign port. The boy cook was terrified at the prospect of being on the open sea in such a craft but he was even more terrified of the ruthless captain.

The next night Stephenson, who had been celebrating his takeover with generous amounts of grog, went below to Millicent's cabin. George was aroused by screams and saw the girl appear in a torn nightdress with the drink-infuriated skipper lurching after her. His treatment of her had been rough for she was bleeding from a wound in the neck while he was covered with her blood.

The deckhand went to the help of the girl but Stephenson managed to knock him out. As he threw the limp body into the sea, Millicent found a knife on the deck and stabbed her kidnapper in the heart. Soon afterwards she too collapsed and died on the deck from the wound she had received in the cabin.

The horror of the boy can be imagined. With two corpses for companions he was lost at sea in a wherry he could not handle. In desperation he put some supplies into the *Mayfly*'s dinghy and cast himself off. For a long time he drifted until thirst and starvation caused him to lose consciousness, and next time he awoke he found himself in hospital in Plymouth where he related his terrifying experience.

Three years later on the anniversary of the tragedy the phantom of the *Mayfly* was seen sailing up Oulton Broad at midnight, a phenomenon which for a long time was said to occur annually.

Another cyclic haunting occurs on the Broads at Horning on the river Bure. Here at five year intervals, on July 21, tradition states that, rather like some historical pageant, there is a re-enactment of the coronation of King Ella by the Abbot of St Benet's Abbey. Ella, who was an Angle, became known in history as the Swan of Peace, and appropriately the best vantage point to view the haunting is a little way downstream from the Swan Inn.

Further on downstream is another inn with a reputation for being haunted. The Old Ferry Inn stands on the site of a mead house which belonged to the abbey centuries ago. It was here that some drunken monks raped a local girl who was unlucky enough to walk past when they had sampled too much of their own brew. She died as a result of their violence and they hid her body in the river. Since then the phantom of the victim has made rare appearances close to the pub.

A previous landlord has described the apparition which he saw on September 25, 1936 when he was sitting up at midnight waiting for the return of a late guest.

"I heard a noise, a rustling," he said. "Not three yards from me, in the passage leading to the staircase, was the frail shadowy form of a girl of about twenty-five. She wore a greenish-grey cloak, but it was her face that most attracted my attention. It was beautiful yet deadly white and had a look of suffering."

He tried to speak to her but she glided towards the front door and vanished into the night. The guest, who was taking a late stroll before turning in, corroborated the landlord's story. He said he heard him cry out and the next moment he was aware of the shape of a girl moving past him to disappear into the water.

Canals have become a passion with me ever since I took my

cruiser *Blue Flame* on to the Grand Union some years ago. To cast off her mooring lines is to escape into a more peaceful century as ninety per cent of Britain's canals wind through unspoiled countryside. The silence is only disturbed by the muffled murmur of the cruiser's engine and the occasional lowing of cattle or the cry of wild fowl. My favourite stretch of water is Fenny Pound which runs north from Bletchley through land now becoming known at Milton Keynes. Often I have taken *Blue Flame* to the end of the Pound, through the locks at Stoke Bruene and on through the Blisworth Tunnel which is three thousand and seventy-five yards of utter darkness, and the longest navigable tunnel in Britain. To cruise through it is an eerie sensation. The sound of the engine and the slap of the oily water against the bows echoes on the damp wall, and unless you know beforehand to put your hood up you are drenched at regular intervals by cascades of water coming down from air shafts in the roof. Once in there is no turning back for the tunnel is little more than twelve feet wide and so long that one only has the craft's spotlight to rely on for illumination. In the old days narrow boats used to be "legged" through by men who lay prone on special boards and pushed the vessels through with their feet. This went out of fashion when steam tugs came upon the scene in the middle of last century but such was the amount of soot that they left on the walls and roof of the tunnel that from time to time a tree was dragged through to clear it.

In 1861 the canal steamer *Wasp*, towing a "cutty", sailed into the northern entrance of the tunnel. The crew found that, because of repair works, a wooden-walled channel or "stank" had been built in the centre which was only wide enough for one vessel. The *Wasp* slowed to pick up a carpenter who had finished his shift, and then steamed forward steadily until it met a narrow boat being legged through from the opposite direction. Before the *Wasp* could slow down there was a collision in the darkness which was made worse by the smoke pouring from the steamer's stack. Unfortunately the engineers had fired the boiler a few minutes previously and the smoke was extra dense.

Within a minute the tunnel had become a smoky hell while choking men fought desperately to disentangle their boats. The *Wasp*'s cutty was cast off and the crew attempted to race the steamer to the open air, leaving behind the unfortunate leggers who had passed out with the fumes. One of the *Wasp*'s crew fainted and fell into the water where he was drowned, another died through suffocation while the helmsman collapsed and fell overboard as the boat emerged into daylight. The water revived him so that he was able to clamber back aboard and close down the steam. Then it was found that the carpenter who had hitched a lift was dead, while the two engineers were sprawled by the furnace door which had given them ghastly burns when they fell against it.

I have learned from folk I have met on the canal that the Blisworth tunnel is haunted. People going through have experienced a sickening sensation of suffocation near the Buttermilk Hall airshaft (which was sunk to give extra ventilation after the disaster), and on occasions choking cries have sounded in the darkness there. As these have been heard when only one boat is in the tunnel there can be little doubt that they are echoes from that dreadful day over a century ago.

There are several other hauntings on Britain's canal system. Early this century a narrow boat Number 471 sank in the Moira Cut of the Ashby de la Zouch Canal, drowning the boatman who was inside the cabin. The boat was later raised to the surface and put back into service. But after the new boatman had experienced odd happenings in the cabin where his predecessor had drowned, word got around that No 471 was unlucky and no one would work it, with the result it had to be broken up.

The two hundred-years-old Harecastle Tunnel between Tunstall and Kidsgrove on the Trent and Mersey Canal is now closed to water traffic which may explain why its ghost has not been seen recently, to the relief of narrowboat people. The phantom is that of a murdered woman whose body was dumped in the tunnel. The appearance of the headless apparition used to presage the drowning of someone working on the canal. By a tragic coincidence the tunnel is now connected to the drainage system where the kidnap victim Lesley Whittle was found dead.

The most renowned ghost on the canal system was known as Spring-heeled Jack. He was a Negro who earned his nickname by being able to leap across the fourteen-foot canal at the lock at Cassiobury Park. Jack was in the employment of the local landowner when the canal was first cut, and once it was in operation it amused him to terrorise the boatmen. Being "as black as the very night itself" he boarded moored narrowboats under the cover of darkness and stole the lock keys (or windlasses) which were used to open the sluices. Superstitious canal folk believed it was a ghost which played such tricks upon them until an enraged skipper caught Jack in the act and killed him with his lock key. When an old hollow tree in the park was struck by lightning some years ago it was found to be filled with two hundred of these keys which the Negro had stolen. It is ironical that black Jack, who enjoyed playing at being a ghost, now has the reputation for being a real one. If you are planning a canal holiday make sure that when you reach beautiful Cassiobury Park you keep a wary eye on your lock key.

6

CLASSIC CASES

For a long time Scotland's most famous phantom was that of
Pearlin Jean. It had all the ingredients of a Gothic melodrama—
a blue-hooded seducer, an innocent convent girl and a vengeful
ghost! The story goes back to the 1670's when young Robert
Stuart left his family home of Allanbank, which stood close to
the village of Allanton in Berwickshire, to enjoy what was known
as the "Grand Tour". A "Grand Tour" was a prolonged excursion round Europe which was supposed to finish the education
of young men of quality and also enable them to sow their wild
oats at a discreet distance from their own doorsteps. After visiting
the museums of Italy, Robert Stuart resided for a while in Paris,
the gay city being a revelation after his stern Scottish upbringing.

He lodged in a house overlooking a convent garden where
morning and evening the young novices would stroll for exercise
after their studies and devotions. One in particular caught his
eye because of her large blue eyes and the hint of blonde hair
beneath her severe head-dress. Her name was Jeanne de la Salle
and she was then a romantic fifteen-year-old who, in a fit of
adolescent enthusiasm, had entered the nunnery only to find that,
despite her most earnest prayers, her mind strayed to more
worldly things than the cloisters could provide. When she looked
up and saw above the high wall the face of the handsome Scot
gazing down at her with a devouring expression, she returned his
look with a glance so ardent that his heart must have pounded
with the thought of making such a Freudian conquest.

Soon they were smuggling notes to each other and within a
few weeks Mademoiselle de la Salle caused a scandal at the

convent by running away and becoming the mistress of Robert
Stuart. They took lodgings together and for a few idyllic weeks
all went as happy as a marriage bell with the exception that
marriage was the last thing that Robert had in mind. He knew
that if he was to safeguard his inheritance he would have to
marry as his father, an autocratic old baronet, dictated.

At last the time came for him to return to Scotland but he
could not find the words to break off the relationship with the
passionate young girl who had so trustingly placed herself in
his hands. Men are cowardly when it comes to the thought of
embarrassing scenes and Robert Stuart was no exception. On the
morning of his departure he said nothing to Jeanne but merely
climbed into a coach in moody silence.

Instinctively realising that her lover was abandoning her,
Jeanne de la Salle ran into the street where she loudly implored
him to stay or take her back to Scotland where they could be
married. Robert Stuart cringed at such a public scene and
shouted to the coachman to drive off. At this Jeanne leapt up
on to the carriage with one foot on the hub of a front wheel,
still entreating Robert to change his mind. As he commanded the
perplexed driver to whip up the horses she cried out : "Robert
Stuart, if you marry any woman but me I will come between
you and her to the end of your days !"

The whip cracked, the coach lurched forward and Jeanne was
thrown to the ground, one of the wheels of the carriage passed
over her head and blood dyed the white lace dress which she
wore.

After this embarrassing scandal, Robert no doubt enjoyed a
sense of relief when some weeks later a carriage was bumping
him over a rough Scottish road to his own home of Allanbank.
Allanton would certainly be dull after the life he had known in
Paris, but he felt that here he would get over the shock of seeing
his mistress die as a result of his selfishness.

Autumnal dusk was falling as he beheld the outline of the
house ahead of him but then to his horror, high on the arch of
a gateway, he saw a figure gazing down at him. It was the
apparition of a woman in a white dress but what made Robert
Stuart faint was the sight of her bloody head. Jeanne de la Salle
had returned with him to keep her parting compact. From then

on her pathetic phantom haunted Allanbank. At times a scream —horribly familiar to Robert Stuart—echoed along the passages of the old house. At other times there was the rustle of a silk dress, accompanied by the sound of invisible footsteps.

Frequently Robert Stuart escaped to Edinburgh whereupon the household was left in peace. In 1687 he was created a baronet and he could not neglect the family seat, but whenever he returned the disturbances would start all over again and, for good measure, poltergeist activity accompanied them. During the night invisible hands hurled furniture about and the household would be kept awake by the slamming of doors which earlier had been securely bolted.

The manifestations came to a terrible climax when Sir Robert brought home a wife who appears to have been of a very cool temperament. He had confessed to her his youthful indiscretion which had ended so tragically and she was determined that no "sheeted shadow of the past" was going to stop her becoming Lady Stuart. Seven ministers of the Church of Scotland were called in to perform a ceremony of exorcism. To Sir Robert's dismay their efforts were futile as Pearlin Jean—as the phantom came to be known locally from the pearlin or lace-like material of her dress—increased her persecution of the newly-married couple.

Then remembering the last words that his ertswhile mistress had said to him, Sir Robert had an idea. He engaged an artist to paint a portrait of Jeanne de la Salle from a description he gave him and this was hung in the gallery between a painting of Sir Robert and one of Lady Stuart so that technically she had come between the couple as she promised. This recognition of her status seems to have satisfied the phantom for peace began to reign at Allanbank and continued until one day, to avoid awkward questions being asked by Sir Robert's young family, the portrait was removed to an attic. Almost within minutes the disturbances began again. Perhaps because she wished to defy her ghostly rival, Lady Stuart did not have the portrait returned and Allanbank continued to be one of Scotland's most haunted houses. Even after Sir Robert and his lady had died the phenomena continued. Many were the stories that were told around the district of the activities of Pearlin Jean whose spectre was frequently seen in the house and its grounds.

In the nineteenth century the old house was pulled down and many thought it would be the end of the jilted ghost, but for a long time after it had been reduced to rubble, Pearlin Jean was glimpsed, particularly at dusk, in the gardens where the house had once stood. On one occasion a young man named Thomas Blackadder, waiting in the orchard for a tryst with a servant-girl, went to a figure as it appeared through the trees. Only when it melted before his outstretched arms did he realise he had made a terrible mistake and had tried to embrace Pearlin Jean.

A classic English haunting goes back to an even more unpleasant event than the death of Jeanne de la Salle. It took place at an old Elizabethan manor house known as Littlecote in Wiltshire which is famous for its collection of Cromwellian armour, period panelling, tapestries and carpets while in its grounds there are walled gardens. It is an ironically pleasant setting for the ghastly crime which took place there in 1575.

Its details are known because of a statement a Great Shefford midwife, Mrs Barnes, made to a magistrate, Mr Anthony Bridges, on her deathbed. She related that one night a stranger rode up to her house in the village and told her that her services were required immediately by a lady of quality. Hinting that she would be paid well for her trouble, he said that the confinement must remain a secret, and therefore she would be blindfolded. He mounted his horse and, with Mrs Barnes on a pillion saddle, set off, travelling for about an hour and often going across country. At length the midwife heard the sound of the horse's hooves on the cobblestones of a courtyard, and here she was lifted down and taken into a long dark passage where the blindfold was removed.

The stranger led her up to a chamber where she saw a masked woman in labour lying in a bed. She did not recognise the lady, but, as her professional services were required immediately, she dismissed the strangeness of the situation from her mind.

When the child was born the man seized it from her arms and, despite a shrieked entreaty from the exhausted mother, threw it into the fire where he held it down in the coals with the heel of his riding boot until it was dead. With great presence of mind Mrs Barnes, perhaps realising that at a future date there would be an enquiry into the infanticide, cut a small piece of material from a bed curtain with her scissors. As she was led blindfolded down the stairs from the hateful chamber, she counted the number of steps. It was a large sum of money which kept her silent until she knew she was dying and felt the need to bring about some retribution to the murderer.

After her confession suspicion fell on William Darrell—known locally as Wild Will—of Littlecote Manor. Tradition has it that when the investigation took place a hole was found in the bed hangings into which fitted the piece of material which Mrs Barnes had snipped away. The trial of Darrell was held under Sir John Popham who acquitted him, though rumours were rife that he had been bribed to do so. Certainly it is known that William Darrell made over Littlecote to Sir John in 1586 though he continued to live there until his death.

One flaw in this account is that Sir John Popham was not a judge at the time though he was Attorney-General and it would have been possible for him to have influenced the acquittal. He did become Lord Chief Justice in 1592, and is remembered in history for presiding over the trial of Guy Fawkes. He took possession of Littlecote in 1589 when William Darrell was flung from his horse when riding past a gate which is still known as Darrell's Stile, and which is still haunted by his phantom.

Melodramatic legend asserts that it was the sudden appearance of a child surrounded by flames which caused the horse to shy.

For generations speculation has been rife as to the identity of the unfortunate mother who saw her child immolated. William Darrell earned his nickname through his amorous exploits, and there are several women who would have fitted the role including Ada Darrell, his own sister. One suggestion is that she was the wife of Sir Henry Knyvett, another that she was a Miss Bonham. A letter was found at Longleat towards the end of the last century, dated January 2, 1578, in which Sir John Thynne wrote to Mr Bonham, then staying at Longleat, asking him "to enquire of his sister touching her usage at Will. Darrell's, the birth of her children, how many there were and what became of them;

for that the report of the murder of one of them was increasing foully, and would touch Will. Darell to the quick."

Whoever the tragic mother was, her phantom has returned frequently to the birth chamber. Some of those who have seen it described her as holding an infant in her arms. Other manifestations going back to that terrible night include mysterious bloodstains which appeared on the floor, footsteps made by some invisible person and the echo of agonised shrieking.

In 1927 Sir Edward Wills saw the ghost of a fair-haired woman clothed in what appeared to be a pink nightdress. She was in the passage which led to the Long Gallery and disappeared into a room where his brother slept undisturbed.

Another of England's classic ghosts is the Brown Lady of Raynham Hall who found fame not through any horrific event in her past but because Captain Marryat discharged a pistol at her. Later a photograph was taken which appeared in the December, 1936, issue of *Country Life*. It depicted a shadowy figure on a staircase and has become one of the most often reproduced phantom photographs. Raynham Hall has been described as one of the best houses of its date in Norfolk, being built in the early sixteenth century—possibly by Inigo Jones—for Sir Roger Townshend whose descendants still reside there.

A portrait of the Brown Lady hangs in the house in which she wears a brown brocade dress and a ruff. She is thought to be Dorothy Walpole who was the daughter of Robert Walpole, member of Parliament for Houghton in Norfolk, and the sister of the famous Sir Robert Walpole. Dorothy fell in love with Viscount Charles Townshend, but her father, the guardian of the boy, refused to allow them to marry in case it should be thought he was trying to gain an advantage by marrying his daughter to his ward. Lord Townshend married someone else but became a widower in 1711. Not long afterwards he married his first love Dorothy.

What he did not know was that in the meantime she had become the mistress of a profligate named Lord Wharton who later fled the country leaving behind a mass of debts. Dorothy was twenty-six when she married Lord Townshend who, when he discovered her affair with Wharton, kept her locked in her apartments at Raynham Hall. She died in 1726, some say of a broken heart but the records state smallpox. An even grimmer legend says that she was found with a broken neck at the foot of the grand staircase at Raynham. It is believed that her spirit returns in search of the children her husband parted her from.

One of the Brown Lady's most famous manifestations took place in 1849. A house guest named Major Loftus who, after a long game of chess with a friend, was preparing to go upstairs to his bedroom. As he said goodnight to his fellow chess-player the man pointed to the figure of a woman standing at a door. The men were surprised because of her old-fashioned costume and as they gazed at her she gradually dissolved. On the following night the major saw her again. This time he met her face to face and recounted afterwards that the horrible thing about her was that her eye sockets were empty. He made a sketch of the phantom which he showed to the other guests including Lucia C. Stone who recounted the incident in her book *Rifts in the Veil*.

When the author Captain Marryat was staying at Raynham Hall he asked Lord Townshend to be allowed to sleep in the room which was reputed to be haunted by the Brown Lady, and in which her portrait hung. He was just about to retire to bed when Lord Townshend's two young nephews came to discuss a gun which would be used in a shooting party next morning. The captain said he would like to see it and went with them to their room. A few minutes later they accompanied him along the corridor to the haunted room—joking that they would protect him from the Brown Lady. Suddenly they saw a female figure advancing towards them, and because they were in night attire Marryat and his companions modestly hid behind a door. As she came nearer he realised that he had seen her before—she was the subject of the portrait in his bedroom. She held a lamp which showed that her dress was made of brown material, and as she passed the three men she glanced at them "in such a diabolical manner" that they were terrified.

As he was not the sort of man to take pot shots at house guests, the captain must have known that he was aiming at something not of this world when he pulled the trigger. His bullet went right through the phantom and was later found embedded in a door. The story of Captain Marryat is told in his biography written by his daughter Florence Marryat.

In 1926 Lady Townshend revealed that her son and a friend had seen the celebrated phantom on a staircase, though at the time they knew nothing of her legend but recognised her from the portrait.

The famous picture of the Brown Lady was taken for *Country Life* by Captain Provand who, with his assistant, had taken a photograph of the staircase. Suddenly his assistant Mr Indre Shira called out that he could see an apparition and told Provand to take another shot. The photographer obliged, though he did not see the ghost in the viewfinder. Mr Shira bet him five pounds that it would appear on the photographic plate, and he won his bet. The negative has been examined by experts who have been unable to find any hint of faking, and I believe the original is still in the *Country Life* photographic files.

The Brown Lady is also said to haunt Houghton Hall which stands a few miles away to the north-west, and which was built by Sir Robert Walpole in the early part of the eighteenth century. There is a tradition that when the Prince Regent was sleeping there he awoke to see her ghost and cried: "I will not pass another hour in this accursed house for this night I have seen that which I hope to God I may never see again."

Scotland's most famous haunted mansion stood in an atmospheric Highland setting close to Logierait in Perthshire. So varied and dramatic was the phenomena witnessed there by scores of people that it could be called the Scottish Borley Rectory. To appreciate its bizarre history fully I think it is best to examine it chronologically.

Ballechin House was built in 1806 on an estate which the Steuart family had owned for three centuries. It was erected to replace an old manor house which was demolished once the new building was ready for occupation. The same year Robert Steuart was born and nineteen years later he went to seek his fortune in the militia of the East India Company. In 1850 he retired with the rank of major and returned to Ballechin House which he had inherited from his father in 1834. As he found it was occupied by tenants, he had a small cottage built on the estate where he lived until their lease expired. His neighbours soon began to regard him as an eccentric for, although he was a Protestant, it became obvious that he had picked up some strange religious ideas in the East, one of his main tenets being a belief in the transmigration of souls.

He filled the house with pet dogs whose company he seemed to prefer to that of human beings. He often declared that he would return after death by taking over the body of his favourite black spaniel. One exception to his misanthropy was his pretty housekeeper, Sarah, who died in mysterious circumstances in 1873 at the age of twenty-seven. Tongues of local gossips wagged over the fact that she had not expired in the servants quarters but in the main bedroom of the house.

Next year old Major Robert Steuart followed her to the grave whereupon his relatives arrived at Ballechin House and shot his fourteen dogs, starting with the favourite spaniel. We do not know whether it was because they hated the "smelly pack" or whether they were forestalling any attempt by the deceased to return as he had prophesied.

After he had been buried in Logierait churchyard beside the grave of his housekeeper, his will was read and it was found that Ballechin House had been left to his nephew John, the son of his sister Mary. John adopted the name Steuart and settled down to enjoy Ballechin House and its huge estate. Unlike his uncle he was a devout Roman Catholic (one of his sons became a Jesuit priest), and he converted the cottage his uncle had built on his return from India into a retreat for nuns. Another Roman Catholic member of the Steuart family was the major's sister Isabella who became a nun under the name of Sister Frances. After her death in February in 1880, she was to play a significant role in the haunting which was soon to follow.

The first sign of this haunting came not long after Major Robert Steuart's death. John Steuart's wife was doing her household accounts one day in the old man's study when she suddenly noticed an unpleasant smell of dogs. It took her back to the time when the major's assorted pets had the run of the house. Some doggy people can live quite happily with the smell given off by their four-footed chums but not Mrs Steuart. She was about to open the window when she felt pressure against her legs as though being nudged by an invisible hound. Her experience was followed by various alarming aural manifestations; the sound of knocking echoed along the passages of the house and with it came reports almost like the firing of guns. Another inexplicable aural haunting was the sound of human voices quarrelling though the words were not distinguishable enough to be recognised.

Towards the end of the 1870's these knockings and bangs became worse, and the Steuart children's governess gave in her notice as a result. Father Hayden, a Jesuit priest who often stayed at Ballechin, declared that these sounds seemed to come from out of the air, sounding like continuous explosions which were sometimes so loud he could not make himself heard. He told John Steuart that it was not only knocking which he heard but a high-pitched noise unpleasantly like a scream, and the noise of some creature—could it be a dog?—which hurled itself against his door. When he flung it open there was nothing there.

John Steuart remained tight-lipped about the phenomena and decreed that there should be no investigation of it. Yet he must have been alarmed by it because in 1883 he had a new extension built on to the house so his children would be beyond the zone of disturbance.

In January, 1895, John Steuart was discussing some estate business with his agent in the old major's study when their talk was halted by three inexplicable thuds, rather like the bangs which traditionally open a French play. It has been construed that these three knocks were some sort of omen for, soon after he arrived in London, the master of Ballechin was run over by a cab.

The estate passed to another Steuart who was an army captain. He showed no interest in living there himself and in 1896 let the place, which had over four thousand acres of shoot-in land, to a wealthy family who wished to spend the grouse season there. Having paid a year's rent in advance they moved into Ballechin House to be confronted with the ghostly manifestations about which Captain Steuart had omitted to warn them. Apart from the usual knocking and explosive sounds, one of the daughters of the family was terrified one night when she heard the sounding of limping footsteps circling her bed.

She called out to her brother who came into the room and agreed that there was something invisible moving around her bed. What they did not know at the time was that the girl was sleeping in the room in which the young housekeeper had died twenty-three years before, and that Major Robert Steuart had returned from India with a game leg as a result of his military service.

In the September of 1896 one of the guests at Ballechin House wrote an account of the terrible knockings and screams which were now being heard nightly and of heavy blows delivered on door panels which, when the alarmed occupants threw them open, had no visible explanation. The hauntings reached such a crescendo that after seven weeks the family were happy to quit the house and forfeit the rest of the year's rent.

By now the reputation of Ballechin as a haunted house had begun to spread although it was not always taken seriously. On January 8, 1897, *The Times* published a light-hearted account of the manifestations which provoked a letter from a Mr Saunders who had been the butler at Ballechin House during the ill-fated grouse season in which he averred the truth of the phenomena which had terrified the servants as well as the family.

The Marquis of Bute, who was fascinated by psychical research, seized the opportunity to investigate the house when it became so dramatically vacant. As he was unable to conduct the investigation himself he turned to two famous researchers, Miss A. Goodrich-Freer and Colonel Lenesurier Taylor who organised an investigation for him which was to be one of the most remarkable and painstaking ever conducted in a haunted house.

The marquis put up the money and Colonel Taylor took out a lease on Ballechin House and on February 3, 1897, Miss Goodrich-Freer, accompanied by a number of servants she had hired in Edinburgh, arrived there to take up residence, and to get the place ready for a house-party of thirty-five guests who had been selected because of their ignorance of the house's sinister reputation. The appearance of Ballechin must have lived up to the investigators' expectations. Covered with snow, it had a look of gloom and desolation about it and having been unoccupied for many weeks "felt like a vault", to quote Miss Goodrich-Freer who kept a journal during her stay.

The resolution of these Victorian researchers has to be admired for in the depth of the Scottish winter they were un-deterred by the non-arrival of the stores they had ordered. Miss Goodrich-Freer noted that on the first night her room "was so cold that we had to cover our faces, and we had no bed linen." With Miss Goodrich-Freer was her friend, Constance Moore, a daughter of the chaplain to Queen Victoria. The two ladies did not have to wait long for the manifestation to start. At three o'clock on their first morning there they were awakened by bang-ing sounds echoing along the passage, followed by the mutter of human voices. The next evening they heard another disembodied voice which they wrote had the tone of a priest conducting a service.

Things improved when a supply of food and linen arrived from Edinburgh and they were able to heat the house ready for the house-party. The guests, once they had got over their sur-prise at the hauntings, entered into the spirit of the investigation with a will and their findings were finally published in a book curiously entitled *The Alleged Haunting of B— House.* Now a rare book, it is irritating because it had the Victorian habit of disguising names with initials. In this case initials were used by Miss Goodrich-Freer and the Marquis of Bute after a quarrel with the Steuart family who, perhaps understandably, wished to play down the supernatural aspect of their property. The book was published by George Redway of London in 1899 and gives a detailed account of the phenomena which they classified under audile, tactile and visual.

The book made little impact on the public because of vague-ness caused by the initials. B— House meant very little to the average reader, although on page 82 the name Ballechin slipped past the editor. Perhaps, too, the cautious word "alleged", that eternal safeguard of the journalist, put readers off. Among the instances of the paranormal reported in this book was Miss Goodrich-Freer's description of two phantom nuns she had seen near a frozen stream close to the house. One appeared to be kneeling and crying, the other stood as though comforting her. It was thought that the weeping nun was Major Robert Steuart's sister who had taken the veil as Sister Frances and died in a convent in 1880.

Another visual haunting seen by one of the investigators was a disembodied hand holding a crucifix over his bed, while two of the investigators saw a hump-backed apparition which appeared to float upstairs before dissolving before their eyes. A Ouija board was introduced and an entity who called herself Ishbel wrote a message telling the investigators to go to the spot where Miss Goodrich-Freer had seen the nuns. Her instruction was followed and Miss Goodrich-Freer reported that a figure of a woman in the black habit of a nun was seen moving slowly up a glen.

The most uncanny happening occurred on the night of May 4, 1897, when Miss Goodrich-Freer's Pomeranian, which she had jokingly named Spooks, woke her up with a terrified yelp. Miss Goodrich-Freer lit a candle and saw that Spooks, rigid with fright, was staring at two disembodied black paws which rested on a table-top close to the bed.

'It gave me a sickening sensation," she wrote understandably.

The servants, too, had their share of ghostly visitants. One maid wakened up to see the spectre of a woman in a grey shawl in her room. What made the girl scream and leave Ballechin House the next morning, was the fact that the spectre appeared to be without legs.

In 1932 the Steuart family sold Ballechin House which in 1963 gave up its ghosts under the onslaught of demolition teams.

The foremost haunted house in Sussex is Brede Place which stands close to the village of that name on the A28, a few miles north of Hastings. When I went to visit it I read in a guidebook that this house, built around the middle of the fourteenth century out of Caen stone, was open to the public and was famous for its sculptures by Clare Sheridan and the Brede collection of war posters. But my information was out of date, for when I arrived at the gate I saw an emphatic sign which announced that Brede Place was no longer open.

There is a curious and uncharacteristic legend connected with Brede which goes that a former Lord of Brede Place, Sir Goddard Oxenbridge, was a monster with a particular appetite for the flesh of babies—rather similar to wicked Lord Soulis of

Hermitage Castle. While such creatures as Lord Soulis are quite appropriate in wild Roxburgshire, they were hard to contemplate in the neat countryside of Sussex. According to the tale the local children, tired of his depredations, gave him drink until he was unconscious and then sawed him in half with a wooden saw.

The author Peter Underwood suggests that this story was made up in the eighteenth century when Brede was a centre of smuggling activity in order to frighten away the over-curious.

The real ghosts of Brede Place include a maid who was hanged in the grounds during Elizabethan times, a priest known as Father John, a decapitated phantom who has been photographed and a lady in an old fashioned dress and ruff. The chapel, which is connected to the house, is a particularly haunted area and when the altar there was being restored in the early nineteenth century the bones of a priest were found beneath it. The theory is that they are the mortal remains of Father John, a priest who may have died for his faith during the Catholic persecution.

During the Second World War soldiers were stationed at Brede Place and officers gave accounts of seeing ghostly monks and experiencing furniture being moved by invisible hands.

One of the most pleasant haunted houses I have visited is Wallington which lies a mile south from Cambo in Northumberland. The present house dates from 1688 and is an intriguing stately home now in the care of the National Trust, perhaps what makes it intriguing is that one does not expect to find such a place in the depths of the Northumbrian countryside. It is famous for decorative work by Ruskin as well as for collections of furniture, pictures, porcelain and a room hung with needlework panels which were stitched by a lady of the house in the early eighteenth century.

I was told when I visited it that its haunting takes on the sound of invisible birds' wings beating against the window panes and—far more sinister to me—the sound of heavy breathing. If ever you have picked up the telephone to hear only the respiration of a phone freak, or a burglar casing your flat, you'll know what I mean. Unfortunately, no one seems to know the story behind this mysterious aspiration which has been heard quite frequently. In some way it may be connected with Sir John

Fenwick, the last of his family line, who was executed in 1697 for planning an assassination attempt on William III. The Fenwick family had long owned Wallington, building a Tudor house on to a medieval pele tower.

After Sir John had been executed his famous horse White Sorrel was confiscated and used by the King until one day the horse stumbled on a molehill and threw William who died of his injuries. Thus White Sorrell avenged his master. The way in which the King was killed gave rise to the famous Jacobite toast, "To the little gentleman in black velvet."

Whatever the reason for the phantom breathing of Wallington Hall, there is definitely atmosphere there in keeping with the best traditions of haunted houses.

Another stately home with several ghosts and open to the public is Levens Hall which stands some miles south of Kendal in Westmorland. It is a fine example of an Elizabethan mansion which was converted from a pele tower where the local inhabitants would take refuge against Scottish reivers. The present house was completed around 1586, and its justly famous gardens were laid out at the end of the eighteenth century, one of their features being shrubs sculptured by the shears of clever gardeners into ornamental shapes.

There are several ghosts at Levens; a pink lady who appears only when children are present, a small black dog which materialises so close to visitors' feet that they lose their balance and the Grey Lady who, in the coaching days, was responsible for near accidents by appearing suddenly before the horses. She carries on the tradition today by materialising in front of cars as they go up the driveway to the hall, causing drivers to slam on their brakes in the fear that they are about to run down an old lady. By the time they have wound down their windows to give her some advice on road usage, they find that she has melted away. One of the Bagot family, the owners of the Hall, once cycled straight through her. She is the most interesting ghost at Levens as she is said to have been an old gypsy woman who cursed the family living there.

The story goes that long ago she turned up at the hall begging for bread, but was turned away by a hard-hearted owner. She died of starvation soon afterwards, but just before she died she declared that "no son will inherit the house until the river Kent ceases to flow and the white fawn is born." Strangely the inheritance of Levens Hall has gone from relative to relative rather than from father to son until 1913 when the river Kent froze over and thus technically "ceased to flow", while an albino deer was born in the deer park. With the terms of the curse thus satisfied a member of the Bagot family, Alan Desmond Bagot, did inherit the Hall from his father.

7

BELLS AND DRUMS

Until the advent of the telephone and radio, man was accustomed to receive messages of warning through the sound of bells and drums. They were also his most dramatic expression of sorrow or jubilation, and it is not surprising that some echoes of these instruments have survived through time to reappear as aural hauntings.

Many are the legends along the Welsh and Cornish coasts of bells ringing from submerged steeples of long-drowned towns, a typical one being the Phantom Bells of Aberdovey where, on quiet summer nights, it is said the bells of this sunken realm can still be heard. Legend tells how long ago the maintenance of Aberdovey's sea dykes was the responsibility of Seithenin the Drunkard. Presumably his nickname was correct for one night, when he was carousing, heavy seas smashed the walls he had neglected and the towns and villages they had once protected were inundated.

The tolling of a phantom bell at the village of Elm, near Wisbech in Cambridgeshire, recalls another case of neglect.

Nearly eight centuries ago a certain Brother Ignatius was appointed as watchman when the area was threatened by floods, but he failed to ring the warning bell with the result that several of his brother monks were drowned. Since then he has tolled a death knell when one of the villagers is about to die, though in recent times the bell has only been heard by the wife of the Rector.

A Saxon town at Bomere in Shropshire is said to have been inundated because its wickedness rivalled Sodom and Gomorrah.

A priest, who had correctly prophesied that its end would be as spectacular as those interesting towns, was drowned while tolling a warning. A dam burst, a sign of divine displeasure, submerged the town and it is the priest's phantom which causes the bell to ring beneath the water on Christmas Eve.

Seven miles out to sea in Cardigan Bay there is a group of rocks called Caer Wyddno which mark the spot where the principal city of the lost Lowland Hundred was before the sea claimed it. Here again it is believed that church bells can be heard ringing faintly from beneath the water. Near Blackpool another ghostly chime comes from the church of Kilgrimod which also vanished beneath the waves.

One of the most unlikely places you would expect to find a mermaid is at lonely Rostherne Mere, now a nature reserve in Cheshire. She is supposed to swim along an underground channel from the Mersey to the lake where she rings a bell at dawn on Easter Sunday. The bell, which once belonged to a church, was being transported close to the edge of the water when it broke free from its fastenings. One of the teamsters swore at it and this caused it to roll into the water where it remains waiting for the annual visit of the mermaid.

The bells of Combermere Abbey, also in Cheshire, have a similar story. After the Dissolution they were being ferried across the lake to Wrenbury church when one fell in and from time to time it is tolled by a ghostly hand. Another story from the Dissolution concerns the now starkly ruined Whitby Abbey in Yorkshire. Its bells were sold and were being sent to London by sea when the vessel suddenly became becalmed and inexplicably sank within sight of the abbey. A good omen for lovers is for them to hear the Whitby bells ring a marriage peal on All Saints Eve.

Yet another sub-aqua peal comes from a set of church bells beneath the coastal waters of Forrabury in Cornwall. New bells were being brought by ship for the local church but the profanity of the captain, who overlooked the sacred nature of his cargo, was such that a violent storm blew up and the ship sank with all its crew.

It was an old seaman's legend that the ship's bell rang just before a vessel foundered, even if the clapper was tied. Perhaps there is a link with this belief and the bell which has been heard to echo in the churchyard of St Leven in Cornwall. It chimes out of the grave of one Captain Wetherell who died aboard his ship. It used to be considered an evil omen if a seafaring man should hear eight bells sound from this tomb as it would signify his long "watch" of life was over.

A more pleasant story was told me by the wife of the proprietor of the Old Silent Inn which stands in the heart of the Heathcliffe country, close to the small village of Stanbury in Yorkshire.

"I often hear the sound of bells," Mrs Brogan related. "They seem to tinkle in the distance like fairy bells. When we first came here six years ago I was very worried because I thought something peculiar was happening to me. Then one day a waitress started work here and, as I could hear them tinkling, she asked: 'What are those little bells I can hear ringing?' 'Thank goodness!' I said, 'if you can hear them too it's all right.'"

Mrs Brogan had no explanation for the fairy sound though after she had thought a while she added: "This tinkling does remind me a little of a bell which the previous landlady had. There are wild cats on the moors and this old lady used to feed them. The ringing of the bell was to let them know when their food was ready. Whatever their cause, if they were to stop I'd really miss them."

One would expect the most spectacular bell hauntings to be connected with tolling bells such as Edgar Allan Poe described so graphically in his poem:

> "In the silence of the night,
> How we shiver with a fright,
> At the melancholy menace of their tone!
> For every sound that floats
> From rust within their throats
> Is a groan."

Yet it was nothing more spectacular than the inexplicable ringing of housebells which swept England with speculation in the last century. These bells, common in all homes where servants were employed, appeared to take on a life of their own and, looking back on the phenomenon, it would appear they were activated by a playful poltergeist. It happened at Bealings House in the village of Great Bealings in Suffolk, and the story broke when a long letter appeared in the *Ipswich Journal* of March 1, 1834. It was from Major Edward Moor, F.R.S., a well-known writer on Hindu mythology and an ex-officer in the East India Company's forces who was then living on a special pension for his distinguished services. As people usually tell their own stories best I will quote from his correspondence. He wrote to the editor:

"Sir, A circumstance of unaccountable nature has recently occurred in my house... It commenced on Sunday, the 2nd inst.; and on Tuesday and Wednesday and Thursday following, I drew up an account of it... On 2nd inst. returning from afternoon service I was told the dining room bell had been rung three times, at intervals, between two and five o'clock. At this, the servants left in the house, a man and woman, were surprised; no personal cause being perceptible, though sought... The next day, Monday, the same bell rang four times in the afternoon— the last time within my hearing, shortly after 5 p.m. This too might have passed; for I fancied I could discern a cause sufficient for such an effect, although the room was not in use, and certainly no one was in reach of the bell-pull: but the proceedings of yesterday (Tuesday 4th), I confess, completely baffled me.

"I left home early, and returned before five in the afternoon. I was immediately told that 'all the bells in the kitchen had been ringing violently.' A *peal* at that moment sounded in my ears. I proceeded thither, and learned from the cook that 'the five bells on the right' had, since about three o'clock, been frequently so affected. There are nine bells in a row, about a foot apart, ten feet from the floor, and twelve from the fire but not over it. While I was intently looking at the bells, and listening to the relation that the rings had occurred at intervals of about a quarter of an hour, the same five bells rang violently; so violent was it that I should not have been surprised if they had been shaken from their fastenings. My son was beside me, also watching: he had witnessed one pulled before; and had heard more than one...

"After about ten minutes, I intently watching the while,

another similar phenomenon was witnessed; but we thought not quite so loud as that preceding, and we were in some doubt if more than four bells actually rung. With an accession of observers, we continued watching during another quarter of an hour, when a third peal by the five, occurred; very like those preceding . . . The five bells, whose pealing I have mentioned, are those of the dining room, drawing room over it, an adjacent bedroom— neither of these rooms in use—and two attics over the drawing room . . . During dinner the same five bells rang, perhaps every ten, twelve or fifteen minutes—and continued to do so, with nearly uniform violence, while the servants, six in number, were at dinner in the kitchen; and, with longer intervals until a quarter before eight when the last peal of Tuesday sounded . . . Now, Sir, is this not a strange relation? At the first gentle, single tinkling I was disposed to think I could account for it. But the boisterous clang and agitation of my first witnessed peal of five, one showed its fallacy. You and your readers may be assured that there is no hoax in the matter. I do not mean by me, but by anyone. I am thoroughly convinced that the ringing is by no human agency . . .

"At *this moment*, 11 a.m., Wednesday the 5th comes a peal. I, my son, and grandson in the breakfast room enter a reporter —of the original peal of five, of usual violence—three or four persons in the kitchen—at *this instant*, an interval of three minutes comes another peal like the last. I go to the kitchen. I return and note that three minutes after, I, intently looking, the five rung very violently; again, in four minutes, more violently than ever. One actually struck against the ceiling . . ."

This phenomenon lasted from February 2 to March 27 when the pealing ceased as mysteriously as it began. During this fifty-four day period, the Major went to elaborate precautions to make sure that the pealing of the bells was not the work of some practical joker, and he wrote later in a book on the subject *Bealings Bells*, published in 1841 and now extremely rare: "The bells rang scores of times when no-one was in the passage, or back-house, or house, or grounds, unseen. I have waited in the kitchen, for a repetition of the ringing, with all the servants present—when no one—hardly 'so much as a mouse' could be in concealment. But what matters?—Neither I nor the servants singly or together—nor anyone— be he whom he may came, could or can, however, work the wonderment that I, and more than half a score of others, saw . . ."

He noted that a curious feature of the peals was the violence with which the bells were agitated and found that this could not be duplicated by ringing them from bell pulls in the normal way. His letter in the *Ipswich Journal* caused a considerable amount of correspondence to which Major Moor replied on various occasions, writing once ". . . my answer to some of their queries —that I keep no monkey—that my house is not infested by rats—that the wires of the five, and of the three, *pealers*, are visible in their whole course, from their pull to the bells, save where they go through walls, in which the holes seem no bigger than necessary . . . I have for many years of my life passed over large arcs of the earth's surface, and have seen divers tricks of distant people. If this be one, it surpasses all that I have seen . . ."

The Major also found from his experiments that the bells could not be rung even by tampering with the wires at a point between the bell pull and the bell. He endeavoured to get the effect by pulling down the wires of the five "pealer bells" at a point where they ran parallel along a passage between the kitchen and the back-house. The results showed that if the wires were pulled thus the bells did not ring at all. After the manifestations ceased, the Major wrote his book on the ringing and on thirty similar cases which he had investigated between 1834 and 1841. Among the various accounts is a typical letter from Mrs Mary Castle who described a similar haunting at Stapleton. She wrote : "One afternoon in July, 1836, the bell of one of the sitting rooms was observed to ring loudly several times; no person having touched it. In the course of half an hour the same thing occurred with nearly (if not, every) bell in the house. Sometimes one would ring singly; then three or four together. The wires were distinctly seen to descend, as if pulled violently.

"I sent for the bell hanger, but before he arrived, the noise had ceased. He examined all the wires, without being able to discover any cause for this singular occurrence; and was about to take his leave, as it was growing dusk, when the bells again began its ring more violently than before. One we particularly noticed at this time, belonged to a room immediately over the passage in which the bells hang. It is pulled by drawing up a little slide against the wall; and the wire merely passes through the floor to the hall below. The slide we watched for more than five minutes. It was constantly shaken; even making a rattling noise, and the bell ringing.

"When it had continued about an hour, I desired the bell hanger to take down every bell, as our only chance of passing a quiet night. The maid servants (who as you may imagine, were a good deal alarmed) assured me that the wires continued to shake through the night; but I cannot vouch for the correctness of this statement ... I think it impossible that there could have been any trick, as I assembled all the servants in one place, and had the house thoroughly searched ... We have always supposed it to have been caused by electricity."

The most celebrated case of drum haunting occurred in the seventeenth century and became famous as the "Phantom Drummer of Tedworth" (now Tidworth), although it was a poltergeist rather than a phantom which caused the disturbances. A local magistrate by the name of John Mompesson had brought before him an itinerant drummer, William Drury, who was charged with extorting money. When the magistrate examined his warrant he found it to be forged and sent him before a Justice of the Peace. The mountebank confessed to his crime but asked for the return of his drum which had been confiscated by John Mompesson and held in his house. This request was refused pending a report from a Colonel whom Drury claimed had been his commanding officer. Then the trouble began.

When Mompesson had to make a journey to London his wife was alarmed by violent knocking sounds about the house. When her husband returned these unaccountable noises turned to the sound of drumming. In the beginning the sound seemed to come from outside the house but later it echoed indoors. Frequently the family was kept sleepless for up to five nights consecutively while the drum beat, sometimes recognisable military tattoos and sometimes just a rhythmic beat.

Neighbours frequently came in and heard the phenomenon, and the fame of the Tedworth Drummer spread so far afield that Charles II sent a Commission to investigate. While it was at the manor house the drum remained silent, though it sounded triumphantly once it had left.

The activity of the poltergeist did not remain confined to the beating of a drum. The children of the house were teased by invisible fingers, a family Bible was apported into a fire, beds were fouled when the contents of chamber pots were poured into them or articles such as iron spikes were hidden under the blankets.

On one occasion John Mompesson, probably nearing the end of his tether through sleeplessness and anxiety, cried out : "Satan, if the drummer set thee to work give three knocks and no more." Whereupon he was answered with three loud drumbeats.

During the disturbances William Drury was in Gloucester jail and after being accused of witchcraft he was tried at Sarum, though later acquitted for lack of evidence, despite the fact that he had once declared : "'I have done it, I have plagued him, and he shall never be quiet until he hath made me satisfaction for taking away my drum." Finally he was sentenced to trans-portation for stealing a pig, whereupon the ordeal of the Mompesson family ceased.

Hurstmonceaux Castle in Sussex—which now houses the Royal Observatory—has echoed to the ghostly tattoo of a phantom drummer who was believed to have been one of the followers of Sir Roger de Fiennes, and who was killed on the battlefield of Agincourt in 1415. His activities are underlined by the fact that in the castle there is a chamber known as the Drummer's Hall.

There is an odd postscript to the story when the castle was owned by a certain Lord Dacre. His Lordship, having developed a morbid enthusiasm for the Church, followed the example of early Christian anchorites by hiding himself away in a small cell where he subsisted on bread, water and meditation. Content for the outside world to believe he had died, he thus concentrated on developing the spiritual side of his nature though, understand-ably, his young and pretty wife found life intolerable. So that men would not try to console his "widow", the old man was still worldly enough to beat a drum at night and thus, by pretending to be the Phantom Drummer, sought to scare strangers away. Finally the frustrated young lady locked him in his cell, and the sound of his drumming became fainter and fainter as he starved to death.

Even more sinister is the drumming which heralded the death of members of certain families. Close to Harpham church in Yorkshire, there is a well known as the Drumming Well and when the sound of a roll echoes from its depths, it is supposed to indicate that death will soon take a member of the St Quentin family. According to the legend a squire of that name was presiding at an archery competition when a drummer called Thomas Hewson, while playing his drum, accidentally collided with the squire and fell into the well. Another version is that the Lord of the Manor actually pushed him into the deep shaft in a fit of temper. Unfortunately for the squire the drummer's mother had the powers of a witch and prophesied that whenever St Quentin's descendants were close to their end, her son would sound a ghostly rataplan.

A similar case occurs in Scotland's Cortachy Castle in Angus where the playing of a long-dead drummer heralds death for members of the Airlie family which has owned the castle since 1625. There are at least three legends to explain this, but the most popular is that there was once a very handsome drummer in service there who cuckolded his master the earl. When the affair was discovered, the enraged husband ordered that the drummer be squeezed into his own drum then rolled from the highest turret.

When the earl went to the foot of the wall he found that the youth was still alive though expiring fast. With his final breaths he managed to curse his murderer and his descendants, declaring that his drumming would be the portent of their deaths.

In Buckland Abbey, near Plymouth, Drake's Drum still hangs on one of the walls. In 1581 Sir Francis acquired this thirteenth-century Cistercian monastery from the Glenville family and, according to the well-known tradition, ordered from his deathbed that his drum, which had gone with him on his voyage round the world, should be taken back there. If it was beaten when England was in danger he would return to the aid of his country. The legend altered until it was believed that the drum itself would sound prior to a war, and it was heard to beat prophetically in 1914.

8

HAUNTED VILLAGES

'I curse thy village... May it sink beneath the earth and may men forget its name, may trees grow above thy streets, and grass above thy roof . . ."

So screamed the old woman as she was hustled from the court which had found her guilty of witchcraft in the village of Culbin which once stood close to the Moray Firth. The year was 1697 and witchcraft was the most infamous crime of the day, a crime which in Scotland demanded punishment by stake and faggot.* No doubt the villagers felt uneasy when they heard the curse of the doomed beldame echo about them, but they must have felt more so when a howling wind from the sea stirred up the ashes from her pyre and sent rivers of sand flowing between their dwellings.

For a week the great tempest raged and so much sand was thrown up by sea and wind that the villagers had to flee before they were inundated. When the wind finally dropped and they returned there was little to tell them where their village had once stood. The landscape had changed and what had once been a thriving village was now buried beneath what are known today as the Culbin Sands.

The tale of Culbin and its curse was never quite forgotten as from time to time contrary winds would displace the sand and, for brief periods, skeletal roofs and twisted chimneys would appear before being buried again.

Stories of the reappearances of the village persisted up until

* The last witch to be burnt in Scotland was Janet Horne, who died at the stake in 1727.

109

the Second World War, but now it would seem that Culbin has been laid to rest for ever. Malcolm Macpherson, of the Forestry Commission at Fochabers, Morayshire, told me that the commission took over seven thousand acres in the Moray Firth district in 1920 which included the ever shifting Culbin Sands. The area was planted with trees which are now mature enough to stop the movement of the dunes. So Culbin has gone and its gables will never appear again, but at least in memory it lingers as one of Britain's haunted villages.

Other haunted villages survive and prosper perhaps because they are haunted by spectres rather than curses. The village of Great Leighs in Essex was also connected with a witch. In the days of witchcraft mania she was executed in the village and buried with a stake through her heart in a plot of land known as Scrap Faggot Green. (Scrap Faggot is an old Essex name for a witch.) A boulder was placed over her grave to make sure she remained decently interred.

During the last war there was an American base nearby and, in 1944, a bulldozer removed the boulder from Scrap Faggot Green, now a small triangle of turf where three roads join in a Y junction, so that heavy military trucks could go straight across it. This released the malignant spirit of the witch and she celebrated her freedom by playing the oddest tricks on the village. Apart from the old witch habits of stopping hens laying and cows giving milk, the church bell pealed by itself, hayricks were overturned and frightening things began to occur in the local pub called the St Anne's Castle. Dennis Higginson, its proprietor, described the sort of things which had happened.

"One farmer had quite a few hens and the chap up the road had a lot of ducks," he told me. 'When they got up one morning the chap who owned the hens found he had ducks in his coop while the duck-owner had the hens. Now you might say it was the work of an ordinary practical joker, but have you ever tried to catch dozens of ducks at night without them making any noise?"

The spirit of the witch now seems to centre activities on the pub and Mr Higginson related how a girl once looked into the empty fireplace and gave a scream. Her friend said: 'What on earth's the matter?' She replied: 'Look at that thing in the fireplace!'" Then she collapsed to the floor in a faint.

"There was nothing there that we could see," said Mr Higginson, "but she saw something which was enough to scare her into unconsciousness. She could never say clearly what it was, just a shape like a queer human figure standing in the large fireplace beneath the chimney. Since that day she has never set foot in this place again." Strange manifestations continue to take place there.

Another well-haunted village is Lytchett-Maltravers, situated near Poole in Dorset. Sir John Maltravers, who was involved in the horrific assassination of Edward II, is buried in the church-yard of St Mary the Virgin and it may be that his presence has something to do with the strange subdued voices which are heard at Whispering Corner which lies on a path between the village and the church. Although the invisible speakers seem to be dis-cussing something urgently, no one has been able to pick out the exact words they use. The village also boasts several haunted houses.

Prestbury, which stands just outside Cheltenham, has several active ghosts. At St Mary's church, in the main street, and at the Old Priory, can be seen occasionally a phantom known as the Black Abbot. The lanes round the village sometimes echo to the hooves of a phantom cavalier bringing news of the Battle of Worcester while Cleeve Corner is favoured by a ghostly strangler. More peaceful is the spectre which appears playing the spinet in the garden of Sundial Cottage, and Walnut Cottage is the haunting ground of a character named Old Moses.

Crondall in Hampshire has an odd mixture of ghosts. Phan-tom soldiers in the uniform of Cromwell's Ironsides are said to approach the church on horseback and in Alma Lane the sound of running footsteps are heard. These are believed to have belonged to a murdered courier who was carrying news of Waterloo to his camp at Aldershot. The strangest manifestation here is a phantom flock of sheep which is not only seen from time to time, but whose supernatural bleating is heard throughout the village.

Burford, which stands on the A40 to the west of Witney in Oxfordshire, has been the site of a frightening manifestation which has been described as a dark mist. Should you encounter it, it produces a feeling of panic. But this is only one of the village's mysterious hauntings. Its ancient priory, where a phantom bell is sometimes heard to sound at two hours after midnight, is frequently visited by a monk in a brown habit. A phantom in the clothes of a gamekeeper carrying an old fashioned gun, and moving through anything that bars his path, has been seen by nuns of the Benedictine order who now live there. Poltergeist activity has been reported at the old rectory as well as the sound of screams echoing from an empty room. There is also a monks' cemetery and from here the sound of chanting has been heard.

Perhaps the most pathetic village haunting occurs at Bramber in Sussex where the phantoms of two ragged children haunt the main street at Christmas time. They hold out their emaciated hands as though begging for food, but if you approach them they fade the moment you speak. They are the children of William de Brayose whose family was starved to death in Windsor Castle in 1210 at the order of King John.

The village which is an El Dorado for people with a taste for ghost hunting is Pluckley in Kent and it well deserves its reputation as the most haunted village in England. It is difficult to tell exactly how many ghosts visit it, but the usual number is reckoned to be at about a dozen. Many of these hauntings are connected with the Dering family who were granted an estate there, by Charles II, for their loyalty during the Civil War. The local story is that Lord Dering was given as much land as he could ride his horse around in a day.

A reminder of the Derings is that many of the houses and the village pub, the Black Horse, have windows whose top, instead of being straight, are like inverted "U"s. This goes back to the Civil War when Lord Dering escaped from the Roundheads by diving out of such a window. When he came to build his manor he said that every window should be shaped like this in memory of his escape.

The Black Horse is haunted by a poltergeist which seems to take delight in playing tricks on the staff by apporting various objects, though Mrs Peggy Whiting, the landlady, declares: "There is certainly nothing malicious about it."

The village church of St Nicholas is haunted by the beautiful Lady Dering who died several centuries ago. Her grief-stricken husband had her dressed in her richest attire with a red rose at her breast and placed in three coffins, one fitting inside the other. She was interred in the family vault beneath the Dering Chapel in the church and it is in the churchyard that her phantom has been seen walking, complete with the flower which was the last gift of her lord. Mysterious lights have been reported shining through the stained glass windows of the Dering Chapel from which eerie knocking sounds sometimes issue. The church is also haunted by a woman in modern dress.

Another member of the Dering family haunts the churchyard and is known as the Red Lady. She is believed to be searching for a lost baby. Yet another Dering phantom glides about the ruins of Surrenden Dering and is simply named the White Lady. The manor house was burned down in 1952 but its ghost still revisits the site.

Pluckley's phantom population includes a monk who haunts Rose Farm, close to the church of St Nicholas, and who was last reported in 1971. Two ghosts have been seen near the crossroads to the Blacksmiths Arms. One is of a woman who sold watercress and who accidentally set herself on fire when she went to sleep smoking her old pipe. Although her actual spectre has not been seen for some years, an unearthly glow has been glimpsed after sunset at the spot where she died.

Near the same crossroads—appropriately called Fright Corner—is the stump of an oak tree which must be of particular interest to the schoolchildren who are brought to haunted Pluckley as a special treat. Here a highwayman made his last stand and, as he stood against the tree defending himself, he was run through the body by a sword which embedded itself in the wood. On bright moonlit nights the highwayman's death scene is re-enacted by phantom figures.

In a lane opposite the Black Horse is the site where a school teacher committed suicide about a century and a half ago. His spectral corpse has been seen in an old frock coat, swinging from the tree from which he hanged himself. Another phantom suicide used to be glimpsed in Dering Woods. It was that of a colonel who, like the school teacher, also hanged himself in the eighteenth century, but since the trees have been cut down he has not been seen.

At full moon, if you should visit Pluckley's ruined mill, there is a chance that you may encounter the spectre of a miller who died there. A ghostly soldier still marches through Park Woods, and at Rose Court a spirit calls to her dogs as she did in life. Another aural haunting has been experienced at the brickworks near the railway station where the scream of a workman who fell to his death in a claypit has brought a shudder to passers-by. As if these manifestations were not enough, villagers sometimes hear the rattle of a phantom coach echoing down the High Street.

9

PHANTOMS OF THE ROAD

When one studies the ghostlore of Britain one finds so many references to phantom coaches that one begins to fear the problem of ghostly traffic congestion. The idea of the phantom coach is very evocative—in one's imagination one can picture a dark, funereal vehicle, its great lamps glowing like spectral eyes while on the box, a luminous coachman—or perhaps a skeleton—lashes coal-black headless horses to a frenzy of supernatural speed.

Before the railways spread their ribbons of steel across the country the coach was the most exciting and magnificent thing that most people ever saw. The drivers of crack mail coaches had a glamour which the airline pilots of today might well envy, and the approaching sound of a coach horn could electrify a village in a way never achieved by the roar of a train or the howl of a jet. And if these conveyances, which, prior to the *Rocket*, were the fastest vehicles known on land, aroused the admiration of hamlet-bound country folk, one can guess how the idea of a ghost coach would catch their imaginations. Although the spectral coach is one of my favourite aspects of the paranormal, space considerations prevent me from listing all the coaches that have come up in my researches, and I shall have to content myself by giving some different examples of these unearthly forms of transport.

Sometimes the ghost coach is a harbinger of death. A black coach has been seen to drive to Caister Castle in Norfolk when a member of the Paston family was about to die. It was a huge old vehicle, rather like a hearse in appearance, which rolled up to the castle as fast as the headless driver could urge his team.

It passed through the gates even when they were bolted, and hurtled round the courtyard several times before vanishing in the direction from which it had come. Another decapitated coach driver whips his team up the drive to Langley Castle close to my home in Northumberland. In this case the midnight vehicle is pulled by headless horses, and it is interesting to note how often phantom coaches are associated with headless drivers and animals.

Hatfield House in Hertfordshire, a stately house famous for its association with Elizabeth I, is haunted by a coach pulled by four horses. It must be one of the most spectacular apparitions ever seen. It careers up the long drive to the entrance of the house, passes through the great door and continues up the stairway. One can imagine the consternation which such a visitation would cause. Wolfeton House, in Dorset, also has a spectral coach which has been driven up the grand staircase.

Another coach which goes through a building is the invisible coach of Queen Mary, the wife of William of Orange, which rumbles right through the Royal Castle Hotel at Dartmouth. Mrs Gwyneth Powell, the landlady of the hotel, told me that the phenomenon is signalled by the sound of an outrider galloping in.

"It is followed by the noise of the coach, the opening and closing of its doors and then the rumble of its wheels as it moves off again," she said. This phenomenon has gone on for many years but is never heard before September 12 and never later than November.*

A ghostly coach accident is re-enacted in the Kent village of Grafty Green. Local people told me that in the old coaching days, a coach-and-four departed from the village bound for Lenham late at night. After the driver had whipped up his horses they took fright for some unknown reason and bolted. When the swaying vehicle reached the bend by the local church, the panic stricken animals charged to the right instead of taking the left fork of the road. As a result they galloped up a driveway into the grounds of the old rectory and crashed into a tree.

The impact killed the horses immediately and smashed the

---

* This haunting is reported in detail in *Haunted Inns* published by Frederick Muller in 1973.

coach to pieces. The driver was catapulted from his seat with such force that he was decapitated on the branch of a tree. Villagers still report hearing the sound of the flying hooves followed by the noise of the collision. A local gardener was walking home from the village a few years ago when, passing the old rectory, he heard these sounds followed by the noise of horses in their death-throes and the screams of the dying passengers.

"The man was completely shaken by his experience and said he had never heard anything so horrible in his life," I was told.

Another ghostly coach crash is re-enacted at Rockfield, in Gwent, where at Ancre Hill a spectral vehicle drawn by four horses strikes a wall head-on.

There is a tradition that the defeat of the Spanish Armada was bought with the soul of Sir Francis Drake. As a result of the pact he made with His Satanic Majesty he is doomed to be driven in a black coach over Dartmoor. This legend may be based on the old belief that the Devil used to send a phantom coach to collect souls of sinners who died unrepentant—a door-to-Hell service.

On the same theme there is a tradition at Breckles Hall, in Norfolk, that one George Mace, the leader of a poaching gang, arranged an illicit meeting on the Breckles estate. He planned that the men should split up into small groups and then meet, when the moon went down, at an outhouse near the hall to share out the game. The poachers duly assembled with their sacks of rabbits and birds, but their leader never turned up. They waited for some time until they heard the sound of coach wheels crunching up the drive which led to the main entrance of the hall. What was frightening about it was that it appeared to glow and, as it pulled up in front of the door, its door opened, steps were lowered by invisible hands, and then the spectral vehicle vanished.

The men were in a subdued mood as they went home for they knew that the phantom vehicle had come to claim a victim. Next day they knew why their leader had not shown up and why the coach had called at Breckles Hall. On the spot where they had seen it, the corpse of George Mace had been found. A local author, Dr Jessop, recorded the affair in his book, *Frivola*, in these words : "There was nothing to show what had killed him. There were no marks of violence on the body nor any signs of sudden illness. His time had come, and he had been fetched away by a Power which even the boldest poacher cannot hope to defy."

A double murder which was committed in the eighteenth century would have probably passed into oblivion by now if it were not revived from time to time by the appearance of a black carriage drawn by a team of black horses. The story goes that one day the squire of Oulton House, at Oulton in Suffolk, returned home after a day in the field to find his wife in bed with a dashing army officer. The squire, a man of spirit, behaved in a way typical of those far off days but the officer, a ruthless man, slew the squire and fled, taking his mistress with him. The squire's young daughter was left behind and subsequently she grew up and fell in love with a farmer.

The night before her wedding was to take place the servants at Oulton Hall saw a strange vehicle draw up out of which stepped a veiled woman carrying a bottle. (Later accounts make the story more picturesque by saying she was actually carrying a cup—but I doubt if the finest sprung coaches of those days would have allowed her to travel without the contents slopping over.)

The unfortunate girl was found dead on her bridal morning, and it was concluded that the veiled woman was her mother who had returned with poison to prevent her revealing to her new husband the identity of the man who had murdered her father.

Another sad wedding story is re-enacted at Great Melton in Norfolk, where a phantom coach has been seen in which are sitting four bridesmaids. A legend tells that they were returning from a wedding late one night when they simply vanished, abducted by some unknown agency into the unseen world from which they occasionally fleetingly reappear.

Yet another coach connected with a tragic wedding has been seen at Potter Heigham in Norfolk. The legend—and in this case one is tempted to think it could have been made up from some normal accident by those who like to season their tales with melodrama—occurred in 1742 when Sir Godfrey Hazlitt took Lady Evelyn Carew for his wife at Norwich. This lady had been so anxious to have Sir Godfrey as her husband that she had made an unholy pact with the Devil who, reluctant to wait until her soul should depart this life naturally, sent a coach with the usual four sable horses to her husband's hall at midnight. Ghoulish passengers in the vehicle seized the bride and abducted her. The team was whipped up and the coach rattled in the direction of Potter Heigham. When it reached the bridge over the river Thurne, it struck the wall and tipped over the parapet into the water below, which does not say much for the powers of evil or the efficiency of infernal coachmen. However, that is the story and it is said that on the anniversary of the wedding, May 31, the diabolical vehicle once again makes its fatal journey.

Phantoms of the road are not confined to coaches. There are endless legends of galloping highwaymen and, more unpleasantly, phantom funeral processions. One of these has been seen occasionally at Lyme Park, a National Trust property, in Cheshire. The ghostly cortege is said to have been that which brought home the body of Sir Peter Legh, who was killed in Paris in June, 1422. Eye witnesses who have seen the mournful procession have noted that the coffin is followed by a grieving lady who, though she was not Sir Peter's wife, was in love with him. She died of a broken heart when she heard the news of his death. In Scotland phantom funeral processions are not necessarily re-enactments. To those with the gift of second sight, which seems synonymous with Celtic blood, they are omens to be feared, usually portending a death in the family of the unfortunate observer.

Road phantoms play an important part in our contemporary folklore, one of the most spectacular of these being a ghostly London bus which was reported in the press in the early 1930's as being the reason for a fatal road accident in Kensington. A phantom motor coach has been reported between Lamberhurst and Frant in Sussex and phantom lorries are now part of the modern ghost scene. One of these, on the A7 between Stow and Heriot in Midlothian, is said to swerve off the road in front of oncoming traffic and continue over rough fields as though it was driving on an invisible road. On the A428, between Coventry and Rugby, motorists have been alarmed to see a huge lorry driving without lights and coming straight for them. It dematerialises just before the point of impact but the effect on the unfortunate motorists can be imagined.

The most widely repeated story concerning a road haunting I have heard concerns a driver who picks up a hitch-hiking girl late at night. She sits silently in the car and when he reaches the town which is her destination he decides out of kindness to take her right to her home. She tells him the address of her parents' house but when he pulls up outside the door he finds that the seat beside him is empty.

Puzzled by this, he knocks at the door. A woman appears who, after listening to his story, tells him: "Our daughter was killed in an accident where you picked her up a year ago."

There are so many variations of this modern legend that I have found it impossible to track down the original source, but it does illustrate that even in this technological age we still have some of the credulity which enabled our ancestors to see their spectral coaches speeding along highways in the glow of hellfire.

10

HALLOWED STONES

An idea prevalent in India concerning ghosts is that stone has the property of absorbing certain vibrations given out by human beings, storing them and then releasing them in the form of psychic emanations. Certainly it seems that stone is a catalyst for a lot of ghostly activity. Modern houses made of less solid material have their share of hauntings but these are usually by poltergeists rather than spirits. And when one looks at Britain's amazing array of ghostlore it is obvious that most of it is connected with ancient stone buildings such as churches, castles and houses whose thick walls have survived over the centuries.

Some readers may remember a remarkable ghost play written by Nigel Kneale entitled *The Stone Tape* which BBC television produced as a Christmas entertainment. Its idea, as the name suggests, was that the stones of a building had absorbed a dramatic situation and then "replayed" it at certain intervals.

I have always been intrigued with the story my father told me which, although it did not take place in Britain, illustrates the theory. In the First World War my father, Ronald Alexander, was a trooper in the 7th Queens Own Hussars. After a spell of duty in France his regiment was shipped out to India where he remained until 1920.

"In those days it was very much like Kipling's India," he said, "and the life of a cavalryman was just as it had been described by him."

At one stage he was posted to a small town on the banks of the Jumna. During the day he was occupied with his military duties which included grooming and exercising his white horse, Snow-

121

ball. Once the velvet Indian night fell, bringing welcome relief from the dusty heat, he and some companions would go for walks along the riverbank which, in the almost startling moonlight of India, appeared as though made of solid silver. One night, when he was on such a ramble, his friends sat down in a clearing to enjoy their pipes and he wandered on by himself. In a clearing he found a derelict stone building close to the lonely river. Around it ancient sculptures lay higgledy-piggledy in the long grass. He said there were dancing girls, warriors, concubines, forgotten gods, all carved in grey stone. In the centre of this field of broken images one statue still stood erect upon a pedestal. Carved from the whitest stone, it was a young man holding a sword. My father said that it was not a sinister being with six arms, on the contrary it was rather pleasing. So intrigued was he by this sole survivor that he sat down on a broken column looking up at its face in the blanched light of the moon.

"I remember becoming aware of a feeling of disquiet," he recalled. "Perhaps there were emanations from the forgotten past which were capable of vibrating human nerves. The air was heavy and oppressive without even the friendly twittering of a cricket to break the silence, and gradually I had a mounting fear that the statue was going to come forward towards me with its sword. The sensation that at any moment it would come to life became so intolerable that I stumbled away."

When he told his friends they reacted the way one would expect of young cavalrymen and mercilessly teased him. The story relieved the boredom of the mess and the jokes were endless. To preserve his self respect and prove his point, my father offered to give a month's pay to any of his fellow troopers who could sit alone in front of the statue for ten minutes.

A kind of game developed, he said. Small parties would make nocturnal visits and leave one of its members alone with the stone man, waiting for him out of sight. A stopwatch, usually used for regimental athletic events, was borrowed to time the endurance of the participant. My father never lost his wager, the longest time spent by anyone before fleeing from the statue was six minutes. He said that of course there were all sorts of explanations, such as plain old fashioned auto-suggestion or a trick of the moonlight on the delicate carving which made the features appear to become animated. Yet a month's pay meant a very great deal to soldiers in my father's day, and if the explanation was that simple I am sure that there would have been at least one individual self-willed enough to have lasted the ten minutes. One wonders what emanation it was which made those tough Hussars flee to the protective company of their mates.

I have found that ancient stone places of worship, whether mosque or cathedral, are filled with peaceful—or what one might dare to term holy—atmospheres compared with modern religious edifices which have no more sympatico with the spirit than railway stations. This is particularly noticeable with Continental cathedrals such as Rheims where, uninterrupted by a Dissolution, centuries of daily prayer has been formed within their walls. Again one wonders whether some essence of this past devotion remains to soothe and uplift the present-day worshipper.

English abbeys, many of which have not been used for religious purposes since Henry VIII's great take-over, still retain something of their past atmosphere and make ideal haunting grounds. It is strange, that Westminster Abbey, that pantheon for illustrious British dead, is not the most haunted spot in England. Considering its history, it is remarkably free of ghosts. I once had the privilege of working there with my camera late at night, the reason being that in daytime with the tourists passing through photography is impossible. And what a different atmosphere I found it took on at night, especially when most of the great transept is in darkness and one is working in a little island of light provided by the duty electrician. Everywhere I seemed to be walking over the graves of those whose names fill the history books, and when the great organ suddenly pealed in practice through the darkness making the very air vibrate I could not imagine a better setting for any amount of paranormal drama. I mentioned this to the electrician who told me that some workmen refused to work in the abbey at night because they found the atmosphere too creepy.

"They say that around midnight there are unaccountable rustlings and sounds as though chairs were being dragged over the stone floor though nothing is ever seen to move," he said. I replied that I expected there would be something more dramatic, at least the spectre of a king or two. He told me that if I wanted a dramatic haunting it was to be found at No 20 in the Dean's Yard, a now empty house which belongs to the Abbey. There a disembodied hand has been seen sliding down the banister, though no one knows any explanation for this phenomenon.

The only other definite ghost I have heard of connected with the Abbey is the phantom of a monk which has been seen gliding a few inches above the ancient stone flagstones.

A more typical religious haunting has been reported from the beautiful ruins of Fountains Abbey, in Yorkshire, where after dusk the sound of male chanting has drifted between the ancient columns and over the green velvet lawns which surround them. Phantom voices are also heard in the ruins of Bayham Abbey in Kent. Not only do invisible monks sing sweetly in Latin, but bells chime and on rare occasions a procession of spectral figures is seen winding through the moonlit ruins. A pleasant aspect of Bayham's haunting is that visitors have frequently noticed a smell of incense in the air. Monks have also been seen in abundance at Beaulieu Abbey in Hampshire and they seem to have about them an aura of peace and tranquillity. Here, as at Bayham, the smell of incense has been noticed.

Such ghosts are what one would expect from the backgrounds of such religious establishments, but not all are haunted thus. Other abbeys have had ghosts grafted on to them since the Dissolution when their buildings were put to secular use. In Sussex, Michelham Priory has a fine gatehouse which is the haunt of a Grey Lady who, one would think, does not date from the time when the monks were in residence. Other ghosts have been seen in a room in the main building known as the Tudor Room. It is haunted by a lady wearing Elizabethan clothing and by a most unusual ghost in a black cloak. He has been seen to descend diagonally from the ceiling to the floor opposite an inglenook fireplace. One theory is that this phantom is following the course of a staircase which was removed long ago.

Battle Abbey was built by William the Conqueror as a thanks offering to God for his victory over the English. It stands on the spot where King Harold fell surrounded by his veteran housecarls who defended his body to the last man. Now a picturesque ruin, its supernatural manifestation is unique. A fountain of blood has been seen to spurt skywards on the spot where the high altar used to stand. This strange vision, symbolic of the blood that was spilled on the field of Senlac below the abbey is still witnessed from time to time.

One of Britain's best haunted abbeys is Newstead, the ancestral home of Lord Byron. Its most famous ghost is the Black Friar whom the poet claimed to have seen and whose appearance was an omen of misfortune to any member of the Byron family who saw it. Byron claimed that he saw the figure before his ill-fated marriage with Anne Millbanks, but perhaps this was a piece of chauvinistic bitchery on his part.

Other ghosts at Newstead include Sir John Byron, who was the first owner after Henry VIII had taken the Priory from the Black Canons, and a phantom dog which in life was Lord Byron's beloved Bos'un who was perhaps the most faithful friend the poet ever had. Byron was broken-hearted when his dog died. He buried it in a grave where once the Black Canons' high altar stood, and left instructions that he was to be buried there himself. After his death at Missolonghi in 1874 his body was returned to England from Greece in a ship with black sails and interred against his wishes at Hucknall Torkard in Nottingham.

Since 1946 the seven-centuries-old Bisham Abbey has belonged to the Central Council of Physical Recreation. The abbey, which stands close to the Thames in Berkshire, is haunted by the ghost of Lady Elizabeth Hoby whose remarkable effigy can be seen above her tomb in nearby Bisham Church. According to legend she haunts the site of the abbey symbolically washing her hands in a basin of water in an attempt to atone for the death of her son. The wife of Sir Philip Hoby, she was a close associate of Queen Elizabeth, a brilliant scholar who wrote poetry in Latin and Greek, and as ambitious for her children as she was for herself. Her one disappointment was her youngest son, William. A poor scholar, he infuriated his mother with his blotted writing. One day, when there were more than the usual number of ink blots on the page of his copybook, she lost her temper and gave him a thrashing, after which she locked him in a small cupboard with his hated books, telling him that he would not be released until he had finished his exercises properly. Soon after a messenger arrived at Bisham saying that Her Majesty required Lady Hoby immediately at court. Doubtless scenting some political intrigue, Lady Hoby left her home in great haste and forgot to mention to the servants that William was locked in the closet.

She must have forgotten about the punishment under the pressure of court business—until she returned several days later and found that William had starved to death.

For the rest of her life, until she died in 1609 at the age of ninety-one, she never forgave herself for her neglect, nor it seems, in her afterlife. Her phantom has been seen at the abbey and even photographed, and at night the sounds of an invisible woman weeping have been frequently heard.

A pathetic sequel to the story came about in 1840 when some renovations were being made in the abbey. Ancient boards were taken up and some faded copybooks were found. William Hoby's name was written on them and the pages were filled with his untidy handwriting. The last page of one of the exercise books appeared to be heavily blotted and smudged with tears.

Another death by neglect which has left a ghostly aftermath occurred at Houghton Castle whose towers look across the north Tyne near Chollerton in Northumberland. The history of the haunting goes back to the days when the lord of the castle was Sir John de Widdrington. At that time the Border was a lawless place made worse by the fact that Lord Dacre of Gilsland had been appointed Lord Warden of the Marches. Instead of pacifying the area, he was known to be in league with freebooting families who preyed on their neighbours. The oppressed local gentry asked Sir John to travel to York to acquaint Cardinal Wolsley of the anarchical situation.

Just before he was to begin his journey his followers captured a reiver named Archie Armstrong. He was summarily thrown into a dungeon and Sir John, his head full of the importance of his mission, rode out. It was only when he reached York that he found the key of the dungeon in his pocket. He realised with a thrill of horror the plight of the prisoner, for it was the only key in existence which could unlock the dungeon door. He immediately began the return journey, galloping so fast that by the time he reached Durham one horse had died beneath him. When he finally arrived at the castle his first words were to ask about the prisoner. The retainers answered that for the first two days there had been a lot of shouting heard from behind the thick oaken door but latterly there had been silence.

Sir John ran to the door, turned the lock and found Archie Armstrong sprawled on the floor dead of thirst. As a protest against his untimely end the phantom of the outlaw returned to Houghton Castle and his despairing cries rang again and again to torment the inhabitants and drive away the servants. A minister was called in to exorcise the vengeful spirit. The ceremony appeared to be successful but the Bible which he had used was kept within the castle as a protection against the spirit's return. Later it was found that the leather binding of the book was crumbling away and it was despatched to London for re-binding. Almost immediately the dying screams of Archie Armstrong were heard in the castle. A messenger was despatched to London to bring back the book after which peace was restored.

1. Newstead Abbey, haunted by a phantom Black Monk which was seen by Lord Byron.

2. No. 50 Berkeley Square as it is today. Towards the end of the last century it was a house of particular evil.

3. The bricked up window at Croglin Low Hall—the large window has been added since the haunting.

4. Calgarth Hall, close to Lake Windermere, where two skulls frequently reappeared to revenge themselves on the wicked magistrate who had brought about their downfall in life.

5. The skull of Theophilus Brome which refuses to be removed from Higher Farm at Chilton Cantello.

6. Sedgemoor Battlefield, still haunted by ghostly rebels, as it appears today.

7. Burgh Castle in Norfolk. From these ramparts unseen hands hurl a white-draped body which vanishes when it reaches the ground.

8. The Culloden Monument by which the ghost of a battle-weary Highlander has materialised.

9. Wallington Hall, in Northumberland, which is haunted by a sound of heavy breathing.

10. The Pass of Killiecrankie where royal troops marched to their defeat by the Highlanders, and where a phantom glow recalls the battle of 1689.

11. Haunted Blisworth Tunnel on the Grand Union Canal.

12. The Black Horse, at heavily haunted Pluckley in Kent, showing examples of the 'Dering windows'. Among the village's numerous paranormal visitants is a poltergeist which plays tricks at this inn.

13. Caister Castle where a ghostly black coach was an omen of death.

14. Hatfield House where a phantom coach drives up to the entrance in front of the clock tower. (Photograph by Simon Alexander)

15. Mist-shrouded Langley Castle in Northumberland is the destination of a spectral coach.

16. No. 20 Dean's Yard, by Westminster Abbey, which is haunted by a disembodied hand.

17. Fountains Abbey, Yorkshire, where ghostly chanting mingles with the dusk.

18. Michelham Priory, Sussex, whose ghosts include a descending man.

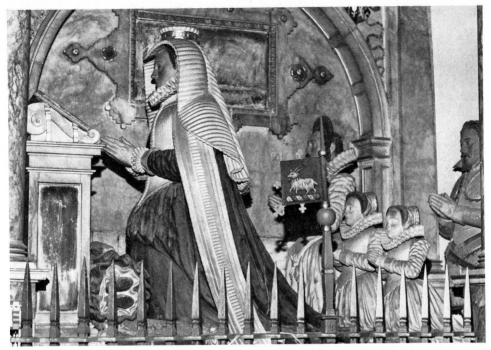

19. The effigy of Lady Elizabeth Hoby at Bisham Church in Berkshire. Her ghost is seen at nearby Bisham Abbey wringing its hands in remorse over the death of her son.

20. Houghton Castle, on the banks of the North Tyne, was haunted by a prisoner who was accidentally starved to death.

21. All Saints Church, Renwick, where a cockatrice was killed with a rowan branch.

In MEMORY OF
John Arundel Radford
(RECTOR OF THIS PARISH)
Who died 28th May 1867,
Aged 63 Years.
AND OF
Thomasine Elizabeth
(HIS WIFE)
Who Died 12th March 1850,
Aged 63 years.

22. Tombstone of a homicidal vicar whose ghost is still peeved at his burial place in Lapford churchyard.

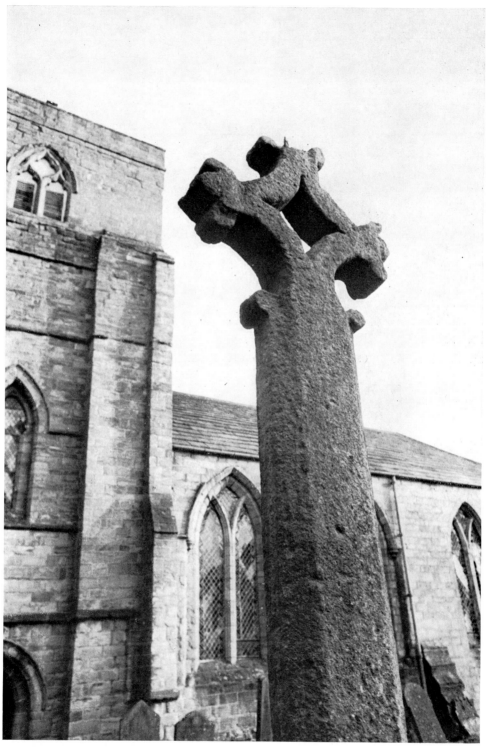

23. This ancient cross marks the burial place of massacred monks at Blanchland
Church.

24. Farnham Parish Church which has been the scene of a ghostly mass.

25. The Greyhound Inn haunted by a mysterious female figure.

26. Mrs Connie Biggs with the witch ball which inspired her experience of a forgotten tragedy.

27. 408 Strand where the author heard the ghostly footsteps of a suicide.

28. The entrance to the Cloisters at Hurley. This Quadrangle was once a monks burial ground and something in its atmosphere causes it to be shunned by birds.

29. The Citadel Restaurant, Carlisle, which is the haunt of a mysterious Grey
Lady.

30. Castle Acre was once the scene of a massive exorcism by a dozen clergymen, in which the ghost played a prominent part.

31. Ghostly footsteps of a Victorian lawyer sound late at night at the Wig and Pen Club.

32. Sandford Orcas Manor House, complete with leering gargoyles. Among its amazing array of phantoms is one which leaves behind it the stench of decomposing flesh.

33. The beginning of the Lairig Ghru Pass, in the Cairngorms, which passes beneath the bulk of Ben MacDhui, and which itself is strangely haunted.

34. The Rufus Stone in the New Forest glade where William II was "shot off with an arrow", and where his restless spirit has been seen to return.

35. Castle Rising, in Norfolk, where the demented ghost of Queen Isabella has been seen walking the ramparts.

36. Blickling Hall, in Norfolk, where the phantom of Anne Boleyn returns dramatically in a spectral coach.

37. Effigy of the Black Prince in Canterbury Cathedral. His ghost returns to Hall Place in Kent.

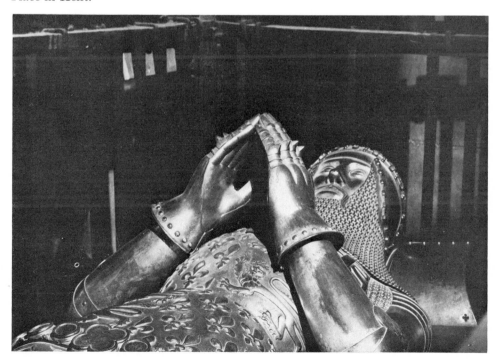

38. Asterly Castle in Warwickshire was once the home of Lady Jane Grey but was haunted by her scheming father Henry Grey, Duke of Suffolk.

39. St. James's Palace haunted by the victim of a royal scandal.

40. The woods at Aylmerton which sometimes echo with cries which come from the mysterious "shrieking pits".

41. The Eldson Gibbet which marks an area haunted by an outdoor spirit known as the Brown Man of the Moors.

42. Sandwood Bay, at Cape Wrath, where the phantom of a seaman has been seen walking over the sand before vanishing.

43. The ruin of Sandwood House, overlooking Sandwood Loch at Cape Wrath, which has echoed to ghostly footfalls and where lonely travellers have experienced more frightening manifestations.

44. The remains of Bramber Castle in Sussex. It was once the home of the children who now haunt Bramber Village.

II

HOLY GHOSTS

Britain is rich in haunted churches, a great many of whose phantoms are believed to date from the Dissolution and appear as priests, monks or nuns earthbound until the True Faith should be re-established. I find it hard to accept that any particular happening in history should produce a larger crop of ghosts than any other, and sceptics can be excused their criticism of paranormal phenomena when it appears to be partisan. Cases of apparitions being tagged with religious or political motives are common, just as some vague spirits are given the identity of important historical personages because they happen to haunt an appropriate area or because it fits in with the wishful thinking of propagandists. (It is interesting to note how often such ghosts belong to a losing side; nothing lingers on as romantically as a lost cause.) This, of course, in no way diminishes the genuineness of the apparition itself.

A simple example of this occurred when some people were convinced that St Nectan—who in the early days of English Christianity miraculously picked up his head after he was decapitated—had appeared at Hartland parish church near Bideford in Devon. The Reverend Harold Lockyear, rector of St Nectan's church, told me: "I momentarily saw a monk in the church aisle about six years ago. The story got abroad that he was our patron saint, St Nectan. Obviously it was impossible to say yes or no to this. To me it was a common or garden monk in a black habit. I was not, one, deluded nor, two, had I been drinking at the time."

Now let us look at churches with more unusual hauntings, and one of the foremost of these is York's Holy Trinity. It has been well-known for its phantoms ever since the Reverend Sabine Baring-Gould, the author of "Onward Christian Soldiers", chronicled eye-witness accounts of its supernatural activity in his *Yorkshire Oddities and Incidents* published in 1874. An unusual feature of the church is that today your attention is drawn to its ghostly reputation by a notice on its information board.

Holy Trinity stands at Micklegate on the site of an earlier church which in the year 1100 was donated by one Ralph Pagnel to the Benedictine Abbey of Marmoutier in France, and which remained under monastic control until the Dissolution. A legend, such as I have just mentioned, purports to give a background to the haunting. When the agents of Henry VIII arrived to take possession of a convent attached to the church on December 11, 1539, the abbess tried to prevent them entering with the threat that they would only do so "over her dead body". Her serene determination goaded the soldiers of the party to frenzy and, after wounding her mortally, they burst into the establishment. The martyred nun just had time to gasp that her spirit would return to the scene of her murder until the authority of the Pope was recognised again, before her eyes glazed in death.

Typical of quite a few "hauntings" which began as a result of Henry VIII's anti-Papal policies, it has no historical basis. On the contrary, it is known that the last Mother Superior of the convent lived out her life peacefully in a house close to Holy Trinity, which she bequeathed to the poor after her death. Nor do any of the three ghosts reported in the church resemble a nun.

A letter quoted in Sabine Baring-Gould's book described the appearance of a phantom in the church thus:

YORK, *March 28th*, 1874.

"Sir,

"Owing to severe illness in my family, I was not able to reply to your note earlier. I will now try and tell you what I have seen of the ghosts at Holy Trinity Church, Micklegate.

"A York lady, now dead, told me she remembered seeing it when a child, and that she once read an account of it in an old History of York: she thought the book must have been published in the seventeenth century . . .

'As I have no faith in ghosts, I have been most wishful to have the matter cleared up. At present I cannot account for the appearance in any way.

"I went many times to the gallery in hopes of seeing the phenomenon, but was repeatedly disappointed. At last, one dull day, hopeless for the purpose as I thought—rain was falling at the time—I was startled by seeing something.

"There are two east windows—one on the right, filled with common green glass, the organ in front of it. From the outside of this window I saw something move, and immediately the graceful figure of a girl of eighteen or twenty years crossed the outside of the stained east window with a light, free step. She was entirely covered with a fine lace veil which, as she walked and met the air, showed the outline of the head and figure; the features I could not distinguish, but could see a shade through the veil where they naturally would be.

"The veil was of a pure white, flowing back as a train as she walked. In two or three minutes the figure returned, the robe flowing back in the same way, and disappeared behind the organ window . . ."

One of the most detailed reports of the Holy Trinity haunting appeared in the columns of *The Chronicle* of May 6, 1876, by a writer who signed himself by the initials H.G.F.T. The widespread—almost familiar—knowledge and acceptance of the church's supernatural elements can be gathered from his opening: "On Good Friday last I went to Holy Trinity Church, York for morning service, at eleven o'clock, and repaired with a friend to the gallery, being anxious to see a certain apparition which is said to haunt the place.

"The gallery is situated at the extreme west end of the building, and faces the east window, from which it is distant some sixty feet or so. It is said that in the aisle and body of the church nothing is ever seen. The gallery was full, but no one seemed to have come there especially for the ghost and though many of them afterwards said they saw it, they were not in the least affected by the apparition, treating it as a matter of course, to which they were well accustomed."

The correspondent continued that although he kept his eyes

fixed on the east window for the hour-and-a-half service, and although others claimed to have seen something, he saw nothing abnormal and left the church believing himself to be the victim of a hoax. But as so many of his friends assured him that they saw the phenomenon every Sunday, he decided to try again. He went to an Easter Day service and half way through it his eyes "which had hardly once moved from the left or north side of the window, were attracted by a bright light formed like a female robed and hooded passing from north to south with a rapid gliding motion outside the Church, apparently at some distance."

H.G.F.T. went on to describe the apparition as being transparent "yet thick [if such a term can be used] with light. It did not resemble linen, for instance, but was far brighter and would no doubt have been dazzling to a near observer."

When the figure passed out of sight, a friend whispered to him it would return, and in five miuutes it did, gliding back the way it had come.

Half an hour later the phantom appeared yet again outside the Gothic window, passing from north to south. It then returned with the figure of a young child before vanishing in front of the last pane but one of the window. The correspondent continued : "I did not see the child again, but a few seconds afterwards the woman re-appeared, and completed the passage, behind the last pane, very rapidly. Nothing more was seen during the service . . .

"It cannot be a reflection on the principle of Peppers' Ghost, which is produced by the figure actually being in a very strong light and appearing reflected on glass in a darkish spot. The lights both inside and outside the church at York, which might be thought to produce the ghost, are precisely the reverse, and any figure required to be produced by reflection on the east window would have to be standing or walking in the centre of the aisle.

"For the above facts I can vouch, and I have no reason to believe that the following are either incorrect or exaggerated.

"It is said to appear very frequently on Trinity Sunday, and to bring two other figures on to the scene, another female, called the nurse, and the child. It is often seen as distinctly on a dark, rainy, or snowy day, as when the sun is shining. When I saw it the sun was not bright.

"The motion is even, not at all jerky. Sometimes it glides swiftly; at other times slowly. It cannot be a mere accidental reflection, from a door or a window, for instance, for the figure faces different ways, according to the direction in which it is going; and it is not always alone, nor do the figures always act in consort.

"One of my friends, with a companion, has watched outside on the wall, where he had a full view of the whole place around, during morning service. The ghost has been seen from the inside, while outside nothing was visible.

"It is said to have haunted the church for 150, 200 and some authorities say 300 years."

When these ghosts were frequently seen the explanation for their appearance went back to an outbreak of plague in York two centuries earlier. Then a child and her nursemaid died of the disease and were buried outside the city walls in a plague pit. The child's mother survived the pestilence, and when she died she was buried normally in the Holy Trinity Churchyard. Here her spirit returned to wait for the phantom nursemaid to bring her daughter to her for a tragically brief reunion before parting until, in some mysterious way, the scene was acted out again.

If you should visit Holy Trinity you will find the church altered since the time when the appearances were commonplace, the east window is not the one through which the nurse and child were seen, and it is not in the same position. After the building of the present chancel in 1886, a critic wrote: "When the restoration of the church took place, the ghost scooted. I cannot blame it. No phantom, with any pretensions to respectability, could have taken any other course."

And yet . . .

From John Mitchell, who is working on a book about the ghosts of York, I learned that there may still be something odd about Holy Trinity. In 1951 a local schoolteacher was showing a friend who was a keen historian round the ancient churches of the city. It was evening when the two ladies reached Holy Trinity and while her friend explored the building, the teacher went to the west end of the church and loitered at the spot where H.G.F.T. sat eighty one years earlier.

The temperature about her suddenly dropped and her surroundings changed to what she described as "earthy and cold, a very charnel house atmosphere of death and decay". It was not until seven years later that she learned of the church's haunted reputation.

The most intriguing haunting of a church that I have encountered took place at the small Cumbrian village of Renwick where, as at York's Holy Trinity, a notice admits a supernatural connection. Among the usual parish announcements pinned on a board inside the door is one guaranteed to catch the imagination with its typewritten heading: "Why the Inhabitants of the Village are called Renwick Bats".

Well away from any highway, on a road which AA map legends dismiss as "other tarred", Renwick nevertheless has an ancient history, having been an important settlement long before the advent of the tribes from Northern Europe. The fells surrounding it were rich in minerals, and it was a defence centre for Celtic hamlets when the Picts and Scots came raiding from the north, and for this reason the centre of the village is still called The Castle. It is the last village before the ascent of the old Hartside Track over the Pennines and its name was derived from Raven's Wick, meaning a wick or vyke (the Anglo-Saxon word for a settlement) on the Raven river which formed the parish boundary.

Renwick's manor, first in the hands of the Staveley family, dates back to 1124. It was later bestowed by Edward III to Robert Eaglesfield, Queen Philippa's confessor, who settled it on his college, Queen's College, Oxford, which has held it since 1341. The church, dedicated to All Saints, and which owes its original foundations to Celtic missionaries in the sixth century, was originally rectoral, but later appropriated to St Mary's, York, and Hexham Abbey. As the centuries went by it gradually fell into decay and when Bishop Nicholson visited it in 1725 he found the chancel 'without floor or glass", and as a result of his inspection it was decided to rebuild it in 1733.

As workmen from the village were demolishing the old building a monster, described as a Cockatrice, flew out and attacked them from the exposed foundations. What interested me was that it should be recognised as a Cockatrice, a creature which in the Middle Ages was believed to be a four-legged cock with a crown, great thorny pinions and a serpent's tail which ended in a hook. It was said to have a deadly gaze, Chaucer writing that it "sleeth folk by the venim of his sighte".

The appearance of this creature not unnaturally terrified the men who all fled except one John Tallantire, who armed with the branch of a rowan tree, fought the monster and destroyed it. "For this act his estate was enfranchised to him and his heirs forever," states the church record.

It is interesting to note that John Tallantire used a piece of rowan wood for a weapon, which is known in some districts as the Witch Tree because of its power of averting the evil eye, goblins and witchcraft. The Druids used its berries in their magical rituals and throughout Britain rowan wood has been used in various ways to prevent ill luck, sometimes being incorporated in agricultural implements, thatched roofs and babies' cradles, and also whips which controlled restive horses. A Yorkshire doggerel went :

> If your whipstock's made of rowan,
> You may ride your nag through any town.

Perhaps it was very lucky for John Tallantire that a rowan tree was handy when the great black creature suddenly rose up before the startled villagers. The surprising thing is that such ancient beliefs should reappear as a factual occurrence in the eighteenth century which ushered in the Age of Reason.

The Reverend J. M. Allen, in whose parish All Saints stands, told me that the story has frequently been repeated to him by local people, but neither he nor I have been able to trace any of the enfranchised descendants of John Tallantire.

The description of the monster as a cockatrice may have been poetic exaggeration at the time, and over the years it has become known as a bat, hence the epithet of "Renwick Bats". This may also be partly due to the connotation that our English bats have innocently gained with vampires, due mainly to the habits of the South American vampire bat and the association that Bram Stoker gave them with Count Dracula. It is an interesting point that one of the nearest villages to Renwick is Croglin where, at

Croglin Low Hall a vampire described as a "tall spindly fellow in a curious cloak" attacked Amelia Cranswell exactly a hundred years ago.

Whatever the thing was that gave rise to the Renwick legend —and legends never seem to come about by themselves—it has refused to stay decently dead. In *Ghosts of the Lake Countries*, published in 1972, Gerald Findler wrote : ". . . records show that since then, even as recently as ten years ago, people say they have seen an enormous black bird-like figure flying around Renwick on certain evenings."

A somewhat similar church-haunting began at West Drayton near Uxbridge in 1749 when a sinister knocking was heard by late passers-by, usually on Friday nights. One theory for the noises was that a murder victim and the murderer, who had afterwards committed suicide, had both been interred in the same vault, and there was psychic disturbance because of this proximity. Soon a different story was being circulated. Three men living close to the church were alarmed one night to hear screams coming from the direction of the building. They hurried over and, following the unearthly sound, finally peered through a grating of one of the vaults. They leapt back as what appeared to be an enormous black bird flew up to the ironwork and tried to peck their faces, the screams continuing as it flapped its sable pinions.

At first it was thought to be a real bird, most probably a raven, which had somehow entered the vault, but the story received a new twist when the men reported its presence to the Parish Clerk. He replied calmly that the ill-omened bird was a phantom which he, his wife and daughter had seen sometimes in the vaults and at others in the chancel of the church.

A little while later a young man saw the bird in the church and ran to tell some bell-ringers who seized sticks and, entering the body of the church, began chasing it as it fluttered over the pews. One managed to give it a blow which knocked it into a corner where it lay screaming. Thinking that he had finally caught a real bird which had given rise to such strange rumours, the bell-ringer bent forward to grab it when it dissolved before his eyes and those of his companions.

The bird was seen on quite a few occasions after that, sometimes perched on the communion rail or flapping about the vaults. The last report of its appearance came in 1869—over a century after it was first seen!—when two ladies arranging flowers in the church saw its eerie shape hunched on a pew back.

In 1883 Mrs de Burgh, the wife of the Reverend R. L. de Burgh who was a former rector of the church, told the Reverend F. G. Lee, a well-known writer on psychic matters in his day, that she had frequently heard fluttering sounds, such as a large bird would make, in the chancel of the church. A Mrs White, whose family lived in the West Drayton area, told the doctor that "the country folk always believed that the Spectral Bird which haunted Drayton Church was the restless and miserable spirit of a murderer who had committed suicide and who, through family influence, instead of being put into a pit or hole with a stake through his body at the crossroad at Harmondsworth, as was the sentence by law, had been buried in consecrated ground". Thus the two versions of the haunting were neatly connected.

I was filled with curiosity as early one bright Sunday morning I followed the A377 north-west from Exeter towards Lapford. I was going to seek out a particular tombstone in the old churchyard—a tombstone which I had been told marked the grave of a murderer whose resentful ghost would not allow it to stand upright.

When my car was parked, its sleek yellow modernity so out of place in the shadow of the lych-gate, I entered the churchyard and found that practically every tombstone was askew. I had never seen such a wildly-angled collection of weathered stone memorials before except in old Hollywood Frankenstein and Dracula films which as a child had filled me with delightful terror. Indeed, should any film director be seeking a location for such Gothic stories I suggest he lead his camera crew straight to Lapford.

But I did find the stone cross I sought, "In Memory of John Arundel Radford, Rector of this Parish", and it turned out to be about the only erect gravestone there. Perhaps the ghost kept the stone upright as an act of protest!

If my information had been wrong, the story behind the stone was still fascinating. Around the 1860's a curate attached to Lapford Church was killed by the rector who was duly charged with murder. At this trial the jury failed to convict him, it was said because they could not bring themselves to hang a parson, and he continued his duties at the church for several years.

Before he died he declared that he wanted to be buried in the chancel of the church, and that if this instruction was not carried out his ghost would return and haunt the village. However, because of the scandal attached to him, it was decided, after his death, to bury him outside by the door of the vestry, and since then his phantom has kept its word and has been seen prowling about the village.

Probably it does not worry the good people of Lapford very much, as their village has a much more ancient haunting to its credit. Two days after Christmas a spectral rider is supposed to gallop through at the midnight hour, and for some strange reason it was believed that this horseman was Thomas à Becket who was assassinated at Canterbury Cathedral on December 29, 1170. Why he should wish to ride through the village two days before the anniversary of his death is as mysterious as the origin of the story of the crooked tombstone.

"Old Calverley, old Calverley, I have thee by the ears,
I'll cut thee into collops, unless thee appears."

This couplet used to be chanted by boys who, holding hands, stamped in a circle round a pile of their caps in Calverley churchyard in Yorkshire. When they tired of this they threw a "magical mixture" of pins and crumbs on the ground, after which the bravest would go to the church door and whistle through the keyhole in order to summon up the church's ghost.

There is a story that on one occasion the phantom obliged, and the boys fled in panic leaving their caps behind them. Knowing the ability of children to set themselves into a state of delicious panic, I would not place too much credence on that story. I remember how, when I was at school in Poverty Bay, New Zealand, the cry of "White Mouse" would cause us to bolt as though pursued by demons, though what White Mouse was

—except that he or it was supposed to be in some way connected with an abandoned house—I do not know. Yet White Mouse was implanted in our childish traditions just as Old Calverley was with the boys who fearfully tried to raise him from the dead.

The story behind old Calverley is a bloody one, and his ghost haunted two churches as well as Calverley Hall and its surroundings.

Walter Calverley, whose father had been a rich man, had a reputation for recklessness which may have reflected a streak of insanity from his mother's side of the family. His natural instability was heightened by the imagined infidelity of his wife (in fact a most virtuous lady if old accounts are to be believed), and nagging money worries.

Everything came to a head on April 23, 1604, when the balance of his mind finally went and he ran amok, killing two of his children with a knife and attempting to murder his wife, who was saved by the blade striking her corset. Thinking her dead, he leapt on to a horse and galloped in the direction of Norton with the intention of slaying his remaining son Henry. Luckily for Henry, Calverley's horse threw him and he was arrested, and taken to York where he was put on trial.

It seems that sanity—and with it remorse—returned to him when he appeared before the judge because he refused to plead, despite the fact that a terrible fate awaited him if he did not. In those grim days the penalty for refusing to plead either guilty or not guilty was known as *peine forte et dure*, which meant death by pressure of weights. Sometimes men preferred this because if they did not plead they could not be found guilty, and therefore their children could not be disinherited and their estates taken by the Crown.

Calverley met his end under a great weight of stones in York Castle, and there is a legend that one of his old retainers tried to hasten his death and was hanged for his compassion. The body of the murderer was then buried at St Mary's churchyard in York which soon gained the reputation of being haunted by Calverley's restless phantom.

After some time rumours spread that his friends secretly disinterred the remains and translated them to the churchyard at Calverley so that his shattered bones could rest by his old home.

In turn Calverley churchyard became haunted, as did the countryside around. There were wild stories told of Calverley appearing as a ghostly rider—perhaps re-enacting his desperate ride towards Norton—and so troublesome was it that the local priest was called upon to exorcise him, though with little success it seems. On other occasions the spectral rider was seen at the head of a band of mounted phantoms which began its wild chase from Calverley churchyard. Once the church bell pealed at one o'clock in the morning, and when the alarmed villagers went to investigate they found that no human hands were hauling the bellrope. Naturally they blamed Walter Calverley.

Calverley Hall, too, received the attentions of the ghost. At the close of the eighteenth century the Reverend Richard Burdsall stayed the night there before preaching in Calverley Church the following day, and he left an account of how he had been awoken by the feeling of an intolerable weight on his chest, after which he was hurled from his bed three times.

"This was about one o'clock," he wrote. "I now put on my clothes, not attempting to lie down any more. I was afterwards told that this very house had been the residence of Calverley, who, in the reign of King James, was tried at York for the murder of his wife and two children and, standing neuter, was pressed to death in the Castle."

Beautifully preserved Blanchland village, which was originally a Premonstratensian Abbey dissolved in 1539, has a church at one end and an ancient stone bridge spanning the Derwent River at the other. It is over this bridge that one passes from Northumberland into Durham and up the steep slope of the Derwent Valley. On the left hand side of the path leading to the church door is a famous thirteenth century cross which marks the mass grave of monks massacred during a raid by Scottish reivers.

It is recorded that a large party of these raiders set out to plunder the Abbey of "Blancalande"—"White Land" after the white wool habits of the monks—and they followed an old drovers' track over the Hexhamshire Common which was its only link with the outside world. Suddenly a thick fog blanketed the landscape and the Scots lost their way to the relief of the monks who had learned that the raiding party was heading in their direction. Seeing the mist as divine intervention, the White Monks sent their bells pealing a Te Deum of gratitude.

It was an ill-conceived thanksgiving as the marauders were able to follow the boom of the bells to the vapour-shrouded abbey where they soon put the monks to the sword. It was a long-held tradition in Blanchland that on the anniversary of the massacre the church bells tolled by themselves and the shadowy figures of the slaughtered monks were seen in the graveyard close to their time-worn cross.

It is also believed that on certain nights the phantom of the murdered abbot can be seen walking over the high arch of the ancient Blanchland bridge.

Next to the church stands the Lord Crew Arms, once the Abbot's Lodging but now one of the pleasantest hotels I know, which is also haunted. In this case the ghost, who usually manifests herself around September, was the Jacobite heroine Dorothy Forster.*

By the time this book is published I believe that Britain's church phantoms will be reduced by one, for by then an embalmed corpse which for centuries has been an object of morbid interest at the London church of St James's will have received Christian burial. The site its restless spirit has haunted stands at the bottom of Garlick Hill, just round the corner from Mansion House Underground Station where a church has stood since the Norman Conquest. The present one was rebuilt by Christopher Wren after the Great Fire of London in 1666.

For those interested in church architecture St James's has a structurally separate chancel, which is an unusual feature in City churches, a graceful spire which rises to one hundred and twenty-five feet and its interior is illuminated by light coming through so many windows that it was nicknamed "Wren's Lantern"—hardly the dark and sinister setting where traditionally ghosts are expected to lurk.

Six medieval London mayors are buried there, but its strangest interment was that of the mummified body of a young man which was discovered beneath the chancel before the Great Fire.

* This story is dealt with in detail in *Haunted Inns*, published by Frederick Muller in 1973.

Who he was—how he got there and how long he had been there, were questions that nobody could answer. Regarded as a curiosity, the body was placed in a glass-panelled coffin, and though the old church was burnt down the mysterious mummy survived. In Wren's new church it was kept on display in the vestibule.

Nick-named "Jimmy the Mummy" or "Jimmy Garlick", it was a macabre attraction to visitors, though it would seem that the spirit of the unknown cadaver resented this treatment of his embalmed remains.

Frequently his shrouded ghost has been glimpsed in the church, the most famous occasion being when the son of an American tourist looked up to the gallery and beheld a figure wrapped in a winding sheet and with its arms crossed over its skinny chest, gazing down at him. It was exactly like the withered corpse the boy had been gaping at a few minutes earlier in the vestibule. The terrified youth screamed and fled into the street.

At other times the ghost has been blamed for inexplicable sounds which have echoed through St James's, and the mischievous apporting of various church objects.

When I went to Garlick Hill to photograph Jimmy the Mummy I found that I was too late. The Rector of St James's, Prebendary D. C. Mossman, O.B.E., told me that it had been decided to give the body a decent burial, and until that took place it had been locked away. Once the burial service has been read over him and he is no longer an object of fun for tourists, I have the feeling that this phantom will cease to haunt St James's—his five-centuries-old protest will be over.

OTHER HAUNTED CHURCHES

ALL SAINTS, *Crondall, Hampshire*: Haunted by a shadowy figure of a Parliamentarian soldier who was believed to have been killed in a skirmish there during the Civil War.

ALL SAINTS, *Faringdon, Berkshire* : At dusk a headless man has been seen walking in the graveyard. A local legend says that he was beheaded during the Civil War.

ASHOVER CHURCH, *Derbyshire* : The churchyard used to be haunted by a headless woman, thought to be the wife of one John Towndrow who murdered his wife and decapitated her before committing suicide in 1841.

AVENBURY CHURCH, *Herefordshire* : From 1919 onwards the sound of ghostly music has been heard echoing from the church when it was locked and deserted. When people have gone to the church to investigate the music fades away and the building is found to be empty.

BURNLEY PARISH CHURCH, *Lancashire* : Legend says that this church was haunted by a spectral dog, but he may have long faded away. The Bishop of Burnley wrote to me that "as far as I know Burnley Parish Church is not haunted. But then I may be taking a partial view because I'm told ghosts tend to disappear when I am around."

CAISTER CHURCH, *Lincolnshire* : Haunted by a monk who enjoys playing the church organ. Some of his music was tape recorded in 1967.

DIGBY CHURCH, *Lincolnshire* : Haunted by an apparition riding a pony. A curious legend says that if you run round a certain grave there the clatter of crockery will be heard within the tomb.

ELLESBOROUGH CHURCH, *Buckinghamshire* : Occasionally a tall phantom in medieval clothing has been seen to glide across the church to one of the memorial tablets before vanishing.

FARNHAM CHURCH, *Surrey*: Haunted by the sound of chanting and the phantom of an old lady. Several people have experienced a vision there which would suggest the celebration of a High Mass being performed as it would have been in pre-Reformation days.

MANNGINTON CHURCH, *Norfolk*: Once the haunting place of a phantom lady whose tomb had been destroyed, and who appeared to be distraughtedly searching for it.

MINSDEN CHAPEL, *near Hitchin in Hertfordshire*: Now an ancient ruin, it has ghostly manifestations on All Hallows Eve (November 1), which start with ethereal music, the music being followed by the appearance of a monk.

ROCHE CHAPEL, *near St Austell in Cornwall*: A ruined fifteenth century chapel where the sounds of an invisible person moving about have been heard and a quickly moving shape has been observed, perhaps the ghost of a Cornish miner.

ST BARTHOLOMEW-THE-GREAT, *London*: Haunted by the footsteps and figure of Rahere, the churchman who suffered malarial fever on a pilgrimage and who, as an act of thanksgiving began the building of St Bartholomew's Hospital and St Bartholomew's Church in 1123.

ST DUNSTAN'S CHURCH, *East Acton, London*: Has been haunted by processions of ghostly monks in brown habits. At various times the haunting of St Dunstan's has had a great deal of publicity and many people have testified to seeing the monks, including a *Daily Graphic* journalist. Harry Price the famous psychic investigator was very interested in the church and believed that the monks appeared at four-yearly intervals.

St Giles, *Camberwell High Street, London* : Haunted by the spectre of an old priest who was last seen in 1971 walking in a churchyard passage which adjoins the church.

St John's Church, *Torquay, Devonshire* : Haunted by the phantom of an organist whose appearances were so frequent he once held up choir rehearsals. He is thought to be the hymn-composer Henry Ditton-Newman who died in 1883, and one theory for his manifestations is that he was writing a piece of music which, because of his death, remained unfinished. According to one tradition the organ played of its own accord at his funeral.

St Magnus The Martyr, *London* : Haunted by the cowled figure which has been frequently seen and who is believed to be either a former priest of the church or Miles Coverdale, the translator of the Bible who was buried there in 1568.

St Mary's Church, *Twickenham* : Said to be haunted by the ghost of Alexander Pope since 1830 when the poet's grave was desecrated and his skull removed. The figure has not been seen recently, but its limping footsteps are still heard.

St Michael and all Angels, *Rycote in Oxfordshire* : Haunted by a Grey Lady, who glides from one of the pews and disappears into a stone wall. She has been seen several times in this decade. (This chapel is unusual in that it is under the care of the Department of the Environment.)

St Michael's Church, *Highworth in Wiltshire* : Here a ghostly figure was reported about sixty-five years ago and was last reported in 1970. The alarming feature about the phantom is its lack of features—where there should be a face there is just a "grey blank".

St Michael's Parish Church, *Linlithgow in West Lothian*: Here, in 1513, a phantom wearing a blue robe appeared to James IV of Scotland to warn him that he would be vanquished at Flodden Field.

———

Weare Gifford Church, *Devonshire*: Haunted by a tall phantom who approaches the church door before vanishing. Some say he is Sir Walter Giffard, who died in the thirteenth century, searching for his lost wife.

IN THEIR OWN EXPERIENCE

Most people know someone who knows someone else who knows somebody who has had contact with the supernatural; it is far rarer to know someone who has come face-to-face with a ghost. Because of my researches I have met more than my share of people with first-hand stories of such experiences. They cover a wide spectrum of the supernatural and in this chapter I am passing on some of these accounts. They have not been published before and come from people whose integrity I trust.

I count myself lucky in numbering among my friends the Reverend Dr Donald Omand, a retired Anglican priest, who is an internationally famous exorcist. Over the past four decades he has performed hundreds of casting-out ceremonies, which have been so successful that his services are constantly in demand by doctors and psychiatrists who have patients whose disturbed states can only be attributed to demoniacal possession.

Dr Omand's first exorcism occurred in Germany in the early 1930's when the ringmaster of a circus begged him to exorcise a lion into which he believed an evil force had entered. The normally gentle animal had suddenly gone berserk and mauled its trainer to death. Before he was hardly aware of what was happening Dr Omand found himself inside a cage with the enraged lion, instinctively intoning the words of exorcism. Even as he spoke the lion quietened and became docile, much to the amazement of the horrified spectators.

This proved to Dr Omand what he had suspected for some time, namely that he had the power of exorcism. It was also the cause of him becoming a circus priest, for he found that although most circus folk are deeply religious, no one took any interest in their spiritual needs at that time. His duties have included the baptism of babies born to circus families, arranging for other priests, when they came into their districts, to visit circuses and the annual blessing of animals. Over the years many press pictures have appeared of him performing this ceremony in front of lions and tigers.

Dr Omand comes from the Orkneys where his mother had the gift of second sight, and perhaps it is some inherited sensitivity which has made him so successful as an exorcist. It has also had the effect of making him very aware of the ghost world and to a man who has spent so much of his life dealing with the spirits of evil, ordinary ghosts are almost mundane to him. To sit in his home at Offwell in Devon and hear him recount his experiences with the supernatural is a fascinating experience, and recently he told me the following story.

"During the last war, between periods in the forces, I spent an intervening period living in London," he said. "During that time I served in the City of Westminster Civil Defence through the London Blitz. I was then living at 33 Longridge Road in Earls Court, having the lower half of the house which had been divided into two maisonettes. I was very friendly with an old Anglican clergyman by the name of Braine who often came to call on me. Among other things he acted as chaplain up at Kingston House where our headquarters were located in what was originally intended to be the garage underneath.

"One day when I was down in the kitchen, the bell rang and I went up to the ground floor which included a beautiful front room which had once been a very palatial drawing room. At the front door I found my friend.

" 'Somebody going to a fancy dress ball?' he asked.

" 'I'm not,' I said, for I had been doing some cooking, or trying to.

" 'Not you,' he said. 'In your front room there, a lady there nodded to me.'

"I said : 'What lady?'

" 'The lady who is going to the ball . . .'

" 'What ball? What lady?' I asked.

" 'The lady dressed as Portia.'

148

" 'Here, you'd better come with me,' I said. We went into the room but there was nobody there.

" 'That's very strange,' he said. 'She was at this window. And she smiled at me. She was dressed as Portia.'

"He had been on the stage many years before, and he knew quite a lot about Shakespeare.

" 'I couldn't be mistaken—it's Portia,' he protested.

" 'You must have imagined it,' I replied, and no more was said about the matter.

"And then one day as I went to that room I suddenly sensed something very pleasant. I thought for a moment that I saw a feminine figure, but very shadowy—just for a second and then it was gone. I began to think of what my friend had said, but this did not look like Portia, it looked more like a lady dressed in clothes worn in the time of Queen Victoria. I never saw anything again but once or twice after that I sensed that there was some-one in the place ... it was a subject I knew something about, and I knew that such things could be.

"A little later someone I knew in Kensington said : 'I read something very interesting about where you live. I'll show you it.' And next time we met he lent me one of the *Ego* books by James Agate. And the interesting thing was that Agate mentioned that when he was a child he used to get pleasure out of going to 33 Longridge Road to meet Ellen Terry. He described how she used to talk to him and take him into the back garden where she had a hammock suspended between two trees. And in that front drawing room, where she loved to sit, she told him about her theatrical experiences, particularly in Shakespeare.

"This absolutely astounded me. And perhaps it stimulated my imagination and I realised that this was the lady my friend had seen as Portia, because after that—although I never saw her—I was conscious of Ellen Terry as an everyday companion.

"Then the time came for me to leave, but before doing so something happened which infuriated me. Two men turned up and began to cut down those trees in the garden. I rushed to the house agent and I told him they were Ellen Terry's trees.

" 'I don't care whose trees they are,' he said. 'They're going to be cut down.'

"Then I found out what was likely to happen to the property, and I thought, 'Poor Ellen—she'd hate all this.' So I did what I would never have done otherwise, because she was happy there and she made it happy for everybody. Before leaving I released her spirit from the house."

Another friend of mine, and a business partner of many years' standing, has the habit of saying goodnight to a phantom every time he leaves his office at 50 High Street in Eton.

Derrick Baker could never be accused of being over-imaginative, the magazines he publishes deal with technology and electronics and his favourite pastime is following the career of his racehorse. Towards the end of 1973 the lease of his City office ran out and he decided to move to Eton. In December he visited the house at 50 High Street with the idea of buying it. Built in 1420 and originally part of a large banqueting hall, its timber frame structure is an essential part of the traditional architecture of the town. It was then owned by a Mrs Lowson who, after showing him over the building offered him a drink in the chapel-beamed upstairs lounge. While they were discussing the possibility of a purchase, the door of the room (which had been closed on a latch) suddenly opened as though by an unseen hand. My friend looked surprised but Mrs Lowson informed him quite nonchalantly that the "pretty ghost" had come to "look him over", and Mrs Lawson hoped that she was satisfied with the prospective owner.

The pretty ghost walks through the house and has been seen on regular occasions at the Cockpit Restaurant, which is on one side of the house, and in the antique shop on the other. Mrs Lowson's experiences with her had always occurred on the stairs which were added to the house in the seventeenth century. She claimed that she had actually talked with the ghost although she never had any response, and described her as being extremely beautiful and dressed in blue clothes as would befit a seventeenth century lady of quality.

Although Derrick Baker's company has moved into the house, the reception rooms have retained their old world character, decorated with antiques and always with an open fire burning. It seems the phantom appreciates the fact that the whole of the building has not been turned over to typewriters and layout tables because Derrick believes he has got on to more familiar terms with his spectral tenant. I asked him how he knew this and he replied that now he has a tremendous but inexplicable feeling of well-being whenever he climbs the stairs and sits in the upstairs room, though he is still looking forward to actually seeing the lady who has brought happiness to the house. He has two dogs, a yellow labrador and a long-haired mongrel, who always come to the office with him. To begin with they both refused to climb the stairs however much they were coaxed, but now Derrick finds that they have either accepted the ghost or more likely she has accepted them for they now go up and down the stairs without any qualms.

The presence of the phantom at 50 High Street, Eton, has become so much a part of life there that when Derrick leaves after a day's work he always says, "Goodnight, Pretty Lady," as he closes the ancient door behind him.

As a result of some articles on the supernatural which appeared in a newspaper, I received a considerable amount of correspondence from people who believed that they had experienced a psychic happening and wanted to tell someone about it without the danger of ridicule. These correspondents fell mainly into two categories; people who had seen some vague shape or figure or those who had experienced poltergeist activity. A more startling incident was related to me by Mrs M. Power who lived in Morayshire. She explained that at Easter in 1973 she went to visit her mother whom she had not seen for eleven years and who was to have her ninetieth birthday that year. Mrs Power's father had been dead for just one year.

"Several times I had noticed Mother gazing into the fire and while she did this she wasn't aware of anything going on around her," Mrs Power wrote. "One evening she said, 'I often go to see your Father and we talk about all of you.' "

Mrs Power put down this statement to her Mother's mind wandering because of her age and thought no more about it. A few days later she took her mother to her great-granddaughter's birthday party.

"During the afternoon photos were taken of the children with an instant camera," Mrs Power continued. "My nephew said he would take a photograph of Mother. He tried quite a few times but the camera just would not work. He said he would try one more time and it worked fine." When he took the photograph out of the Polaroid camera and they looked at it, Mrs Power described it as "awful".

"Mum's hat and coat were clear, so was the outline of the chair but there was no face or hands!"

Mrs Power had noticed that when the picture was taken her mother was gazing into the fire just as she did when in her mind she thought she was back with her husband.

"I told my nephew to wait a while then take another photograph of Mother. This time it came out perfectly but she was not gazing into the fire on this occasion. When we got back to Mother's house she said, 'Your father thinks you smoke too much.' I asked her how she knew and she said, 'He told me so this afternoon.' "

A more traditional experience was related by Mrs V. Gerrard who lives in Northenden, Manchester. She said that the first home that she and her husband shared in the late 1940's was the attic of a very old house at Chorlton-cum-Hardy, situated close to the convent and the church of St Clements.

"To say it was dilapidated was to put it mildly," said Mrs Gerrard. "The floors were riddled with woodworm, and in one room, the rent in the roof revealed the sky and was not to be considered as a bedroom in wet days, however we were desperate . . .

"One day I was washing up at the sink when I realised that somebody was standing in the open doorway behind me. I turned quickly just in time to see a man in robes disappear. I ran to the door wondering how he had got up the stairs so quietly and what he wanted. Nobody was there—not a sign that anyone had been there. I put it down to a trick of the light as it was an old house with plenty of shadows.

"Some weeks later, exactly at the same time and in more or less similar circumstances, the robed figure again stood in the open doorway, only this time I had a definite feeling of fear. Again the figure disappeared but this time I ran downstairs and knocked at a neighbour's door. 'Good gracious, have you seen a ghost?' she asked. 'You look scared.' I explained that I thought

I'd seen somebody lurking in my flat so she came up and helped me investigate. I did not tell her that I had seen a 'robed figure' but let her think it might have been a prowler.

"Nothing further happened to me and shortly afterwards we moved to a ground-floor flat in the same building which was an improvement on the attic. The young couple who took over the attic were delighted with some improvements that we had made and said how pleased they were to have found it. But they only stayed a short time, leaving after the girl had woken her husband up one night screaming. They never said *why* they moved almost within a day.

"Four years later I was speaking to a lady in the house next door when she asked me if I knew I lived in a 'haunted house'. By then I had almost forgotten my experience and asked her 'What is it supposed to be haunted by?'

"She answered that the building was once used as a religious retreat where monks frequently came and stayed. On one night two of these brothers quarrelled so bitterly that one murdered the other, hiding the body under a flagstone in the cellar.

" 'A monk is supposed to be seen wandering about from time to time,' my neighbour told me. 'I don't know anybody who has actually seen him, but that's the story.'

"I said nothing about my experience but I will always remember that house. At the time of my experience I tried hard to explain it away as a trick of the light, from the peculiar position of the windows. One doesn't think of ghosts in the middle of a bright sunny day when one has just come in from work. But for a fraction of time a robed figure did stand in the doorway and a sensation of fear was projected, and I had the awful feeling it was deliberately and maliciously intended."

A friend of mine, Mrs Nancy Newberry, once told me how on an occasion when her mother and father were courting they were interrupted by the sounds of a phantom horse. Later I met Nancy's mother, Mrs Langstone, and she told me that the experience had occurred on a summer evening forty-four years ago near Hemel Hempstead.

"We were standing by a gate in a road near the turning of a narrow lane," she explained. "Suddenly we heard the clip clop of a horse's hooves coming up the road. It got closer and closer until it sounded as though it was level with us, then it began to fade as though it was going away, but still we could see no sign of the horse or rider. My husband looked in the fields on either side of the empty road but there was no living thing to be seen in any direction. We were completely mystified and left with an uncanny feeling.

"Suddenly we remembered the story of the young woman who had been murdered there. She was a local girl who had been to fetch milk from a farm when a young man rode up on a horse and attacked her. It was said that he got away and left England never to return, but as a result of the killing the lane earned its name of Murder Lane."

It is an interesting speculation as to whether certain events can generate a psychic power which is absorbed into inanimate objects, to remain there until some catalytic effect recalls the original impression. An example of this seems to have happened in the case of Mrs Connie Biggs of Streatham.

"My daughter was passing through Torquay when she saw a witchball in a secondhand shop," she related. "Knowing I had always wanted one she bought it for me as a present. According to an inscription on the metal at its apex it had been made in France in 1721. I was so delighted that I put it on a table by my bed so that I would have the pleasure of seeing it when I woke up in the morning.

"I went to sleep quite normally but after some time I was suddenly conscious that I was in a glade in some woods. Lying on the grass was a dead soldier, his fair hair blowing in the breeze. He was dressed like an officer in white breeches and a blue tunic. I was filled with a sense of desperate sorrow because I knew he was my husband.

"The vision or hallucination was so real that I could feel the texture of the clothes I was wearing, a green dress of soft wool and a greenish brown cape. Nearby in some scrub his chestnut horse was standing having carried him from a battle. I could not see any sign of blood or a wound, but he may have been shot in the back.

"Suddenly another officer galloped up in a similar uniform.

He was riding a white horse and, when he saw me, he reined up and cried 'You must get away! They are coming!' I did not want to leave, I just shook my head. Again he told me to flee, then spurred his horse and rode off.

"Then I woke in a terrible state and found myself gazing straight at the witchball beside my bed. It was 4.45 in the morning. I lay there with tears streaming from my eyes still feeling the shock of seeing my husband dead. I can't explain why but I just knew it had happened in the year 1745, the year of the Jacobite uprising. In some way I do not understand the witchball had taken me back through time. Perhaps in the past it had belonged to a woman whose soldier husband had been killed in the way I had seen and it had reflected the sorrow from her to me down through the ages."

It is well known in the dreaming Thames-side village of Hurley that uncanny things happen at The Cloisters. As the name suggests, they surround the quadrangle of an old Benedictine monastery beside the Church of St Mary the Virgin. What was once the refectory of the Priory of St Mary has now been converted into flats, and it is here that supernatural manifestations frequently take place. It is thought that the pleasant garden between The Cloisters and the church was once a burial ground for monks, and that this has something to do with the haunting. People living there have noticed a curious thing about it—no birds ever alight there. It seems that the most tempting worm will not induce them to fly down from the surrounding roofs.

Mrs Vera Wates, an investment executive, spent a year in a flat at The Cloisters, and was very relieved to go at the end of that period.

"Many strange things happened there," she told me. "One night my mother—who had come on a visit—and I were sharing the same bed. She went up first, and when I went to get into bed later she was completely huddled under the bedclothes. I elbowed her and said 'Come on, what's up?' Then I found she was absolutely terrified.

" 'Can't you see it?' she said.

" 'What?' I asked.

" 'Up there,' she said pointing to the ceiling. 'A blue face. Surely you must see it.'

"Although I didn't see it, my daughter, who was seven at the time, saw it when she slept in that particular room. It made her cry with fright, and though it happened several years ago she still remembers that weird blue face which seemed to float above her vividly. She mentioned it only the other day.

"There was always a strange atmosphere in the place. I remember trying to look after a friend's Boxer bitch there. The poor thing didn't get a wink of sleep. On the landing next to the haunted bedroom it howled and scratched so much that I had to take it back the next day.

"The downstairs door was also very disturbing when it opened itself—the flat was filled with cold air, apart from the fact that anyone could walk in. There was no accounting for the way it opened. At first I thought it must be a faulty lock, so I had a locksmith along who stripped it down and then told me that it was in perfect condition. I used to check it every night to make sure that it was fastened, but every so often the door would open of its own accord.

"I was telling one of my psychic friends about it, the author Richard Wade, and he came and stood in the garden outside and after a moment he declared, 'Something terrible has happened here.'

"When I was there some young pilots lived in another part of The Cloisters. They treated the idea of a haunting as a bit of a giggle at first, but soon they were convinced that they were haunted by a child of between thirteen and fourteen. Three out of the five saw her, but all heard her footsteps. Sometimes they felt something invisible brush past them on the stairs. I must confess that although it is a beautiful place I was never happy there."

Close to The Cloisters is the site Ladye Place, which was once the farmhouse of the priory and which is also impregnated with the supernatural. The present house which bears the name was rebuilt in 1903, and twenty-one years later it was bought by Colonel Rivers-Moore whose great interest in archaeology caused him to begin excavating in the hope of finding the tomb of Editha, the sister of Edward the Confessor. According to an ancient manuscript she had been buried in the priory, and it is believed that it is her ghost which is known as the Grey Lady of Ladye Place. It seems the digging triggered off a series of paranormal happenings. The Colonel's brother-in-law had an alarming experience when he saw a ghostly monk wearing a black Benedictine habit. A little later a guest saw the same figure, and as the excavating continued monkish spectres almost became commonplace. Great interest was aroused in the work and members of the Society for Psychical Research came to help with the digs. A medium was called in to hold seances in order to get spirit advice of the direction the excavations should take. Under this guidance the foundations of the old priory were uncovered as well as several graves of long-dead monks. The work continued until 1944, and when it ceased the hauntings died down with it.

The original house called Ladye Place fell into ruin after its owner, Admiral Kempenfelt, died in 1782 in the sinking of the *Royal George* in Portsmouth Harbour. His brother was the last person to reside in the house and there is a curious story connected with two thorn bushes the brothers had planted, and in which they took great interest. Walking in the garden late one August afternoon, Mr Kempenfelt discovered that the bush which his brother the admiral had planted had mysteriously withered although his own was still perfectly healthy.

"I feel sure this is an omen of my brother's death," he declared. Soon afterwards came the news of the tragedy.

About seventy years ago a new owner of Ladye Place employed some workmen to make some alterations to an existing building there. As the men came from London they slept on the premises, but after the second night they left, swearing that the room they used was haunted. In the middle of each night they had been woken by the sounds of a struggle followed by a terrible shriek. Local workmen were called in, and as they were not there after nightfall, the work continued smoothly until they removed some panelling in the room in which the Londoners had slept and found a skeleton in an upright position. A knife was still buried between its ribs.

When it is known that I have written books and articles about hauntings, I am invariably asked if I have ever seen a ghost. I have to confess that, although I have slept in quite a few haunted bedrooms, I have never yet glimpsed one, perhaps because I am not psychically developed enough. But I certainly have sensed things and experienced some odd happenings when going about Britain in search of material, and on one occasion I believe I heard a ghost. I know to *hear* a ghost does not sound particularly exciting in comparison to other hauntings described in this book, yet when I realised what it was, I experienced a brief but memorable feeling of sheer terror and I can confirm that the hair on the back of your head does rise.

The story goes back to the autumn of 1959 when three journalist friends of mine invited me to join them in a publishing venture. The idea was to publish a weekly trade magazine for the television industry which we called *Television Mail*. It was an exciting adventure and we plunged in with the confidence that comes through lack of experience. After the euphoria of seeing the first issue come off the printing presses, we suddenly realised that we had to produce another magazine for the following Friday and so on. Our financial resources were pitiful and for our editorial and advertising offices we could only afford two small rooms on the third floor at 408 The Strand, one of the oldest buildings in the street.

My experience occurred one Wednesday, which was the day before we went to press. This meant that, because of our lack of staff, I would be working very late sub-editing material. At that time our reporter was a friend named David Wisely, with whom I had worked on a New Zealand newspaper. He kindly said that, although he had to go out that evening, he would return about midnight to help me finish the final copy.

At twelve o'clock I heard footsteps echoing in the stairwell which rose from landing to landing of offices similar to ours. The steps were extremely slow and laboured, and I thought that Mr Wisely, having perhaps looked upon the wine when it was red, would probably not be in a condition to be very helpful.

The heavy steps continued to resound in the stairwell and then paused at the landing outside my door. I looked up, expecting it to open and for Dave to wander in with a typically cynical remark about the trade press and *Television Mail* in particular. To my surprise I heard the footsteps suddenly continue, slow and measured, up the final staircase which led to an accountants' office above us.

It was obvious someone from that firm was going up to burn some midnight oil. At the time I did not think it was a burglar because one would expect somebody following that profession to be suitably light-footed. It seemed as though the person whose footsteps they were had all the cares of the world on his shoulders. I carried on with my work, envying the absent Mr Wisely who had presumably found something better to do. Three or four minutes later I heard the steps again, just as slow and measured. They came down the stairs, paused outside my door and then continued down the stairway.

This time a nagging voice at the back of my mind told me I ought to investigate. I knew it was unlikely to be a prowler as the front door was always heavily locked. Yet for some reason I remember a certain reluctance to do so. Summoning up my determination, I went to my door, flung it open and stepped out on to the landing to find it in complete darkness.

Whoever had been coming up and down had not needed the lights which were placed on every landing. The steps were still sounding on the stairs as I pressed the switch which illuminated the stairwell from top to bottom. As the yellowish lights came on it seemed that the footsteps faded away, and as I gazed over the banisters, I realised with that feeling of shock that I was alone in the building. The stairwell was deserted, the lights shone on the blank doors of locked offices. I went down the stairs and tested each office door and the front door. It was securely locked. I returned to my desk with mixed feelings, rather like the little boy who saw an elephant for the first time and declared: "I don't believe it."

I thought of the usual things: was it the creaking of old wood-work, had my ears been playing tricks? But no, the memory of those footsteps was too vivid and detailed.

The next day I went up to the office above in the hope of finding some explanation. Speaking to one of the accountants I inquired if his office had been burgled or if there were signs of anything unusual having taken place. He said he had found the door locked when he came that morning and nothing had been disturbed.

"Have you been hearing things?" he asked. I replied that I certainly had and told him about the footsteps.

"Oh, you're not the first to hear those," he said. "I can't explain what they are but I think in some way they are related to an incident which took place a few years ago—a man committed suicide here in the attic . . ."

To continue on a personal note. I believe that my grandfather on my mother's side reappeared at his old home as a ghost. His name was Frederick Poole and he was a well-known sportsman in Waterloo, which looks out over Liverpool Bay between Crosby and Seaforth. Therefore it was particularly tragic when he was partially paralysed by a stroke in the prime of life, prior to the First World War. At that time he lived in a large house, No 12 Wellington Street. His particular pride was a stretch of lawn which he kept as smooth and green as the proverbial billiard table. As a little girl, my mother was not allowed to play on it, and I can imagine his frustration at not being able to tend it as he had prior to his illness.

He died in October, 1920, and following a decline in family fortunes my grandmother was forced to let her home while she and my mother lived in more modest accommodation.

At the beginning of the 1930's the tenants occupying No 12 Wellington Street were a Mr and Mrs Bold. In 1931 Mr Bold, who was a keen gardener, dug a round flowerbed in the centre of the lawn in which he planted a lot of bulbs. To his chagrin the expected green spikes never appeared. He dug up the bulbs and the following year planted a new selection but with the same result.

One day Mrs Bold was looking out across the garden through the French windows when she saw a grey-haired gentleman leaning on a stick by the circular flower-bed. She told my grandmother that he looked "very sad and gentle and was shaking his head". She then went on to describe my grandfather perfectly, although she had never met him. She even gave details of the clothes he was wearing which my mother and grandmother well remembered.

Having seen the figure in the garden, Mrs Bold told her husband to grass the flowerbed over as she realised nothing would grow there except grass. Mr Bold did so, returning the lawn to something of its original condition in the hope of appeasing the gentle ghost. The grass seed sprouted and once more there was a stretch of greensward which had meant so much to my grandfather. Although Mrs Bold was known to possess some psychic powers, she never again saw Frederick Poole who was no doubt content that he had got his message across.

13

HAUNTED HOSPITALITY

The haunted inn is an integral part of British ghostlore and, unlike the phantoms which patrol castles or glide between tombstones, the inn ghost is often companionable and sometimes downright jolly in a Dickensian way. Frequently it delights in teasing the publican and his staff by apporting keys and playing tricks with beer glasses. Perhaps because many inns have built up an atmosphere of jollity over centuries, the inn phantom is seldom melancholy or vicious though, of course, there are some exceptions. It is my experience that the landlord and staff of haunted inns do not stay in awe of their uninvited guests long, often bestowing affectionate nicknames upon them and treating them with a familiarity which would amaze serious ghost hunters.

Having visited the inns and pubs with the most interesting hauntings for my book *Haunted Inns*, I discovered others with reputations for being haunted though the details of which had either been forgotten or never properly known. An example of this was the fine old timbered Greyhound Inn at Chalfont St Peter where I stayed after having been assured by a friend that it was haunted. The staff agreed it had such a reputation, but despite all my researches the most I could find out was that its phantom was a white lady who was reputed to walk between the inn and the nearby church. No other information could I elicit from local people, the local public library or old records.

Such apparitions hardly make a paragraph in a book on specific haunting. When I looked into the question of haunted restaurants and cafes, I found the situation to be even more difficult. It seems ghosts prefer the hard stuff because the ratio of haunted restaurants is low compared with inns, and where there are hauntings it is usually the work of poltergeists who, though they might create drama in the kitchen, are rather dull compared to proper phantoms.

One of my favourite eating places in London is the Wig and Pen Club which is housed in a Tudor building, opposite the Law Courts, 230 Strand, and which was one of the few buildings to survive the Great Fire of London. Framed front pages from famous editions of newspapers line the walls, and its erratic collection of rooms are crowded with journalists discussing their latest story over gins and tonics, or lawyers arguing about their cases against a background of old-world hospitality and comfort. It is almost to be expected that this establishment is haunted. Late at night have been heard the footsteps of a man walking along a ground floor passage. One would expect them to be from some unseen phantom dating back over the centuries, but the tradition is that the ghostly sounds are caused by a lawyer who died there in Victorian times.

The Citadel Restaurant in English Street, Carlisle, is a pleasant friendly place and when I visited it I found that one of the talking points there was the Grey Lady. She has been glimpsed several times since 1966 when a sighting was first reported in the *Carlisle Journal*. A waiter told me that the staff believed that there was some connection between the phantom and Carlisle Castle. There is an old tradition that tunnels led from the site of the Citadel—which was built a century ago as a temperance hall, and which, I hasten to add, is no longer so puritanical—to Carlisle Castle. I was told that a while ago a number of these tunnels had been bricked up, and it is possible that they may have been an escape route from the castle in the days when there was always a danger of the wild Scots coming down and laying siege. This happened on several occasions, and during the Civil War it surrendered the besieged garrison to a Scottish army, being faced with starvation after having tried to survive on "rats, linseed meal and dogs". Later it was captured by the Jacobites in the '45 uprising.

The Grey Lady of the Citadel Restaurant may have a connection with a mysterious discovery that was made when the castle was being altered and renovated in 1835. When a wall was being demolished in the second storey of the keep a long niche was found in which lay the skeleton of a woman dressed in silk tartan and with valuable rings on her fingers. No one has ever been able to suggest her identity or why she should be sealed in such a place or whether she was alive when she was bricked in. Her phantom was seen by a soldier of the 93rd Regiment in 1842 when he challenged her in the precincts of the keep. Receiving no reply he advanced and the figure melted in front of him with the result he collapsed with shock and, after recovering long enough to relate the story, died several hours later. Whether the Grey Lady of the Citadel has any connection with the phantom lady of Carlisle Castle we may never know but it makes an interesting speculation.

Another mysterious ghost has been seen at the Blinking Owl Restaurant, a picturesque black-and-white beamed building which stands on the A30 close to Donhead St Mary's in Wiltshire. When I pulled up there for lunch with a companion I had no idea that there was any ghostly association but when we went into the bar my companion, who is not normally psychic, said to the proprietor, Bill Bickley: "You have a ghost here, don't you?"

"Good heavens," he said, "how on earth did you know?"

My friend answered: "I just suddenly had a feeling that this was a haunted place."

Mr Bickley then told us how he and his wife Jan had taken over the Blinking Owl about two and a half years ago after returning from Africa, a point borne out by the wall decorations of assegais, animal skins and African carvings. He described a mysterious presence which had been seen by himself and his wife independently in a bedroom in the upper part of the building.

"When I saw it, or perhaps sensed it is a more accurate term, I did not tell my wife for fear of alarming her," he said. "But later she experienced the same thing and told me about it. Her description tallied with mine."

The presence has only appeared to each of them once. He added that his father-in-law had seen it and that it had had such an affect on him that he had taken to his bed for a fortnight. In the three instances it was a drop in temperature which had caused the witness to wake up and see a vague luminous shape. But it was not the visual aspect which impressed the Bickleys so much as the sense of something supernatural being close to them. In spite of checking with local people and looking through old records, Mr Bickley has found no explanation for the phenomena.

Another Grey Lady, or at least another apparition in a grey dress, has been seen in Farnham, Surrey, at the Lion and Lamb cafe which was built about five centuries ago as the stables of an inn next door before being converted to its present form. Apparently this Grey Lady does not give off any ghostly aura as members of the staff have actually walked up to her with a menu before she vanishes.

In 1971 the *Surrey Comet* printed a story of how one of the rooms of the Castle Restaurant at Sunbury on Thames was kept locked. The proprietor at the time had seen a white apparition in the kitchen and living quarters but the reason the room was locked was because anyone who entered it was struck by a "ghastly feeling". The ghost is traditionally believed to be that of a girl who was killed by Parliamentarian soldiers during a brawl in the Civil War, and the room where the sensation of fear is experienced was long known as The Soldiers' Room.

A famous London restaurant to be haunted is Sheppeys in Mayfair. In the middle of the eighteenth century it was a coffee house with its upper rooms serving as accommodation for young men-about-town, the most celebrated of these being Beau Brummell. Another lodger was a high-living highwayman who was believed to have hidden his ill-gotten booty in one of the cellars. It is his ghost, "tall and thin, dressed in a long black coat" which has been glimpsed in the bar of the establishment. In the past an effort was made to exorcise him but it must have failed as his phantom continues to visit the restaurant.

The publicity which followed the film *The Exorcist*, which included television programmes in which real exorcists appeared, underlined how many exorcisms are still carried out annually. The modern method is usually simple and free from the mumbo-jumbo of the bell, book and candle, and seems remarkably effective in ridding victims from possession by an evil force. One of the strangest forms of exorcism was described in *Notes and Queries* in 1918 when a correspondent referred to services performed, in Castle Acre in Norfolk, to lay a ghost early in the nineteenth century.

"This consisted of requisitioning the services of the neighbouring clergy who read in rotation verses of Scripture, the ghost also reading and keeping pace with them" the correspondent wrote. "If the cleric managed to get a verse ahead, their power was established and the ghost laid. The recess in which the spirit was put to rest (in the Castle) had two candle ends thrown in, from which I presume they were lighted through the ceremony . . . The recess was an object of dread in my boyhood."

OTHER HAUNTED HOSTELRIES

BELL HOTEL, *Thorpe-le-Soken in Essex* : Haunted by some poltergeist activity and a shadowy lady who is thought to be the phantom of an eighteenth-century bigamist buried in a churchyard close to the hotel.

———

THE BELPER ARMS, *Newton Burgoland in Leicester* : Visitors have experienced a sensation of an invisible hand being placed over their faces, accompanied by a sudden drop in temperature. No explanation has been put forward for the phenomenon which occurs where an old spiral staircase used to stand.

———

THE BERKELEY ARMS, *Tewksbury* : Such was the reputation of the tapping ghost that the top floor area of this ancient pub was sealed off some years ago. The tapping, however, continues.

———

THE BLUEBELL INN, *Belmesthorpe in Rutland* : The inn used to be served by a deep well which is now covered over. The spectre of a hunchback has been seen by various local people, and by the wife of the landlord, close to the site of the well.

———

The Blue Lion, *Cwm near Rhyl, Wales* : Haunted by the ghost of one John Henry who was murdered there in 1646. Apart from his apparition having been seen, there are accounts of mysterious footsteps.

The Brocket Arms, *Ayot St Lawrence in Hertfordshire* : Haunted by a monk in a brown habit who was believed to have committed suicide by hanging himself when, in the old days, the inn was a pilgrims' hospice.

The Bull Inn, *Henley-on-Thames* : Part of the bar is sometimes pervaded by the ghostly smell of burnt candles, and this may have some distant connection with a cowled figure which was once seen in one of the bedrooms.

The Castle Hotel, *Castleton in Derbyshire* : Long ago in the hotel a wedding breakfast was prepared but never eaten. The reception was cancelled because the bride was jilted at the altar. Since then her white veiled figure has been seen in the passage leading to the dining room.

The Chequers Inn, *Burry End in Buckinghamshire* : This ancient hostelry was once used as an overnight prison for seven religious martyrs before they were burned at the stake for their faith. A previous landlord left the place after being kept awake night after night by inexplicable groaning sounds. The spectre of the martyrs' gaoler has also been seen.

Cowick Barton Inn, *Exeter* : Built on the site of a monastery dedicated to St Thomas, the pub is occasionally visited by the apparition of a monk. Sometimes he has been glimpsed in daylight in nearby fields.

THE CROWN HOTEL, *Alton in Hampshire*: Haunted by the phantom of a dog once killed by a drunken customer. The animal's body was disposed of in an old fireplace, and a previous landlord described to the press how his two dogs would "start howling and scratching at the fireplace" whenever they entered the room.

THE CROWN INN, *Great Staughton in Huntingdonshire*: Here a poltergeist is active from time to time, playing tricks on the publican and his staff. Local tradition associates it with a previous landlord who died while his wife was pregnant.

THE GOLDEN FLEECE, *Brentwood in Essex*: Built on the site of a twelfth-century priory, the phantom figure of a monk has been seen in the pub from time to time. Once a guest saw it in a mirror, turned in amazement to see the cause of the reflection only to find the room empty. Looking back in the mirror she saw the reflection of the apparition was still there.

THE JACK AND JILL INN, *Lillington in Warwickshire*: Haunted by the spectre of a former landlord. First seen three years ago, it was described as looking like a "reflection on glass", only there was no glass on which it could be reflected.

JAMAICA INN, *Cornwall*: This old smugglers' inn, made famous by Daphne du Maurier's novel, reeks with atmosphere and it is not surprising that it has a ghost. A long time ago a man was lured out of the building and killed. Since then his silent spectre has been seen seated on a stone wall nearby.

THE LADY IN GREY, *Shardlow in Derbyshire*: This pub is actually haunted by a lady wearing a grey dress of the last century.

THE MERMAID, *Rye* : One of Britain's most picturesque inns, it was once reputed to be haunted by the ghost of a smuggler who came to an untimely end. I understand from the landlord that nothing paranormal has occurred lately, so perhaps like so many phantoms the spectre of the Mermaid has faded away.

THE NEW INN, *Backwell in Somerset* : Haunted by the ghost of an alcoholic landlady who committed suicide in the cellar. When Jim Tonkin became the landlord recently he told the *News of the World* : "My wife and I are terrified. It's even worse after the bar closes. The ghost seems to stagger around, slamming doors and dropping things."

THE OLDE WHITE SWANNE, *Eastgate in Lincolnshire* : This five-centuries-old pub is haunted by a figure wearing a white cape which occasionally materialises close to midnight.

THE PESTLE AND MORTAR INN, *Mere in Wiltshire* : Here a female figure dressed in white has been seen to move through one of the rooms late at night.

THE POPLAR FARM INN, *Abbotts Ann in Hampshire* : Haunted by the sound of footsteps and invisible hands which slam doors.

THE RED LION, *Ockley in Surrey* : Haunted by the victim of a hunting accident who was carried into the inn and died there.

THE ROEBUCK HOTEL, *Reading* : Here the sound of footsteps made by some invisible entity sound in the passages late at night. They are thought to belong to the ghost of a naval officer who died at the hotel over two centuries ago.

THE ROEBUCK, *Richmond-on-Thames*: A misty white column has materialised in one of the bedrooms accompanied by a dramatic drop in temperature.

———

THE ROYAL HOTEL, *Hoylake*: Haunted by an unidentified ghost which was investigated by Harry Price in the 1920's. Since then a ghostly figure wearing a cap has been glimpsed near the ballroom.

———

THE SHIPWRIGHT'S ARMS, *near Faversham in Kent*: A lonely inn, close to one of the Swale's creeks, which is haunted by the phantom of a sailor in an old fashioned reefer jacket.

———

THE SMUGGLERS COTTAGE GUEST HOUSE, *Portreath in Cornwall*: A smuggler haunts this aptly named house. A twist was given to the story in the 1950's when alterations uncovered a secret room in which a skeleton was found to be seated at a table. Beside it was a chest and an antique sword, since given to the museum at Exeter.

———

THE VOLUNTEER, *Baker Street in London*: Haunted by a phantom in seventeeth-century costume who has been identified as the Royalist Richard Nevill. A certain amount of poltergeist activity accompanies the spectre.

———

THE WHITE HART INN, *Blythburgh in Suffolk*: Haunted by the phantom of an old man who has been described as being garbed like a monk.

———

THE WHITE HART, *Hemel Hempstead*: Haunted by the ghost of a young man who was killed when a press-gang tried to take him into military service. Customers of the pub, which goes back to the early part of the sixteenth century, have experienced a sensation of sheer terror when close to the stairs where the tragic fight took place. The visual aspect of the ghost is that of a disembodied face with an expression of extreme fear.

———————

THE WHITE HART, *Minster Lovell in Oxfordshire* : Haunted by a veiled phantom called Rosalind who has been seen sobbing close to where an old spiral staircase used to lead to the loft. According to local tradition she committed suicide as the result of an unhappy love affair.

———————

WILLIAM IV INN, *Ewell in Surrey* : Haunted by the creaking of a coach, the jingle of a harness and the hoofbeats of a team of horses which leave the pub in the direction of London.

14

AT THE HOUR OF DEATH

The appearance of a phantom of a person who has just passed away at some distant place is an intriguing aspect of supernatural lore and one that has been well documented. I have known people who have told me that without any conscious reason they have suddenly been aware that someone close to them has died, and the sighting of a person's ghost at the hour of his or her death could be a dramatic magnification of this. It seems to have occurred particularly in the days of our past Empire when many British people were scattered about the globe and letters often took weeks in transit, suggesting that the newly dead made some supreme effort to acquaint their loved ones of their decease.

The following are a selection of cases which were widely believed when they were reported, though there are many other examples which it would be repetitious to quote.

Because of their high position in military circles and public life, the experience which befell General Wynyard and Sir John Sherbroke received much publicity. It happened in 1785 when the 33rd Regiment, of which they were officers, was stationed at Sydney on Cape Breton Island which is separated by a narrow strait from Nova Scotia. In those days George Wynyard was a lieutenant and John Sherbroke a captain. Both men were of a serious turn of mind, enjoyed a mutual taste for literature and tended to spend much of their time together rather than joining in the pursuits of their brother officers which included a considerable amount of drinking in the mess.

Around four o'clock on the clear afternoon of October 15 of

the above year the two friends were reading and drinking coffee in the small living room in Lieutenant Wynyard's quarters, which were situated in a new barracks block. This room had two doors, one opened into a corridor while the other led into the lieutenant's bedroom from which there was no exit. Suddenly Captain Sherbroke glanced up from his book and saw, at the door which opened into the passage, the figure of a tall young man of about twenty whose white, gaunt features suggested he had been ravaged by some serious illness. He appeared to be dressed in clothing more suitable for England than the autumn conditions of Canada.

Surprised that he did not recognise the intruder, Sherbroke turned to his friend and nodded in the direction of the door. Wynyard glanced up and a look of horrified amazement crossed his face. Later Sherbroke said: "I have heard of a man's being as pale as death, but I never saw a living face assume the appearance of a corpse, except Wynyard's at that moment."

Neither officer spoke. It seemed that Wynyard had been struck dumb while Sherbroke did not wish to interrupt the drama which was being played out. Meanwhile the figure crossed the room and, having looked hard at Wynyard with an expression of "melancholy affection", as it was later described, disappeared through the open door into the bedroom.

At this Wynyard appeared to come out of his trance and muttered: "Great God! My brother!"

"Your brother!" exclaimed Sherbroke in astonishment as he was aware that Wynyard's brother, John Otway Wynyard, was a lieutenant in the 3rd Regiment of Foot Guards which was stationed in England. "What can you mean, Wynyard? There must be some deception. Follow me."

He went quickly into the bedroom, followed by his shaken friend but it was empty. The figure had vanished despite the fact there was no way out it could have used.

Wynyard repeated that it was his brother John he had seen, but Sherbroke was convinced that they were the victims of a hoax, it being the sort of trick that lively young officers might play on two such as they who seemed to prefer Plato to port.

They made a thorough search of the room, and were assisted by Lieutenant Ralph Gore, who had come to pay them a visit and had immediately realised there was something odd afoot. Nothing was found which gave any hint of an explanation, and Wynyard remained convinced that he had seen his brother while Sherbroke held to the view that it had been an elaborate trick. Lieutenant Gore suggested that they should take down the time and date of the occurrence, but agreed not to mention it to the other officers as Wynyard felt it was a personal matter while Sherbroke did not wish to give satisfaction to any practical-jokers.

As the days passed Wynyard appeared so worried, talked so much about his brother's state of health and looked forward to the next mail from England with such anxiety that it became clear to those about him that he was greatly troubled, and in the end they forced the story from him. To Sherbroke's chagrin nobody owned up to being the perpetrator of the joke.

According to an account written by the author T. M. Jarvis and published in 1823: "The story of the silent and unbidden visitor was no sooner bruited abroad than the destiny of Wynyard's brother became an object of universal and painful interest to the officers of the regiment; there were few who did not inquire for Wynyard's letters before they made any demand for their own, and the packets that arrived from England were welcomed with a more than usual eagerness, for they brought not only remembrances from their friends at home, but promised to afford the clue to the mystery which had happened among themselves. By the first ships no intelligence relating to the story could have been received, for they had all departed from England previous to the appearance of the spirit."

The officers' speculation livened up the dullness of life in the garrison, and doubtless a number of bets were laid on the outcome of the affair. The likely arrival for correspondence posted after the appearance of the alleged apparition was calculated, and as the time came near the excitement mounted. At length the vessel bringing the expected mail berthed and the officers' letters were distributed in the mess that evening. When it was seen that Wynyard had received no mail at all there was universal disappointment, and though the obituary notices in all the English newspapers were scanned for the name of Wynyard, there was nothing to give the story reality.

Captain Sherbroke had worked through a pile of letters until only one remained. He broke the seal, glanced at the first lines of writing and then rose and silently led his friend Wynyard out of the mess hall.

One can imagine the impatience with which the other officers waited for Sherbroke to return, but he did not appear for an hour, and when he did he walked over to the fireplace and solemnly announced the death of Wynyard's brother. He then read his letter aloud: "Dear John, break to your friend Wynyard the death of his favourite brother . . ." Then followed the time and date of the death which, allowing for the time differential, coincided with the hour and date noted by Lieutenant Ralph Gore.

The story has a strange footnote recorded by T. M. Jarvis who claimed that his manuscript had been read by a relation of General Wynyard who stated that "it is strictly true". Some years later John Sherbroke was in London and one day, when walking down Piccadilly with a couple of friends, he saw a man on the other side of the street who appeared to be identical to the apparition he had seen in Wynyard's quarters. Hoping that he was going to clear up the mystery at last, he ran over and accosted the stranger, explaining the occurrence at Sydney and demanding that the man should tell him if he had any connection with it. The stranger replied that he had never been out of England, but that he was another brother of John Otway Wynyard who had died in 1785.

A similar experience befell Captain Frederick Marryat, the English naval officer who in 1830, at the age of thirty-eight, gave up the sea to become a novelist and is probably best remembered today for *Mr Midshipman Easy* and *Masterman Ready*.

In 1825 he had command of a small ship which saw a considerable amount of action in the Burmese rivers. One evening when his vessel was at anchor he saw the outline of a stranger appear in his cabin. Thinking that such a stealthy entry meant that he had a dacoit to deal with, he leapt from his bunk and tried to seize the intruder. Then, in the beam of tropical moonlight which came like a silver shaft through the porthole, he recognised the features of his brother.

"Fred, I have come to tell you that I am dead," the figure said in a low but distinct voice, and then disappeared. The captain immediately opened his log and wrote down the details of his experience while it was still fresh. On his return to England the next year he learned that his brother had indeed died on exactly the same hour as he made his ghostly appearance in the cabin.

An account of another military apparition was given in *The Life and Letters of the Reverend Richard Harris Barham*—the author of the *Ingoldsby Legends*—which was written by his son R. H. D. Barham and published in 1870. It concerned Captain Edward Blomberg who was serving with his regiment in Martinique and whose wife died when his little boy was only two years old. Following his bereavement he was sent with dispatches to a remote part of the island.

Shortly after his departure a fellow officer, who was sharing a room with a comrade, was awoken by a sound from his door and, opening his eyes, he saw through the mosquito netting the figure of Captain Blomberg standing over his cot.

"Why, Blomberg," he said in surprise, "what on earth brought you back so soon?"

"This night I died," came the low voice of the visitor. "I have come hither to beg you to take charge of my little orphan boy." He then proceeded to give the astonished officer the address of the child's grandmother in London and begged that he be sent to her as soon as possible. He also gave details of certain documents which would establish the boy's right to some property of which he was now heir.

As his words died away the figure disappeared, leaving the officer wondering whether he had dreamed the whole episode. He called to his friend who was in a cot on the other side of the room: "Did you see anyone come in just now?"

"Yes," was the reply. "It was Blomberg, wasn't it? What did he want?"

"Didn't you hear what he said?"

"No. I could hear that he was talking to you, but what he said I was unable to make out."

The officer explained the strange conversation, and when he repeated it in the mess the next morning there was a certain amount of laughter at his expense. But that evening a message arrived stating that Captain Blomberg had died of fever around the time his apparition had been seen at headquarters.

"No time was lost in seeking out the child," wrote Mr Barham, "who was found and despatched to England, where he appears to have been somewhat coldly received by the grandmother. His story, however, happened to reach the ears of Lady Caroline Finch, the Queen's governess, who repeated it to Her Majesty. The Queen, struck by the interest attached to the boy, declared that little Blomberg should never want for a home; and immediately sending for him ordered that he should be brought up in the Royal nursery. She afterwards provided for his education, and saw to the settlement of his property. In addition to this, when the lad reached the age of nine years, the Queen employed Gainsborough to paint his portrait, and subsequently presented the picture to the original. This lad, brought up at the palace, became in due time chaplain to George IV and residentiary of St Paul's."

A double mystery occurred in the extraordinary case of Sir George Tryon who became Commander-in-Chief of the British Mediterranean Fleet in 1891. Two years later, on June 22, he commanded a routine naval exercise off the coast of Syria while, at his home in London's Eaton Square, Lady Tryon was preparing for one of her famous receptions. The British fleet left Beirut at 10 a.m. with Sir George in his flagship H.M.S. *Victoria* which was then the most powerful and modern battleship in the world. With it steamed a dozen ironclads.

At 2 p.m. the Admiral ordered a manoeuvre which entailed the fleet moving in two parallel columns, one of which was led by the *Victoria*, the other by H.M.S. *Camperdown* the flagship of Rear-Admiral Markham. Sir George ordered the two divisions to steam at six cables, or one thousand two hundred yards, apart. This order caused some surprise as it was usual when ships sailed in two lines for enough room to be given to allow them to turn round in each other's direction without danger of collision, and six cables certainly did not allow for this.

On the *Victoria* an officer respectfully asked Sir George if he had really meant six cables, to which the Admiral replied that he did and actually wrote down the order so that there could be no mistake. The signal was sent, and though the captains of the other ships shared the surprise which had been felt on the *Victoria*, such was Sir George's reputation as being the best naval tactician of his day that the order was obeyed implicitly.

At 3.15 p.m. he ordered two more signals to be made, one directing the *Victoria* to turn to port 16 points with the ships she was leading to do likewise, and the other ordering the *Camperdown* to lead its column in a right-about turn. It was obvious that if these signals were obeyed there would be a terrible series of collisions, and Rear-Admiral Markham immediately questioned the order. The reply was another signal from the *Victoria* asking him what he was waiting for. So with blind faith in their Admiral the ships' captains replied, "Your signal is seen and understood," and the course was set for disaster.

In broad daylight, on a perfectly flat sea, the *Victoria* and *Camperdown* turned towards each other while Sir George watched impassively until it became obvious that the inevitable crash was only seconds away. Captain Bourke on the *Victoria*, on his own initiative, ordered full speed on one engine so that the ship might make a tighter circle and perhaps miss the *Camperdown* which was heading straight for it. On the latter ship Captain Johnstone gave exactly the same command, followed by "Full speed astern both engines."

It was too late for such manoeuvres. With a ghastly rending of metal the *Camperdown* ploughed into the starboard bow of the *Victoria*, forcing it to heel over several degrees with the shock. The two great ships remained locked for several minutes, then the engines of the less damaged *Camperdown* managed to haul her clear while the shattered bow of the *Victoria* began to settle.

By now the other ships had hove to and were lowering their boats, but on his bridge Sir George calmly sent a signal commanding them not to be sent. The dazed captains could only think that his intention was to try and beach his damaged ship in shallow water, and this seems to be his idea for he ordered the helmsman to head for the coast, but the rudder was out of action although the engines still propelled the stricken ship forward.

Meanwhile Captain Burke had been told to go below to check that all watertight doors were closed and to report on the extent of the damage. He observed that there was "no panic, no shouting, no rushing about" as, with an incredible example of naval discipline, the men behaved as though they were still on some exercise. The ship's doctor had his patients brought up, among them being the fever-stricken Commander of the Ship who later achieved fame as Admiral of the Fleet Earl Jellicoe. Men without special duties were ordered to fall in on the deck four deep and facing inward. Thus they stood at attention while their ship died beneath them.

On the bridge Sir George remarked to his Staff Commander, "I think she is going," and ordered another signal which read: "Have boats ready but do not send them."

This was followed by an order to the ranks of seamen to "turn about and face the sea" which they obeyed with superhuman stoicism. Suddenly the *Victoria* lurched to starboard, and above the noise of crashing debris came the voice of the ship's chaplain, the Reverend Samuel Morris, encouraging the tumbling crew with the song "Steady, men, steady".

Thirteen minutes after the impact, the *Victoria* turned turtle and sank beneath the blue waters, the last sight of her being her propellers spinning madly which was a grim indication that her engineers and stokers had remained at their posts to the death. As an armada of small craft sped from the other warships many of the *Victoria*'s crew were sucked down after her or devoured by her racing screws. Two hundred and ninety-one officers and ratings were saved; three hundred and fifty-eight were drowned, among them Sir George who just before the final plunge remarked to his Flag-Lieutenant: "It was all my fault."

One of the great mysteries of the sea which will never be solved was why did Sir George Tryon, of whom it had been said "the skilful manner in which he handled squadrons of ships extended far beyond the Royal Navy", make such a tragic blunder?

The other mystery concerns his wife's party which was being held in London. Being one of the most fashionable gatherings of the season, the Eaton Square house was filled with guests with no other thought than exchanging gossip and enjoying themselves.

Suddenly, in the main reception room, some of the guests drew back to let a tall, haggard-faced figure in naval uniform pass. They were surprised to see that it was Sir George Tryon for, as far as they knew, he was supposed to be with the fleet in the Mediterranean, and certainly Lady Tryon had mentioned nothing about him coming home on leave. But just as those who were making way for him began to exclaim in surprise the figure vanished. Only later came the news of the sinking of Britain's mightiest battleship.

One of the most extraordinary instances of an apparition appearing at the time of his death relates to Thomas, Lord Lyttleton—known as "wicked Lord Lyttleton"—because it is two ghost stories in one. Even that factual work of reference *Chambers Biographical Dictionary* states that he died "three days after a death-warning dream". On November 24, 1779, His Lordship was asleep at his house in Hill Street, London, when a fluttering sound awoke him and he saw by his bed the ghostly form of a woman who told him that his death was near. With great presence of mind he asked the phantom whether he would live for another two months, but she replied that he would be dead within three days.

Lord Lyttleton told some house guests about the dream, and there was some speculation as to whether the ghost was that of Mrs Amphlett whose daughters the wicked lord was supposed to have seduced.

On Saturday November 27, he went to Epsom to stay at his house, known as Pitt Place, where just before retiring he told some friends that he felt fine and was sure he would "bilk the ghost". But just before midnight, as his valet William Stuckey was assisting him to undress, he collapsed and died.

A week earlier Lord Lyttleton had told his friend Peter Andrews that he would spend the weekend with him at Dartford, though later he had changed his plans—perhaps because of the spectre's prophecy—without informing him. On the same Saturday Peter Andrews had gone to bed early, to awaken between eleven and twelve o'clock to see Lord Lyttleton standing in his room. Thinking that his friend had arrived late, Andrews told him that unless he left him to have his sleep he would throw his slippers at him.

To this badinage Lyttleton replied: "It's all over with me," whereupon Andrews did throw his slippers at him. At this the figure disappeared into a dressing room attached to the bedroom, but when the startled host followed it in there he was amazed to find the room empty.

He roused his servants who denied any knowledge of Lyttleton's arrival, but still Peter Andrews was under the impression that his friend had played some devious trick upon him. In order to pay him back he told the servants that when he did return to the house he was to be locked out for the night. It was only the next day that he learned that the warning his friend had received had come true, and that he had died just before Andrews had thrown the slippers at his phantom.

In John Aubrey's quaint *Miscellanies*, published in 1696, there is a story of how in 1647 the eldest son of Lord Mohun appeared to his lover after death.

A reckless young man-about-town, the youth quarrelled with Prince Griffin and a duel was arranged to take place in Chelsea Fields one morning. Young Mohun was an accomplished swordsman, and he probably had few fears about the outcome of the encounter as he rode to the appointment. But as he passed Ebury Farm he was attacked by footpads who shot him dead.

The attack took place at ten o'clock in the morning and at that time his mistress, in her house in St James's Street, woke up to see him looking down on her. He then turned to go, ignoring her invitation to stay. Puzzled at such untypical behaviour, she called her maid to inquire where he had gone, but the maid replied that nobody could have entered the room as she had the key to the front door.

The girl was not puzzled for long, soon London was buzzing with the news of the young blade's murder.

In the latter part of the seventeenth century an action was brought before the Court of King's Bench by a widow who demanded £1,000 damages from a man who claimed that he had seen the apparition of her husband. There is an almost humorous element to the case, but it is an interesting curiosity.

On May 14, 1687, Captain Spink recorded in his ship's log that, in company with three other captains—namely Bristo, Brian and Barnaby—he arrived at the Italian island of Lucera where he anchored in twelve fathoms of water.

The following day he wrote: "Captains Bristo, Brian, and Barnaby went on shore shooting colues off Stromboli; when we had done we called our men together, about fourteen minutes after three in the afternoon, when, to our great surprise, we saw two men run by us with amazing swiftness. Captain Barnaby said, 'Lord bless me, the foremost man looks like my next-door neighbour, old Booty,' but he added that he did not know the one that was behind him. Booty was dressed in grey clothes, and the one behind him in black. We saw them run into the burning mountain in the midst of the flames, on which we heard a terrible noise, too horrible to be described. Captain Barnaby, then desired us to look at our watches, pen the time down in our pocket-books and enter it in our journals, which we accordingly did."

On October 6 the Captains brought their ships into Gravesend where Mrs Barnaby and Mrs Brian came to welcome their husbands. Than, according to Captain Spink's account, "Captain Barnaby's wife said, 'My dear, I have got some news to tell you, old Booty is dead.' He swore on oath and said, 'We all saw him run into hell.' Some time afterwards Mrs Barnaby met with a lady of her acquaintance in London, and told her what her husband had seen concerning Mr Booty. It came to Mrs Booty's ears, and she brought an action against Captain Barnaby, assessing £1,000 damages. He gave bail, and it came to trial at the Court of King's Bench, where Mr Booty's clothes were brought into court. The sexton of the parish and the people that were with him when he died, swore to the time when he died, and we swore to our journals, and they agreed within two minutes. Twelve of our men swore that the buttons of his coat were covered with the same grey cloth as his coat, and it appeared to be so."

The jury asked Captain Spink if he had ever known Mr Booty when he was alive, to which the captain replied that he had never seen him until he had watched him run into the burning mountain.

Judge Herbert declared : "Lord grant that I may never see the sight you have seen : one, two or three may be mistaken but twenty or thirty cannot." After this the jury found in favour of the defendant.

15

THE MOST HAUNTED HOUSE?

Borley Rectory, until it was burnt down in 1939 in fulfilment of a psychic prophecy, had the reputation of being "The Most Haunted House in England". Today I believe that description must surely belong to a classic Tudor manor house at Sandford Orcas in Dorset. It is reputed to be haunted by over a dozen ghosts, and has become the happy haunting ground of psychical research groups and television camera teams alike. When I entered its ancient gateway (where one of the current ghosts hanged himself from a pulley still to be seen), I found the appearance of the house to be exactly right for the part. Built of grey stone, it has deep mullioned windows, tall Elizabethan chimneys and high gables, each surmounted by a leering gargoyle the shape of an ape.

Perhaps it is significant that the coat-of-arms of the present occupant, Colonel Francis Claridge, has the motto "Fear nought but God". It seems to me that if the manor had only half its complement of ghosts there would still be a lot to fear.

Sandford Orcas goes back into the roots of history. Originally it was a settlement developed beside a sandy ford, and later, during the reign of Edward the Confessor, the land here was held by the Saxon Brithic, about whom there is a curious legend.

It is recorded that Brithic, who was the master of many Wessex manors besides Sandfordia, as it was known then, was sent as an ambassador to the Count of Flanders by the English King. Here, at the court of Baldwin V, the Count's daughter Matilda was greatly attracted to the arrogant Saxon who, to her dismay and chagrin, showed scant interest in her. About the same time William, Duke of Normandy, sought her in marriage. At first she spurned the young Duke because of his antecedents. It was well known that he was the bastard child of Robert the Devil, Duke of Normandy, and a girl called Arletta. It was not that he was a bastard that mattered but the fact that his mother was the daughter of a tanner.

Matilda made it perfectly clear that she had no interest in the grandson of a humble hide merchant, and it was only when Duke William galloped to her father's castle and, throwing protocol to the winds, took her forcibly by the hair that she realised there was something so attractive and masterful about him that the stigma of "trade" in his family could be overlooked.

When William became the Conqueror of England, and Matilda the Queen of the sullen country, she remembered the Saxon who had rejected her. After his lands were sequestered by the victorious Normans, Queen Matilda arranged that Brithic Algarson should spend the rest of his life imprisoned in Winchester.

In the reign of Henry I, Henry de Orescuilz held the manor which was handed down to his son and grandson, Richard, who lived in the early part of Henry III's reign. As he died childless the estate was divided between his two sisters, the elder receiving a house known in the village as "Jerrards" while the younger Alice took the manor house as her share, and the estate was to be thus divided for nearly six centuries. After this the records are blank until the manor house passed into the hands of the Knoyle family around the beginning of the fifteenth century. Again they are vague when it comes to dating the building of the present manor house though most authorities put it at *circa* 1540.

We know that at the end of the sixteenth century the manor was in the possession of one Edward Knoyle because there is a letter preserved which was written to him by Sir Walter Raleigh. His son William was twice married, his second wife being Grace Clavell. A Roman Catholic, she brought the influence of her faith to Sandford Orcas—an influence which seems to have resulted in an ebb of family fortune during the anti-Catholic times of the seventeenth century.

The slow decline of the Knoyles ended in 1748 when James

Davidge, a tenant farmer, became the occupier of the manor house. Davidge was the first of three such farmers to live in the house for the next one hundred and twenty years. It is considered that the financial problems of the Knoyles during the latter part of their ownership, followed by the occupation of these tenant farmers, is the reason the house has remained in such an original state.

In 1918 it passed to the Reverend Sir Hubert Medlycott who was succeeded by his son, Sir Hubert, two years later. He lived there until he died in 1964, and the present owner of the house, Sir Christopher Medlycott, leased the house to Colonel Claridge.

Before showing me around Sandford Orcas manor, Colonel Claridge explained: "When my wife and I took a lease on this property we were not informed that it was haunted. In fact, if I'd known what we were going to experience we wouldn't have taken the place. Since then the house has been featured on television and we have received many letters from both ex-staff and others confirming many of the various apparitions."

A former footman and his wife, who once was the housekeeper, Mr and Mrs J. A. Allen, have stated that they had the impression that the gargoyles above the porch appeared to laugh in the moonlight, and they were often scared to retire upstairs on their own. They added that from the church opposite the manor house there came the rattle of chains and "footsteps came running down the steps as though someone was being chased".

A Taunton lady slept in the nursery wing when visiting Sandford Orcas and declared that she saw a phantom swaying at the foot of her bed. He appeared to be in evening dress, and she could see him silhouetted against the window.

"His face appeared evil-looking," she said. "He stood there for what seemed quite a while, then disappeared."

Mr A. W. Daniell, who had lived at the manor with his parents in 1900, when he was aged about ten years, has described how "a very nice old lady" visited him on numerous occasions whilst sleeping in the solar which was his bedroom. Colonel Claridge told me that two young ladies related an identical story about the woman with the shawl and who had appeared to them when they too had slept in the solar as girls.

There was a considerable amount of publicity about Sandford

Orcas in the mid-Sixties, and after Christmas, 1966, a BBC television team visited the house, one of whose members said that she saw a ghost of a man in an old-fashioned farmer's smock and hat passing and repassing a window.

A group from the Paraphysical Laboratory at Downton investigated Sandford Orcas and, in 1967, reported in the *Journal of Paraphysics* that "a reasonable *prima facie* case had been made out for the hauntings". They had traced five verifiable cases of hauntings experienced by others other than members of the Claridge family, over the previous sixty years.

Colonel Claridge described the ghosts to me as he conducted me around the manor with its many treasures of period panels, woodwork, armour, collections of silver and china, and furniture which includes a huge and amazingly carved bed in which Catharine of Aragon was born. In one room he showed me a collection of photographs in which it is believed apparitions have been caught. I wished to copy one of these with my Pentax, but the Colonel told me that it was useless to try and take a picture in that particular room. There was something about its atmosphere which made photography impossible, so we removed the photograph to the living room where the operation went quite smoothly.*

"I do not know why it is, but there is something about that room which makes film come out blank, though the frames exposed in other parts of the house are quite all right," the Colonel said. "I have experienced this myself, and so have professional photographers who have come to take pictures of the furniture and the objets d'art which it contains."

Because of the large number of ghosts which I was told about at Sandford Orcas, I shall describe them as follows:

The Gipsy Woman: One evening, after the tourists had finished visiting Sandford Orcas manor at about five o'clock, Colonel Claridge was standing outside the house looking over the lawn when he suddenly saw a woman, wearing a dirty mackintosh and

* I had an experience once of not being able to take a photograph of an old tombstone built into a fireplace wall at the Choughs Hotel, Chard, where photographers more seasoned than I had also met with failure. See *Haunted Inns*, published by Frederick Muller Ltd in 1973.

looking rather like a Gipsy in appearance, come from the gate and walk on the lawn. He was rather put out that she ignored him and walked on what was a private lawn without bothering to ask for permission. Deciding to ask who she was and what she wanted, the Colonel stepped forward on to the lawn, but as soon as his foot touched the grass the figure melted away before his eyes.

The Knoyle Phantoms : When a photograph was taken from the lawn outside the house, it was seen after the negative had been developed and a print made that one of the Knoyle sons, complete with his Stuart hat, had been photographed at the Great Hall window.

On another occasion the ghost of one Edward Knoyle was seen, and recognised from a sketch made by a visitor.

"This occurred when a stained glass window (which has now been sold and gone to Australia) was standing in a room after being twenty-five years behind the altar of a Roman Catholic convent," Colonel Claridge informed me. "It was naturally impregnated with incense, and one of the visitors coming round saw Edward Knoyle (the only one who lived to be old) standing looking at the stained glass. The visitor was so intrigued that he asked me for some paper and made a quick sketch of him. The drawing, on which the visitor signed his name and address, depicted Edward Knoyle who lived to be seventy-five and went bald, as was shown in the drawing."

The Lady in the Silk Dress : On several occasions an elderly lady —described as a "dear old lady with white hair"—has been seen on the main staircase. She always appeared in a beautiful red silk hand-painted dress from the Georgian period. Sometime later, when the colonel and his wife were searching the house for some lost article, they came across a chest in the priesthole in which a similar dress had been carefully put away. When they unfolded it they found the name and the date of the death of its owner had been carefully stitched into it.

The Little Dog: About this spectre Colonel Claridge has written: "On the 15 of September (1972) when I was in the Great Hall a little rough haired fox terrier came into the room wagging his stump of a tail. He went across the room and vanished. I then realised I had seen a ghost dog, and after making careful inquiries I found out that he died in a passage outside the Great Hall in 1900, and was the pet of a mother whose child was born in the house. This little dog only appears on the anniversary of his death, at other times he can be heard running about in the old nursery."

The Little Girl in Black: On one occasion two visitors to the house turned to Mrs Claridge and asked if they should pay their entrance fee to the "little girl in black at the foot of the stairs". Mrs Claridge looked but could see nothing, though three weeks later she and her husband did see the apparition just as it had been described by the visitors. They said that she looked to be a thirteen-year-old and wore a long black Victorian-style dress.

The Moor: A phantom which appeared in the Claridges' bedroom was the figure of a man who materialised briefly for seven nights running. Each time the Colonel woke to see him, he appeared to be gazing down on the four-poster before vanishing. When the week was up he did not return for twelve months. Intrigued as to who he was, and armed with a clue as to the anniversary date, Colonel Claridge consulted old records until he came to a murder which had been committed at Sandford Orcas and which tallied with the date of the appearances. The man who appeared looking down on the centuries-old bed was a Moorish servant who had killed his master while he slept by pressing a wire across his throat.

The Screamer: In the back wing of Sandford Orcas manor is a door with an observation hole cut in it. It was said to be the room where a maniac was held, and during the period from the new moon to the full moon his screams still echo in the wing.

As a boy he had been sent to Dartmouth College to join the Navy, but while there he killed another cadet. Found to be insane, he was sent back to Sandford Orcas where, during the waxing of the moon, he was restrained.

There is a legend that he died at the age of twenty-seven and was buried secretly in a hidden passage behind the Great Chamber.

"A young man who, with his girl friend, had been round the house on several occasions, asked if he could see a really bad room," Colonel Claridge told me. "As we entered this room I stood by the door and felt a most horrible sensation which I could not explain. Then the boy walked in and almost immediately he rushed out in a terrible state of shock and fright, and both I and his girl friend could not get a word out of him for twenty minutes. Then he managed to say that 'the man flew at me and tried to kill me'. We eventually calmed him down but when he went home after an hour he was still trembling."

The Stinking Man : The most repulsive phantom which haunts Sandford Orcas is that of a man who, during the hour between ten and eleven o'clock at night, moves from the gatehouse and goes through the house to the staff wing where there are four bedrooms. Here he can be heard during the rest of the night, tapping on the bedroom doors five and seven times. He is accompanied by the sounds of bodies being dragged on floors. Colonel Claridge told me that the ghastly thing about this apparition is that when he has passed his quarters he leaves behind him the stench of decaying flesh.

Soon after the Claridges moved into Sandford Orcas, Colonel Claridge's daughter, then aged twenty-five years, decided to sleep in a room in the staff wing in order to try and discover what the tapping was about. She went to sleep all right, but was awakened by being thrown to the floor. She had the sensation of fingers on her throat, and after struggling free from this invisible force, managed to race out of the room. She now refuses to enter the house after dark.

Infra red photography has caught the form of this phantom, showing him to be of the Georgian period and seven foot tall.

"This man's pastime in life was raping the maids," Colonel Claridge told me. "He will not materialise to any woman who is not a virgin."

The Suicide : The phantom of this man, who hanged himself from a pulley in the arch of the gatehouse, is said to be visible on a photograph taken on the lawn of the manor. I have seen a blow-up of the picture, which was a typical family snap and which, because of the lack of definition one gets in such pictures when they are enlarged, looks a little blurred. Nevertheless, I found it easy to make out the figure of a man wearing an old fashioned white milking smock in the background—a figure which, I am assured, was not visible to the person who clicked the shutter. The ghost is said to belong to one of the tenant farmers who took over the house after the Knoyles' long occupation of the manor house came to an end. So called "spirit" photographs should be regarded warily for there is nothing easier to fake, yet the spectre of the hanged farmer does not depend on the snapshot only for his authenticity.

Colonel Claridge said that the phantom of this man is often seen walking about the garden.

"On one occasion a lady came with her husband in their car to see the house, and she asked him if she should pay the man sitting in the stables in a white smock," said Colonel Claridge. "The husband replied that he could see nothing, and when they came into the house and told us we realised at once that they had seen the farmer."

It was this ghost which was seen by a member of the BBC television team who felt quite ill with fright when she became aware that it was the suicide's spectre she had seen.

The Wicked Priest : Colonel Claridge has stated that on several occasions he was awakened to see the figure of a priest bending over the great old fashioned bed in which he and his wife sleep. The phantom seemed to be holding a cloak out as though he was about to smother them. This apparition no longer troubles them since the Colonel attached a crucifix on to his bedroom door.

I asked him what he thought the significance of this manifestation was: he replied that he believed that at one time the house had been associated with Black Magic, which might account for so much supernatural activity. He believed that the phantom priest had been connected with the performance of the Black Mass. To lend strength to his argument, he showed me some very curious panels of stained glass set in a window which lights one of the main stairways. The scenes included the portrayal of a goat in a way which would have been hard for conventionally-minded Christians to accept a few centuries ago.

Minor Hauntings: As well as the spectacular hauntings just listed, Sandford Orcas has its share of minor manifestations some of which suggest a poltergeist-like agency.

One day Colonel Claridge's daughter was leading her two bay horses to the stable. No doubt impressed by the sight of the fine animals against such an old world setting, a visitor declared: "What a beautiful white horse standing between those two bay ones." The Claridges did not own a white horse.

On another occasion they saw a procession of six cowled monks cross their room on the day of St Francis' Feast presumably from a small room which, during the time of Catholic persecution, was used as a priesthole.

The Colonel said that usually the ghosts of Sandford Orcas appeared only once "to make themselves known", though what the Colonel referred feelingly to as "nasty" hauntings tended to recur.

He also told me that, in order to keep his grandchildren out of a store room, he bought an extra-large staple and a padlock to secure the door. Some little time later there came the sound of a crash and when he went to investigate he found the staple *broken*, not just pulled out of the wall. Six months later he needed to secure the door again, and again there was a crash and a shattered staple.

"After that I just tied up the door with rope," he said with a laugh.

Phantom Britain

There is also a door which, from time to time, unlocks itself even though the key is in the Colonel's pocket or beside his bed. This is worrying for him when one remembers the material treasures which Sandford Orcas contains.*

* During a visit to Woburn Abbey the Duke of Bedford told me that a similar manifestation took place there, and that door handles had been seen to turn at the touch of invisible hands.

16

THE HAUNTED MOUNTAIN

The mysterious bulk of Ben MacDhui rises to 4,296 feet and is the highest mountain in the Cairngorm range which surrounds it, being only 110 feet lower than the summit of Ben Nevis, Britain's highest mountain. If it only just misses out on this claim to fame, it has another which was the reason why I described it as "mysterious", for Ben MacDhui is the only haunted mountain in this country. Its manifestations are remarkably varied—some enthusiasts of the Aetherius Society even believing that it is a base for visitors from Outer Space—but the phenomenon for which it is most famous is known as the Big Grey Man.

My research into the mountain and its haunter was stimulated when my friend Bill Simpson, a well-known figure in the Trade Union movement, told me that when he had been instructing commandos in alpine work during the war on the mountain, he found that at one shelter a book was kept in oiled silk and contained details of the mystery for the edification of climbers. Presumably they could add their own experiences if they encountered the mountain's spectre. The strange thing is that the story thus preserved does not go back very far; most outdoor paranormal occurrences have traditions which span centuries.*

* In 1831 Sir Thomas Dick Lauder claimed in the *Edinburgh New Philosophic Journal* that he and some companions had witnessed a "Spectre of the Brocken" effect on Ben MacDhui, but this did not give it the ghostly reputation it was to gain in this century. It must be remembered mountaineering is a relatively new sport, only really going back to the middle of the last century (the Matterhorn was not scaled until 1865), and therefore the desolate summit of Ben MacDhui had few visitors until recently.

For example, the Loch Ness Monster was mentioned in Adamnan's *Life of Saint Columba* which was written at the beginning of the eighth century. Yet it was not until the beginning of this one that the Big Grey Man received any publicity, and then it was only in distant New Zealand when Norman Collie, the first Professor of organic Chemistry at the University of London, told some climbing companions there of an uncanny episode he had experienced on Ben MacDhui in 1891. A local newspaper headlined the account "A Professor's Panic", but nothing was heard of that panic in Britain until 1925 when the Professor gave a speech at the Annual General Meeting of the Cairngorm Club at Aberdeen.

"I was returning from the cairn on the summit in a mist," he told his surprised audience, "when I began to think I heard something else than merely the noise of my own footsteps. For every few steps I took I heard a crunch, and then another crunch as if someone was walking after me but taking steps *three or four times the length of my own.*

"I said to myself : 'This is all nonsense.'

"I listened and heard it again but could see nothing in the mist. As I walked on and the eerie crunch, crunch sounded behind me I was seized with terror and took to my heels, staggering blindly among the boulders for four or five miles nearly down to Rothiemurchis Forest.

"Whatever you make of it I do not know, but there is something very queer about the top of Ben MacDhui and I will not go back there again by myself I know !"

Naturally such a statement was a gift to pressmen and the "Ben MacDhui Ghost" received generous linage. Some—no doubt delighted to be in the position to criticise an eminently respectable professor—scoffed at the story and suggested a variety of natural causes ranging from the effect of the wind in crevices in the rocks to a fit of nerves. But others were less sceptical, and more accounts of odd happenings began to appear. One of these, and the first to suggest an enormous figure, related to the famous mountaineer Dr A. M. Kellas, who died on the 1921 Mount Everest Reconnaissance Expedition. Apparently Dr Kellas had earlier heard of Professor Collie's experience through the New

Zealand newspaper story and wrote to him describing how he had seen a "big grey man" on Ben MacDhui.

Although he left no written account of his experience when he died, his story was told in the form of a letter published in the Aberdeen *Press and Journal* in December, 1925.

The author, Mr W. G. Robertson, wrote: "The correspondence in your paper on the subject of the Ferla Mohr* has encouraged me to state the story as given to me by the late Mr Henry Kellas, my lifelong friend, with whom I once climbed Ben MacDhui.

"He and his brother, Dr Kellas, had been chipping for crystals in the late afternoon well below the cairn, and were together on the slope of a fold of the hill. Suddenly they became aware of a giant figure coming down towards them from the cairn. They saw it pass out of sight in the dip on the side of the fold remote from themselves, and awaited its reappearance. But fear possessed them ere it did reach the top, and they fled. They were aware it was following them, and tore down by Corrie Etchachan to escape it.

"Mr Kellas said there was a mist on part of the hill, but refused to believe that the figure could be the shadow of either his brother or himself, causing an optical illusion. He asked why not *two* figures if that had been the case. But he never spoke of 'crunching' or of footsteps being *heard* by either himself or his brother.

"No one who knew Mr Kellas or heard him relate his story could doubt his complete faith in his experience . . ."

Since the story of the Big Grey Man broke publicly at the end of 1925 reports of the Am Fear Liath Mor and inexplicable happenings on the haunted mountain have greatly multiplied. A typical example of the panic which people experienced on the mountain happened in 1945 to a mountaineer named Peter Densham who had been employed on aircraft rescue work during the Second World War. One morning in May, 1945, he reached the summit of Ben MacDhui at midday, having set out from Aviemore.

The morning had been clear and fine, but as he sat eating

* A corruption of the Gaelic "Am Fear Liath Mor", meaning The Big Grey Man.

197

some food he had brought for his lunch, a heavy mist suddenly descended on the mountain—a not infrequent occurrence in the Cairngorms—and for a short while he was in a white, swirling world of clammy silence. Then he began hearing things. Naturally he had heard strange tales of the mountain, but he had never believed them and now he put down the noises, which came to him through the fog, as being caused by the contraction of rock or stones. As he finished his light meal with a piece of chocolate he suddenly had the impression that there was someone close to him. As this is a feeling not unknown to solitary climbers he ignored it at first . . . until he heard a crunching noise coming from the direction of the cairn to his left.

Later Peter Densham recalled that he began to think of the Big Grey Man and the sound his footsteps were supposed to make. Still he was not frightened, in fact he thought the experience would be rather interesting. But when the apparent source of the crunching seemed to be only a few feet away in the mist wraiths, he was engulfed by a wave of apprehension and all he wanted was to get off the mountain.

He began running wildly—and realised that he was heading in the direction of Lurcher's Crag—a route which would end with him toppling to his death over its edge. He tried to halt his headlong flight but found it almost impossible, it was as though something was pushing him. With a supreme effort of will he managed to change direction, racing between the left of the Lairig Ghru and Coire an Lochain, and continuing down a ridge to the Allt Mor Bridge and on past Glenmore. He said he only stopped running when he was safely on the other side of the loch.

Peter Densham had a different but equally strange experience on Ben MacDhui in company with a friend Richard Frere, a mountaineer with over a decade's experience of climbing in the Cairngorms and author of *Thoughts of a Mountaineer*. The two men were sent in search of an aircraft which had gone missing in the area. It was a little after mid-afternoon when they rested by the cairn on Ben MacDhui's summit and gazed at the surrounding mountains.

"I was then surprised to hear Frere apparently talking to himself," Densham later recalled. "I had the impression that he was talking to someone on the other side of the cairn. I went round myself and joined in the conversation. It was a strange experience which seemed to have a psychic aspect. We talked to someone invisible for some time, and it seemed we had carried on this conversation for some little time when we suddenly realised that there was no one there but ourselves. Afterwards, neither of us, strangely, could recall the purport of this extra-ordinary conversation."

Understandably he concluded that Ben MacDhui was the most mysterious mountain he had ever been on.

Richard Frere also had a mystic experience when he was alone on Ben MacDhui which he described in the now defunct magazine *Open Air*. As he went up the high Lairig Ghru Pass he began to get the feeling that he was not alone.

"Very close to me, permeating the air which moved so softly in the summer's wind, there was a Presence, utterly abstract but intensely real," he wrote. Nevertheless, he continued on his way and when he was above the pass he was struck by the sound of a high singing note, "a sound that was just within the aural capacity, which never rose or fell". At first he thought it was due to the effect of lowered air pressure on his eardrums, but he dropped this explanation after a few tests.

"The sound it seemed was coming from the very soil of the mountains," he wrote. "I am not an unimaginative person by any means, but in most spheres of life I limit my imagery to flights of a very whimsical fancy; when I go to the mountains, however, logic remains behind. Two hours later at the massive cairn on MacDhui's devastated summit, the metaphysical phenomena were still with me. There was no other of my species on the hill. Certain I am though that I was not alone. The thin whine of the ethereal music still came to my ears; whether it would have been audible to others I cannot say."

A vivid albeit second-hand account of the actual Big Grey Man has also been given by Richard Frere. It concerned a friend of his who wished to remain anonymous. This mountaineer went to spend a January night camped beside the Ben MacDhui cairn to prove, for the purpose of a bet, that he would be equal to the harsh winter conditions of the mountain coupled with its latent hostility. During the night he awoke with a strong start

of fright and the sensation that although he wanted to move he
could not. As he thus lay in his sleeping bag his eyes focused on
a thin shaft of moonlight which came through a crack in the
tent's fly-sheet and threw a patch of whiteness on the opposite
fabric wall. As he watched he saw that the edge of this projected light began to "blur brownly", warning him that *something* near at hand had moved between the moon and his tent.

Feeling that he was in the presence of some extreme danger,
he lay—to use a hackneyed but very apt phrase—hardly daring
to breathe. And as he continued to gaze spellbound at the
ominous shadow it dissolved as whatever it was moved its position. In some way this released the tension which had paralysed
him and, with curiosity now mingled with his fear, he crawled
out of his sleeping bag, parted the fly-sheet of the tent and gazed
out at the wild moonlit scene.

He declared to Richard Frere that at a distance of twenty
yards he beheld a huge brown creature 'swaggering" down the
slope with great measured steps. He said it looked as though it
was covered with brown hair, that its large head atop a massive
neck was out of proportion to its body, He thought it was a
male because of the narrowness of its hips compared with the
awe-inspiring width of its shoulders. He was certain that it was
not of the ape family as its arms were not of the usual simian
length. The "creature" vanished from his sight and he returned
to his sleeping bag, trying to console himself with the thought
that his senses might have been deceived by the unlikely appearance of a fellow climber swathed in heavy alpine clothing.

In the morning he tried a simple experiment to determine the
height of the prowler. There was no snow in the gully down
which it had marched so there was no question of finding footprints, but he remembered that he had not been able to see the
creature's feet when it had passed a certain boulder which lay
on the slope. This gave him some indication of the distance it
had been from his tent, and by pacing it out carefully he
reckoned it to be twenty-five yards. He then returned to the
opening of the tent and assumed the kneeling position he had
taken when he first saw the nocturnal visitor and found that the
boulder was clearly visible from this point. He then went back

to the boulder, planted his ice-axe beside it and returned to his tent.

When the creature's feet had been obscured by the boulder, its head had still appeared silhouetted just above the level of the horizon. Thus, by making a comparison between the length of the ice-axe, which rose three feet from the ground beside the boulder, and the horizon he was able to roughly estimate the height of the creature.

"Try as I would I could not make it less than eight lengths of my axe," he declared. "Twice I made it ten. So you see, my creature must have been anything between twenty-four and thirty feet in height—which is exactly what I thought at the time."

This story may sound fantastic but the report of an encounter with the Big Grey Man by Alexander Tewnion is even more so —he actually shot at it. An experienced mountaineer, photographer and naturalist, Mr Tewnion described in *The Scots Magazine* of June, 1958, how in October, 1943, he had gone climbing by himself in the Cairngorm Mountains. In the hope of being able to shoot some game to eke out his meagre wartime rations he took his revolver with him.

Mist formed across the Lairig Ghru Pass on the afternoon he reached the top of Ben MacDhui, and with it a rising wind began to moan among the rocks on the plateau. Anxious to avoid a storm in such an exposed region, Mr Tewnion began to descend the Coire Etchachan track, and it was here that he heard footfalls in the mist behind him—footfalls with strangely long intervals between them.

"I am not unduly imaginative, but my thoughts flashed instantly to the well-known story of Professor Collie and Fear Liath Mor," he wrote. "Then I felt the reassuring weight of the loaded revolver in my pocket. Grasping the butt, I peered about in the mist here rent and tattered by eddies of wind. A strange shape loomed up, receded, came charging at me! Without hesitation I whipped out the revolver and fired three times at the figure. When it still came on I turned and hared down the path, reaching Glen Derry in a time I have never bettered.

"You may ask, was it really the Fear Liath Mor? Frankly, I think it was. Many times since then I have traversed MacDhui in mist, bivouacked on it in the open, camped on its summit for

days on end on different occasions—often alone, and always
with an easy mind. For on that day I am convinced I shot the
only Fear Liath Mor my imagination will ever see."

Over the years reports of actual sightings of the Big Grey Man
have multiplied, though there is not space to reproduce any more
as there is enough material available on the paranormal aspects
of the mountain to fill a book, and indeed one has been devoted
to the subject.*

One explanation for the variation of experiences on the mountain may be the possibility that the senses of psychic people
interpret the supernatural in different ways, some visually, some
aurally and some by inner sensations. So now let us examine
other phenomena which have affected people on the haunted
mountain.

In 1941 *The Scotsman* published a letter from George
Duncan, a highly respected Aberdeen advocate and a veteran
member of the Scottish Mountaineering Club. In it he related
an experience which happened to him following a climb in the
Cairngorms in the autumn of 1914 when he was travelling down
the Derry road in a dog-cart, and sitting in such a position that
he had a good view of the mountains.

He wrote : "All at once, I got the shock of my life by seeing
before me a tall figure in a black robe—the conventional figure
of the Devil himself, waving his arms, clad in long depending
sleeves, towards me. I got such a shock that I felt what I have
never felt before or since, a cold shiver running down my spine.
In a minute or two the dog-cart turned a corner and the figure
passed from view . . ."

In her book *Time Out of Mind* the writer Joan Grant (perhaps best known for her *Winged Pharaoh*) described a frightening incident she experienced in the Rothiemurchus Forest, close
to Ben MacDhui. One fine summer day in 1928 she was walking
there with her husband when she was suddenly assailed by a
sensation of horror.

"I was seized with such terror that I turned and in panic fled
back along the path," she wrote. "Leslie ran after me, imploring
me to tell him what was wrong. I could only spare breath

* *The Big Grey Man of Ben MacDhui* by Affleck Gray, published by
Impulse Books.

enough to tell him to run faster, faster. Something utterly malign, four legged, and yet obscenely human, invisible and yet solid enough for me to hear the pounding of its hooves, was trying to reach me. If it did I should die for I was too frightened to know how to defend myself. I had run about half a mile when I burst through an invisible barrier behind which I was safe. I knew I was safe now, though a second before I had been in mortal danger; knew it as certainly as though I were a torero who has jumped the barrier in front of a charging bull.

"A year later one of my Father's professors described an almost exactly similar experience he had when bug-hunting in the Cairngorms. He was a materialist, but he had been so profoundly startled that he wrote to *The Times*—and received a letter from a reader who had also been pursued by the 'Thing'."

Joan Grant then related a sinister sequel to her adventure: "Some years later, when I was living at Mackerach, the doctor told me that two hikers, for whom search-parties had been out three days, had been found dead. He showed me the exact spot on the map. It was the place of my terror. Both men were under thirty. One came from Grantown, the other from Aviemore. The weather was fine. They had spent a good night under the shelter stone, on the highest ridge, for they had written to that effect in the book which is kept up there. They were found within a hundred yards of each other, sprawled face down as though they had fallen headlong in flight.

" 'I did a post-mortem on them both,' said the doctor gravely. 'Never in my life had I seen healthier corpses: not a thing wrong with either of the poor chaps except that their hearts stopped. I put "heart failure" on the chit, but it is my considered opinion that they died of fright.' "

In her book *The Secret of Spey* Wendy Wood also told of an attack of panic in the Lairig Ghru Pass. Although in the book she mentions the experiences of Professor Collie and Dr Kellas, she pointed out that at the time she had no idea of the odd things they had encountered on Ben MacDhui. In her case she seemed to hear an enormous voice echoing about her, a harsh voice which sounded like Gaelic, though she was too startled to pick out actual words.

At first she looked for some natural causes; perhaps it was the barking of a deer magnified by some freak echo. But when the sound seemed to come from beneath her feet she dismissed this theory, and she began searching the snow in a widening circle in case some injured climber should be hidden beneath its surface. There was no one, and the fear that had been growing inside her erupted and her only wish was to get away from the area. As she hurried from the spot she had the uneasy sensation that something was following, taking the same gigantic strides which had frightened Professor Collie. Stumbling desperately down the pass she fled from the crunching footsteps, not pausing until she found herself close to Whitewell.

She ended her account thus: "After all the evidence that can be gathered, we are no nearer a reasonable solution of the identity of the huge being who is felt, seen, and heard by persons of such widely different proclivities in the same vicinity. Are such things the concretion of the imaginings of the race, clinging to a particular place, discernible only to those whose racial sensitiveness is open to receive the primal impression and fears of a bygone day? Or is the day not bygone?"

It would be tempting to place the Big Grey Man of Ben MacDhui in the same category as the Abominable Snowman of the Himalayas, the Sasquatch of British Columbia or Big Foot of the Californian wilderness; to suggest that he is the lonely survivor of some unknown race of large man-shaped creatures whose remnants long ago hid themselves away in remote corners of the earth. If one is inclined to this view one would find support for it in the fact that strange footprints have been seen—and photographed—in snow in the Ben MacDhui area. On the other hand, what such a being would find to eat on the desolate plateau in the Cairngorms poses an almost unanswerable question—unless the Big Grey Man is the ghost of some such creature which died in an earlier age.

17

BORLEY RECTORY YET AGAIN

"Ghostly figures of headless coachmen and a nun, an old-time coach, drawn by two bay horses, which appears and vanishes mysteriously, and dragging footsteps in empty rooms. All these ingredients of a first-class ghost story are awaiting investigation by psychic experts . . ."

This introduction to a *Daily Mirror* article, which appeared on June 10, 1929, was the prelude to the most publicised and controversial case of supernatural activity in Britain. Borley's reputation as "the most haunted house in England" has been so well known that when I planned this book I decided that there would be little point in reviving it. Then I met Edward Rowling who told me of an incident he had experienced at the site of the burnt-out rectory which, until now, has never been chronicled.

Mr Rowling, who is on the staff of the Admiralty and who lives at Woodingdean in Brighton, has family connections with the Borely area, and as a boy was sent there to his grandparents to recuperate after an illness. One day when he had recovered he went to explore the deserted ruins of the building with a friend.

"There had been a fire at the rectory and I know I had been forbidden to go near the house," he explained to me. "Nevertheless I and one other did on one occasion pay a visit and walked up the drive—not a long drive as my memory serves me—to the rectory. We were looking through the front door which was either open or we had opened it after arrival and the staircase was facing us. After peering about for a time, without warning what appeared to be a brass candle-stick came hurtling down the stairs. The immediate action of myself and my companion was to put as great a distance between ourselves and Borley Rectory as we could in the shortest time. On regaining our breath I remember being horrified at the suggestion made by my companion that we should pay the rectory another visit later that day after it was dark. Needless to say I declined the offer and took no part in any further visits."

Mr Rowling's story of this poltergeist-style episode stimulated my interest and I read through the huge amount of Borley literature, later paying a visit to the site. I was surprised at the large number of people who claimed to have experienced paranormal happenings at the rectory. One article concluded: "In all, over two hundred people witnessed these happenings and everyone who lived at the Rectory for any length of time experienced them. Surely over two hundred people could not have imagined seeing or hearing strange things." Borley Church, which stands opposite the rectory site, also has an impressive reputation for being haunted, a reputation which in the past has been overshadowed by the more formidable fame of the house.

I read so much evidence for Borley's phantoms that I gained the impression that it must be almost impossible to visit there and not experience something; a frivolous idea I admit but one which caused me to make a midnight vigil in the Borley churchyard. Though it was as eerie as any graveyard at night, I must confess to feeling cheated when nothing aberrant occurred.

There was something so fascinating about the overgrown site of the now vanished rectory—perhaps because it was here that so much dramatic activity and investigation had taken place over the last century—that I decided it would be ridiculous to write a book on Phantom Britain and not have a chapter on Borley, an inclusion for which I now make no apology. And added to the history of supernatural happenings there is the equally intriguing Great Borley Controversy.

Borley Rectory, which came under the Diocese of Chelmsford, was sited on the foundations of at least two earlier buildings, and within its first three years the occupants were experiencing uncanny manifestations. Situated on the outskirts of Borley village about two-and-a-half miles from Long Melford and the same distance from Sudbury, it was built in 1863 by the Reverend Henry Dawson Ellis Bull, M.A., on the opposite side of the road to the twelfth century Borley Church. The rector seems to have been a true Victorian paterfamilias and as his family increased—there were fourteen children in the Bull family—he added on to the rectory so that it became a rambling building almost enclosing a courtyard with a well in one corner. In old photographs its gloomy appearance suggests exactly the popular impression of a haunted house.

Although large, it had few facilities and running water was not one of them. Its big garden ran parallel with the Sudbury road for a distance of about six hundred feet, and at the far end of this was a summerhouse which was said to have been built so the rector and his wife could sit out and watch for appearances of a phantom nun. She was said to materialise on the long path which ran along the south boundary of the garden and which became known as the Nun's Walk.

The Reverend Bull apparently learned of the legend of the nun from his parishioners. The story was that a monastery had once stood on the rectory site and that one of its members had fallen in love with a young novice in the nearby convent at Bures. In the traditional way the lovers tried to elope in a coach driven by a fellow brother. The runaway couple were caught, the young monk hanged and the novice bricked up alive somewhere in the foundations of the monastery.

It is a satisfying tale for a haunting, but one which is not borne out by a scrap of historical fact as there is no record of a monastic building ever having stood at Borley. Later, as a result of seances held at the rectory, it was believed that the Borley nun was in fact a girl named Marie Lairre who had come from France and had been murdered by drowning at Borley in 1667 by Lesley Waldgrave, a member of a once famous local family whose splendid memorial is the showpiece at Borley Church.

Whatever the story behind the phantom nun, the fact remains that her appearances were well known to the Reverend Bull's family. His death occurred in 1892 and he was succeeded by his son, the Reverend Harry Foyster Bull, whose sisters *simultaneously* saw the nun's robed figure gliding along the Nun's Walk in 1900. The apparition alarmed the three sisters who were in the garden. Two remained standing by the summerhouse, but the third ran into the house and called to another sister who came out and, believing there was nothing supernatural about the figure, advanced towards it whereupon it melted away.

The Reverend Harry Bull also believed he saw a phantom coach drawn by two horses. He frequently spoke of his psychic experiences and it was said of him that he "could hail a spectre as easily as most people can hail a friend." He seems to have been a genial man who kept between twenty and thirty cats, all of whose names he remembered when they prowled behind him in the garden. When he died on June 9, 1927, and like his father was buried in Borley churchyard, he was genuinely mourned by his parishioners.

The next incumbent was the Reverend G. Eric Smith who, with his wife Mabel, took up residence at the rectory on October 2, 1928. They only stayed there nine months, but it was through them that fame came to Borley.

The lack of amenities in the sprawling two-storey house was a disappointment to Mrs Smith, but she was much more worried by the curious happenings which took place there and which finally caused her husband to contact the *Daily Mirror* in the hope of obtaining some advice for allaying them. The newspaper sent along V. C. Wall, one of its staff reporters, to look into the story and his sensational article appeared on June 10, 1929.

Two days later, at the request of the *Daily Mirror* editor, Harry Price, the well-know psychic investigator and writer, went to the rectory to conduct a more professional examination of the affair. The Smiths told him of "sibilant whisperings", mysterious footsteps and an unaccountable ringing of bells, while an upper window appeared to light up although there was no illumination in the room behind it. It was also reported that two maidservants who had been employed there had seen apparitions, one claiming she had glimpsed the coach and horses which had been first seen by the Reverend Harry Bull. Poltergeist activity included keys shooting out of locks and the destruction of a vase which unaccountably flew from an upstairs window ledge and hurtled down the stairs in the manner of the candlestick later witnessed by young Edward Rowling. Seances held at the rectory, attended by the two Misses Bull who came over from their new home at Great Cornard, had some spectacular results. Mrs Smith graphically described the appearance of lights in the air during a sitting.

The Smiths claimed later it was the inconvenience of the rectory, rather than its ghosts, which caused them to leave so soon, and for six months the house stood empty. Then on October 16, 1930, a cousin of the late Reverend Harry Bull, the Reverend Lionel Foyster and his wife Marianne, took possession of the rectory where they lived for five years. It was during the Foyster incumbency that the phenomena there became really sensational. It seemed to centre round Marianne Foyster, a strange young woman who was much younger than her husband.

On the walls scribbled messages appeared addressed to her asking for "Mass", "light" and "prayers", while poltergeist forces rang bells and apported showers of stones. Marianne described the ghost of the Reverend Harry Bull, and nine months after moving in her husband invited two Anglican priests to exorcise the place. This they did on March 11, 1931, but the ceremony seems to have had little effect.

There were now so many manifestations that the Reverend Foyster began to keep a diary of unusual events with the idea of circulating it among his family. He entitled it *Fifteen Months in a Haunted House*, and later gave Hary Price permission to quote from it.

The Foysters moved from Borley in October 1935, and the ugly uncomfortable house was left to its ghosts until May, 1937, when Harry Price rented it for a year. He advertised in *The Times* for a number of investigators—people of leisure and intelligence, intrepid, critical and unbiased—to make observations at the empty rectory. Out of two hundred applications he selected forty people and worked out a rota system for them to stay at the house. These were not spiritualists nor did they have previous psychical research experience, a factor for which Price was later criticised. The chief of these investigators, whose reports added a great deal to the Borley dossier, was Sidney H. Glanville. Using a planchette device his daughter Helen obtained details of the murdered novice whose name came across as Marie Lairre.

Harry Price's tenancy of the rectory ended in May, 1938, and the house remained empty until December of that year when a Captain Gregson acquired it. He and others experienced various psychic phenomena until on the night of February 27, 1939, a lamp was upset in the hall and the rectory was gutted by fire in line with a spirit prophecy. But it was far from the end of the Borley story. Even during the fire mysterious figures were seen at the upper window of the blazing building, although it was only occupied by Captain Gregson at the time the fire broke out.

Soon afterwards there were reports of phantoms at the site and the sound of invisible horses' hooves as well as other phenomena (including the appearance of the nun-like figure) witnessed by casual passers-by and psychic investigators, too numerous to be detailed here.

In 1943 Harry Price began excavating the cellar of the burnt-out ruin and when the dig reached the depth of three feet in the entrance passage parts of a skull were found. Dr Eric Baily, M.R.C.S., M.R.C.P., the Senior Assistant Pathologist of the County Hospital of Ashford, identified it as being human and added that it was possibly the skull of a woman. These remains were interred in Lyston churchyard in 1945—could they have belonged to Marie Lairre?

Since then there have been more excavations which bear out that Borley Rectory, and Herringham Rectory which preceded it, had been built on the site of a much earlier building.

In 1944 demolition work began on the ruins and today they have completely vanished. Yet reports continue to be made of paranormal activity in the vicinity.

And now we come to the controversy!

Soon after Harry Price's death in March, 1948, a *Daily Mail* journalist, named Charles Sutton, accused Price, with whom he had visited Borley in 1929, of fraudulently manufacturing phenomena. This long-withheld disclosure appeared in the 1948 *Inky Way Annual,* and in it the reporter described how an apported pebble hit him on the head at the rectory during an investigation. He wrote: "After much noisy 'phenomena' I seized Harry and found his pockets full of bricks and pebbles. This was one 'phenomenon' he could not explain . . ."

While it is not my object to enter into the Harry Price debate, I cannot help thinking that his deceit must have been rather obvious if he had *bricks* in his pocket, and that—for a man who was recognised as a skilled amateur conjurer—it was odd that he should risk his professional reputation as a psychic investigator so carelessly.

This revelation was reinforced by statements made earlier by Mrs Mabel Smith who with her husband, the Reverend G. Eric Smith, had lived at Borley Rectory from October, 1928, to July, 1929. Her husband died in August, 1940, and in 1945 Mrs Smith wrote a letter to the *Church Times*. It followed a review of Harry Price's *Poltergeist Over England*, and in it she stated: "As I was in residence for some time at Borley Rectory . . . I would like to state definitely that neither my husband or myself believed the house haunted by anything else but rats and local superstition."

In 1948, two months after Harry Price's death, Mrs Smith sent a similar letter to the *Daily Mail*.

Those who are in the pro-Harry Price camp suggest it is peculiar that Mrs Smith should make this statement twenty years after she had lived at Borley. Added to this was the fact that it was her husband who had started the whole business by writing to the *Daily Mirror*, and that the first part of Price's book *The Most Haunted House in England* was based on information supplied by the Reverend and Mrs Smith.

Be that as it may, the doubt over Harry Price and the whole question of the haunting of Borley Rectory crystallised into a book published in 1956 under the auspices of the Society for Psychical Research, though in the foreword the President of the Society declared that "the Society does not hold or express corporate views, and the responsibility both for the facts and the reasoning in the report, as in all papers published or sponsored by the Society, rests entirely with the authors."

This book was entitled *The Haunting of Borley Rectory** and was written by Dr Eric J. Dingwell, Kathleen M. Goldney and Trevor H. Hall. It was a massive examination of the Borley

* Published by Gerald Duckworth & Co. Ltd.

evidence which should have ended the reputations of Harry Price as an honest investigator and Borley Rectory as a haunted house. But reputations die hard, and in 1965 the Society for Psychical Research made a grant in aid of expenses for one of its members, Robert J. Hastings, to reopen the Borley files and make a new report. This appeared in March, 1969, and while some saw in it the re-establishment of Price's integrity, others disagreed.

The arguments continue, and there is a certain fascination in studying them, though it would take the whole of this book to go into the pros and cons of the case. Should you be infected with this "Borley fever", I suggest you first read Price's two books, *The Most Haunted House in England* and *The End of Borley Rectory*, then the critical *The Haunting of Borley Rectory* and finally *The Ghosts of Borley Rectory** published in 1973. The latter was written by Paul Tabori, who was the literary executor to the Harry Price estate, and Peter Underwood who has investigated the Borley case over the last thirty years. In its introduction the authors wrote: "We believe that the Borley hauntings represent one of the most interesting, most cohesive and varied chapters in the history of psychical research and that they contain, as if in a microcosm, the whole range of psychic phenomena".

Because Harry Price was so closely linked with Borley Rectory any criticism of him reflects on the authenticity of its ghosts. Yet if he was a charlatan who used his ability as a conjuror, coupled with psychological suggestion, to hoax investigators and public alike, Borley would still have a solid reputation based on what happened there before Price arrived on the scene in 1929, and what has happened there since his death. Many of the latter incidents are described in *The Ghosts of Borley Rectory*. They include mysterious footsteps which have approached a witness and then faded away without any visible cause, the appearance of a spectral cat which was seen by several different people at different times, and the nun-like figure which has been glimpsed on various occasions. One of these sightings took place early on a July morning in 1966 when the phantom was seen by Gerard Kelman, of Buckhurst Hill, Essex, and two companions.

* Published by David and Charles.

In 1970, three investigators, led by Mr G. Croom-Hollingsworth of Harlow, Essex, visited the site. At 1.50 a.m., on June 20, Mr Croom-Hollingsworth, who was standing in the old rectory garden, saw an apparition, with a shrouded head, move over the rank grass to vanish in the direction of the gate.

He immediately used a walkie-talkie to contact his two companions, Mr R. Potter and Mr F. Connell, who were standing in the roadway near the church. He warned them that the figure was moving in their direction and to watch out for it. Mr Potter and Mr Connell ran along the road and, when it did not appear, Mr Potter went to join Mr Croom-Hollingsworth in the garden. When he did so he saw his friend *and* a figure which appeared to be draped in some grey material. As he watched it turned and passed through a fence before vanishing.

Haunting continues at Borley Church. There have been many reports of disembodied footsteps, appearances of a shrouded shape and the inexplicable moving of objects when the church has been locked up. There has also been the sound of organ music issuing from the empty building, some of which was tape recorded by Mr Croom-Hollingsworth and his fellow investigators in 1970.

18

BLOOD ROYAL

"The king is but a man; royalty is the gift of God."

So wrote Alexandre Dumas in his novel *Twenty Years After*, and it is a sentiment with which I am in full agreement. The institution could be considered archaic in the twentieth century, yet paradoxically, of the countries I have visited, the ones where I sensed the greatest stability were the ones with royal families. Historians find rich material in the various royal houses which have ruled Britain, and so should psychologists, for our sovereigns seem to have reflected every facet of human strength and weakness. Some have been double-dyed villains, others have been charming heroes; and it is not really surprising that the crowned and anointed of this island have left behind their legacy of phantoms.

The earliest of these goes back to William Rufus, the second son of William the Conqueror who was known throughout his unhappy realm as the Red King because of his ruddy complexion. He was crowned in 1087. The following year many nobles revolted against him · in support of his elder brother Robert, Duke of Normandy. In order to stay in power, the Red King appealed to the English, offering them a relaxation of the hated Forest Laws and crippling taxation in return for their support. This he received but, when the danger was over, his promises were forgotten and the Forest Laws were enforced more harshly than before. He quarrelled with the Church, selling ecclesiastical benefices or keeping them vacant so he could take their revenues.

Thus he had alienated most sections of society when, on

215

August 2, 1100, he joined a hunting party in the New Forest, that great tract of land which his father had laid waste so that he could enjoy deer hunting. The party split up and the King found himself alone with Sir Walter Tirel. The next time the hunting party saw William Rufus he was lying dead with Tirel's arrow protruding from his body.

Whether it was an accident—some say the arrow glanced off a tree—or whether it was deliberate is one of the mysteries of history, but Sir Walter wisely did not let the matter be put to the test. He fled the country while the members of the hunting party departed with equal speed to safeguard their estates and possessions under a new regime. Henry, the Red King's younger brother, raced to Winchester where he seized the Royal Treasury, knowing perfectly well that his future as a sovereign depended on his being able to back up his claim with cash.

It was left to a poor charcoal-burner named Purkiss to transport, on his cart, the body of the dead monarch to Winchester, and it was said that as the corpse jolted along between the trees of the New Forest, it left behind it a ghastly trail of blood. Such was the universal dislike of the King that when he was buried at Winchester Cathedral not a prayer was said nor a bell rung, and when the roof of the building later collapsed, it was blamed on his malign influence.

The glade in the New Forest where, to quote the Anglo-Saxon Chronicle, "the King was shot off with an arrow" is close to the A31 near Stoney Cross. It was marked by a stone monument which, in Victorian times, was preserved in an iron casing. According to an old tradition William Rufus returns to this spot on the anniversary of his death, after which his ghost follows the path which, eight hundred and seventy-five years ago, was marked with his blood.

Perhaps the local people were not surprised that the King should die in the New Forest for, ever since William had razed villages and destroyed churches to make this great hunting domain, it was regarded as accursed, another of William the Conqueror's sons having been gored to death there by a stag.

Apart from his appearances at the Rufus Stone, there was a belief which lasted for many centuries that William's spirit wandered in the forest close to Stoney Cross. Another anniversary manifestation was supposed to occur at the site of nearby Castle Malwood which the King had used as a hunting lodge. Here a pond was credited with turning crimson once a year because Sir Walter Tirel had paused in his flight there to wash the blood off his hands. People who believed this must have been very credulous as it is obvious that an assassin does not get bloodied hands if he shoots somebody with an arrow.

Chronologically the next King to leave ghostly reminders of his tragic life was Edward II who died one of the most horrible deaths in history at Berkeley Castle on September 21, 1329. Strangely enough, he himself left behind no unhappy phantom, but his favourite and companion from childhood, Piers Gaveston, has returned again and again to the ruins of Scarborough Castle where he was captured by his enemies in 1312.

Edward II's Queen, Isabella, has been seen running dementedly on the ramparts of Castle Rising in Norfolk where her son, Edward III, banished her for her part in the downfall of his father. The other ghost connected with Edward's unhappy reign is that of Roger Mortimer whose footsteps have been heard in England's oldest inn, The Trip to Jerusalem, which is partly hewn out of the rock upon which Nottingham Castle stands. The echoes of someone pacing restlessly within a confined space are thought to come from a natural dungeon in the rock which is still called Mortimer's Hole. Mortimer, the paramour of Queen Isabella, who had ordered the murder of the abdicated Edward II, was imprisoned here when young Edward III seized power.

The eldest son of Edward was also destined to become a phantom. He was also christened Edward but better known in history as the Black Prince because of the colour of the armour he wore when he fought so valiantly at the Battle of Crecy. The site of his haunting is Hall Place, which still stands near Bexley in Kent. Here he stayed before departing to fight in France. When he has made his rare appearances at the great house, now an educational establishment, he has come as a harbinger of doom, warning when England is endangered, or when some disaster is going to befall the owners of the manor. Wearing his sable armour, his phantom has usually been seen at twilight and accompanied by what sounds like faint medieval music. Lady Limerick, who resided at Hall Place some years ago, claimed that she had seen him on four occasions prior to tribulation coming to her family. There are also stories that his phantom has been seen before British setbacks during wartime.

It is interesting to note that there is another ghost at Hall Place. This is Lady Constance, who was married to Sir Thomas Hall, who owned the manor seven centuries ago. When he was accidentally killed, she threw herself off the tower in an agony of suicidal despair.

In 1483 the uncrowned Edward V and his younger brother Richard were taken to the Tower of London, after which their fate remains a mystery. Edward's uncle Richard was crowned in his place after John Stillington, Bishop of Bath and Wells, revealed that these children of Edward IV were bastards because at the time their father secretly married their mother, Elizabeth Woodville, he already had a pre-contract with Lady Eleanor, the daughter of the Earl of Shrewsbury, and that consummation had taken place.

For centuries history—with no other evidence other than a verbal account given by Henry VII, nineteen years after he had won the crown from Richard III—has regarded Richard as the wickedest uncle of all time, the tradition being that he gave orders for the princes to be smothered. Whether he actually murdered his nephews or not, and the question has become a classic historical argument in recent times, the fact remains that the boys were never seen again outside the Tower. Over the past five hundred years there have been reports of their pitiful wraiths being glimpsed in the Bloody Tower where they were supposed to have been murdered. Unfortunately they give no hint as to their mysterious fate and unless some new and dramatic evidence is discovered (comparable to the finding of evidence given at the inquest of Christopher Marlowe), it seems the question of Richard III's guilt will never be settled.

The pro-Richard faction argue that such an act was against everything that is known of Richard's character. Furthermore, what was the point of killing them once he had the crown on his head—especially as he would have had to continue with more assassinations if he had wished to remove all those with some claim to the throne? The Tower of London keeps its secrets well and is the scene of other royal hauntings which have been described fully in *Haunted Castles*, as have been the royal ghosts of Windsor Castle.

Our next ghosts date to Tudor times, and in particular to Henry VIII whose associations with Hampton Court have left it with the reputation of being dramatically haunted. Although it was never used by a monarch after the death of George II in 1760, the palace with its crenellated walls, turrets of time-mellowed brick and formal gardens overlooking the Thames is the most picturesque and impressive of England's royal residences.

Though many kings and queens have lived there, it is with Henry VIII that it is most closely associated. Built in his reign by Thomas Wolsey, Archbishop of York, it stands on a site he acquired in 1514, the year before he became a cardinal and the Lord Chancellor of England. The most powerful and richest of Henry's subjects, Wolsey made Hampton Court the symbol of his success. His household there numbered five thousand and nearly three hundred furnished rooms were always kept in readiness for guests. It is recorded that when a treaty was signed between France and England in 1527, the Lord Chancellor entertained the French Ambassador and his retinue of four hundred in splendour there.

This magnificence was not to last for, in 1529, after losing favour with the King, he was stripped of his privileges and in a desperate bid to win back royal favour he presented Hampton Court and all its contents to Henry. This gesture did little good for on October 30, 1529, his lands were declared forfeit to the Crown and in 1530 he was arrested on a charge of High Treason. He died while being brought down to London to stand trial. One can imagine the feeling with which he made his most famous remark just prior to his death: "Had I but served God as diligently as I have served the King, he would not have given me over in my grey hairs."

Delighted with his acquisition, Henry began to enlarge it and make it one of the most luxurious palaces in his Kingdom. It was here he brought Anne Boleyn, Jane Seymour, Anne of Cleves, Catherine Howard and Catherine Parr, and later his three children were all to hold court there.

One would expect that the foremost ghost to haunt Hampton Court would be that of Cardinal Wolsey grieving for his lost palace and yet over the centuries there was no report of his phantom having been seen until 1966. During a *Son et Lumiere* production at the palace the figure of Wolsey was noticed under one of the archways and at the moment of being seen was thought to be an actor. When it was realised that no actor was playing the part of the Cardinal, nor would have been in that position during the performance, the real identity of the figure was guessed.

The other ghost that one would expect to find there would be that of Henry himself, but the nearest I could find of anything supernatural relating to him was a vague story of irregular footsteps that suggested of one leg dragging. (In later life Henry was to suffer terribly with an ulcerated leg.) Such an insignificant haunting hardly befits a King who altered the whole course of English history and had such a traumatic personal life.

It was at Hampton Court that Henry's third wife, Jane Seymour, bore him a sickly son and then died seven days later. Dressed in white and carrying a candle, her phantom has been seen to glide from the old Queen's Apartments, through the Silver Stick gallery and down the stairs into the large Clock Court where, during the daytime, tourists enter through an archway named after her predecessor—Anne Boleyn's Gateway.

Marwell Hall in Hampshire is also reputed to be haunted by Jane Seymour for it was there in May, 1536, that she married Henry secretly in one of the upper rooms. Joyously she made preparations in the old house for her wedding with the King while Anne Boleyn was waiting to meet the headsman in the Tower of London. Ironically she little realised that her own death was only a year away, though she did succeed in giving Henry a live male heir who became Edward VI.

A much more dramatic royal ghost is that of Queen Catherine Howard. In the same month that Anne of Cleves was divorced she became Henry's fifth queen, but in November of the following year, 1541, Archbishop Cranmer accused her of having had sexual relations with a relative, a musician, before she married Henry. On February 13, 1542, she was beheaded.

When she was arrested at the palace she managed to break free from her captors and run along a gallery—to this day known as the Haunted Gallery—to the chapel where Henry was at prayer. She beat on the door and screamed to her husband for mercy but Yeomen of the Guard seized her and she was dragged away, still screaming. Apparently Henry did not allow his wife's cries to interfere with his devotions. In the past her ghost has been seen and heard re-enacting this dreadful scene on the anniversary night of her arrest. Eye witnesses who have seen her have described her as a figure running with her long hair streaming behind her but who dissolves almost as soon as she is observed.

Another well authenticated ghost of Hampton Court is that of Mistress Sybil Penn who was the foster mother of Henry's sickly son, Edward VI. Because of the devotion she had shown to the boy, she was given apartments at Hampton Court when he died at the age of sixteen. She died there of smallpox in 1562, and was interred at the old church of Hampton-on-Thames where an elaborate monument was erected, proving the esteem with which she had been regarded. A long poem extolling her virtues was carved on it, the first lines being :

Penn here is brought to home, the place of long a bode
Where vertu guided hathe her shipp into the quyet rode
A myrror of her tyme, for vertues of the mynde
A Matrone suche as in her dayes the like was herd to find . . .

There was nothing to remind the world of Mistress Penn except this monument until 1829 when the church was pulled down and her grave descrated, the memorial being moved into the lobby of the church which replaced it. Soon afterwards the ghost of Mistress Penn returned to the apartments at Hampton Court where she had lived so long ago. By now the rooms were occupied by a family called Ponsonby who reported hearing the sound of a woman's voice and the noise made by a spinning wheel which appeared to come through one of the walls. These sounds caused such interest that the Board of Works authorised a wall to be demolished and behind it was found a room which had been sealed up for centuries. Under the covering of dust was found a spinning wheel which it is possible was once used by Mistress Penn who, during her lifetime, had been noted for her spinning. People unfamiliar with the Penn monument in Hampton Church described the ghost as wearing a long straight dress and a close fitting headdress such as was fashionable with Tudor matrons—they could have been equally describing the effigy which laid with its hands pressed together in prayer on Mistress Penn's tomb. One witness who knew nothing of Mrs Penn was Princess Frederica of Hanover who, when she saw Hampton's Lady in Grey, gave a description identical to that of the effigy.

A little over a hundred years ago Lady Hildyard lived in grace-and-favour apartments overlooking Fountain Court, a beautiful colonnaded square in the heart of the State apartments. She was disturbed by the sight of two ghosts there, as well as by unexplainable tapping sounds. She complained to the Lord Chamberlain about the manifestations but nothing was done. It is easy to imagine her being regarded as a crank. Then, in 1871, when workmen were excavating in Fountain Court opposite her apartments, two skeletons were uncovered which were thought to be the remains of a couple of cavaliers from the time of the Civil War—Lord Francis Villiers and a friend who were killed in a skirmish with Roundheads.

Another version of the story suggests they were two soldiers from the time of William III, but no doubt Lady Hildyard felt some satisfaction at this vindication of her story.

Other Hampton Court ghosts include the White Lady who has been seen on the Thames bank where once the royal barges used to berth; the alleged phantom of Archbishop Laud who lost his head on Tower Hill in 1645 for "endeavouring to subvert the laws, to overthrow the Protestant religion, to act as an enemy to Parliament."

A party of unrecognised ghosts was seen late one night in February 1907 by a police constable with twenty years' experience in the Force.

"On this particular night," he reported, "I went on duty at the east front of the Palace at ten o'clock and had to remain there until six o'clock next morning. I was quite alone, and was standing close to the main gates, looking towards the Home Park, when suddenly I became conscious of a group of figures moving towards me along what is known as the Ditton Walk. It is a most unusual thing to see anyone in the garden at that time of night, but I thought it probable that some of the residents in the Palace had been to a party at Ditton, and were returning on foot. The party consisted of two gentlemen in evening dress and seven or nine ladies. There were no sounds except what resembled the rustling of dresses.

"When they reached the point about a dozen yards from me I turned round to open the gates to let them in. The party however altered their course and headed in the direction of the Flower Pot Gates, to the north of the gardens. At the same time there was a sudden movement amongst the group; they fell into processional order, two deep, with the gentleman at the head. Then, to my utter amazement, the whole crowd of them vanished; melted, as it seemed to me, into thin air. All this happened within nine yards of where I was standing, the centre of the broad gravel walk in front of the Palace. I rushed to the spot, looking up and down, but could see nothing or hear nothing to explain the mystery." And indeed the mystery has remained unexplained.

Two of Henry VIII's other wives find different venues for their haunting. After Henry VIII's history-making divorce from Catharine of Aragon, the lady spent the last two years of her life at Kimbolton Castle in Huntingdonshire where she led an austere and devotional life prior to her death in 1536. The castle, which is open to the public at certain times, has been frequently visited by the shade of this sad lady and, although part of the building collapsed at the beginning of the eighteenth century, the Queen's Chamber remains intact. It was here that Catharine would supervise the cooking of her food as she lived in mortal fear of being poisoned.

Without doubt the most sensational ghost who emerged from Henry's tortuous marital relationships was that of his second wife, the vivacious and tragic Anne Boleyn who while Henry's divorce negotiations over Catharine of Aragon were dragging on, became his mistress before being secretly married to him in

January, 1533. By May, Archbishop Cranmer declared her to be the King's legal wife and she was crowned in the midst of magnificent pageantry in Westminster Hall on Whitsun of that year. Yet within three months Henry's passion for her—which such a short while ago had been the inspiration of his poems to her beauty—had ebbed away. When in September, 1533, she bore him a daughter christened Elizabeth, she found her royal husband's affections failed to revive. It would seem that by bearing a still-born son in January, 1536, she further disappointed Henry of his desire for a male heir and her fate was sealed. On May Day the King suddenly left her side at a tournament being held at Greenwich and the next day she was taken to the Tower of London where a secret Commission investigated charges of adultery with her brother, Lord Rochfort, and four commoners. Her own uncle, the Duke of Norfolk, presided over the trial and pronounced her sentence.

On May 19, she was beheaded at Tower Green and the next day Henry married Jane Seymour. Since then there have been stories of her ghost appearing in different parts of the country with strong Boleyn associations but one of the most dramatic sightings of her has been at the church of St Peter ad Vincula in the precincts of the Tower of London where her body was buried.

One night an officer of the Guard saw the church lit up and looking through the clear windows he saw a procession of people in old-fashioned costume walking down the aisle. At their head was a woman who resembled the portraits he had seen of Anne Boleyn. He watched the phantom promenade for several minutes before it vanished and the church returned to its normal darkness.

Anne Boleyn has been reported on Tower Green, where she was one of the seven special prisoners who were given the privilege of being executed on this sad spot. Her ghost returns to her old home at Hever Castle in Kent, where at Christmas Eve her spectre has been seen to walk over the bridge which spans the River Eden in the castle grounds.

Bollin Hall in Cheshire claims to be the birthplace of the unhappy Queen and there have been accounts of her being sighted there, but apart from her appearance at the Tower of London it would seem that Blickling Hall in Norfolk is the setting for her most dramatic reappearances which take place on the anniversary of her death. Then she has been seen to ride in a coach drawn by four headless horses up the avenue to the main door in the lovely old red-brick house. Here Queen and equipage vanish.

According to some accounts the coachman is headless and so is the Queen within the spectral vehicle. The apparition was first reported when the news was carried to Norfolk of the execution of Anne and Lord Rochfort. Then, four headless horses were seen galloping across the countryside dragging the corpse of a decapitated man behind them, obviously Anne's unfortunate brother. Since then the manifestation has been more sedate with the carriage ride up to the door of the Hall.

The folklorist Christina Hole wrote just prior to the Second World War: "The occupants of the house are so used to her annual appearance that they take little notice of her."

The next in the long procession of Tudor phantom is Lady Jane Grey—"queen for a day", although in fact her reign lasted ten days. A cousin of the young King Edward VI, she was the eldest daughter of Henry Grey, Marquis of Dorset and afterwards Duke of Suffolk. A remarkably talented scholar she was forced at the age of fifteen to marry Guildford Dudley, the son of the Duke of Northumberland. He saw his son winning the throne through Jane's royal blood ties. The wedding took place on May 21, 1553, when King Edward agreed to make her "heirs male" his successors. When Edward died on July 6, 1553, Guildford Dudley wasted no time in presenting his young wife to the Council and claiming that the late Edward had named Lady Jane as his successor, not just her "heirs male". He backed this with forged evidence. The Council accepted the statement and four days later Jane was taken down the Thames by a royal barge to the Tower of London where she issued a proclamation announcing her own succession. At the same time Henry VIII's eldest daughter, the Princess Mary, made a counter claim that she was the rightful heir to her half-brother. The Council still continued to regard Jane as the true sovereign and the Crown Jewels were presented to her by the Lord Treasurer.

Meanwhile Guildford Dudley tried to persuade his wife to proclaim him as King but, although she had been a puppet in these political manoeuvres, she refused this, saying that only Parliament could do so.

Princess Mary rallied her supporters at Framlingham Castle and with thirteen thousand of them behind her marched to London where, riding a wave of short-lived popularity, she was proclaimed Queen. It was obvious that Jane's brief career was at an end and, in one of the most shameful acts of betrayal in English history, her father actually welcomed Princess Mary at the gates of the Tower of London.

At first Queen Mary, who in the past had been a firm friend of Lady Jane, merely confined the young usurper to the home of the Lieutenant of the Tower and, though she was found guilty of treason and sentenced to death, it was believed that this was a mere formality, and that she would be retired to private life. She probably would have been if not her foolish father, changing sides yet again, had become involved in a plot against the new Queen.

Seeing that Jane could be a focal point for rebellion, Mary allowed the death sentence to stand and on February 9, 1554, Jane and her husband were beheaded on Tower Hill. Their remains were interred in St Peter ad Vincula and it is here, close to the scene of her execution, that the ghost of the tragic seventeen-year-old Queen has been seen. It was last reported in 1957.

Jane's father, Henry Grey, Duke of Suffolk, gained nothing by his political machinations. After his final conspiracy against the Queen, he fled to Astley Castle in Warwickshire where he remained hidden until he was given up by his park-keeper. He suffered the same death as the daughter he had so heartlessly betrayed, and in 1849 his head was discovered at a church in London's Minories, several cuts on its neck testifying to the headman's lack of skill. The castle, which is now a hotel, was haunted by Suffolk's headless phantom for many years.

The ghost of Queen Mary, known in history as Bloody Mary, returns to Sawston Hall in Cambridgeshire where she took shelter in 1553. In a plot against her the Duke of Northumberland sent a courier with a message which stated that her brother Edward was seriously ill. In fact he was already dead, and the Duke hoped to seize the heir to the throne when she came to London so that the way would be clear for Lady Jane Grey.

The princess' jeweller managed to find her before she reached the capital and warn her of the conspiracy. She immediately fled to Sawston Hall, the home of an ardent Catholic named John Huddlestone who was only too pleased to give her shelter. Early the next morning the household was roused by the drumming of hooves as a band of Northumberland's men galloped towards the house. Mary managed to escape disguised as a milkmaid, and in frustrated anger the ruffians razed the house.

"Let it burn," the princess told Huddlestone as she rode away from the glow of the conflagration. "When I am Queen I shall build a finer one there."

Bloody Mary's phantom has been seen in the house and grounds right up to present times. It has been identified because of a portrait, attributed to Guillin Stretes, which hangs there. In the room where she slept that fateful night three knocks herald the appearance of a "grey lady". Although the Queen's life was full of bitterness and tragedy—for herself as well as many of her subjects—her apparition at Sawston has been described as having a peaceful expression, perhaps because it was here with her Catholic friends that she had some happy moments. Sawston Hall, famous for its portraits and tapestries, is unfortunately no longer open to the public.

When Cumnor Place was demolished in 1810 a two hundred and fifty-years haunting by the tragic phantom of Amy Robsart came to an end. In 1550 she had been married to Robert Dudley, Earl of Leicester, who soon afterwards began to neglect her in favour of Elizabeth I. It was widely thought that the Queen would have married him if it had not been for the fact that he was married already. As it was he kept his wife hidden in the country while he spent all his time with Elizabeth at court, and even before Amy's death there were rumours that she was to be poisoned.

In 1560 she was staying at Cumnor Place, Berkshire, which was the house of Anthony Forster, who has been described as "a creature of her husband's". On September 8 of that year she sent her retainers to Abingdon Fair, and when they returned they found their mistress lying with a broken neck at the foot of the great staircase. Despite the fact that a verdict of accidental death was given, rumours continued to link Amy's death with her husband and even with Elizabeth herself. One story which was repeated the length of England was that she had been poisoned first and then thrown downstairs to make her end look natural.

The effect of her death was that Dudley and the Queen never married. Elizabeth was shrewd enough to realise that if she married her favourite after the death of his wife, it would give confirmation to the rumours. The English Queen was too hard-headed to make the same mistake as Mary Queen of Scots, who lost her throne because she married Bothwell whom Scotland believed responsible for the assassination of Mary's husband, Darnley.

The belief that Amy Robsart had been murdered was strengthened by reports, circulating soon after her death, that her phantom had been seen on the fatal staircase at Cumnor Place. She is also believed to have appeared to Dudley at Cornbury Park in Oxfordshire. Her apparition materialised before him while he was hunting in Wychwood Forest and predicted that he would be dead within ten days. Sure enough, on September 4 of 1588, he suddenly died, and this time it was whispered that he succumbed to poison intended for his wife.

Another scene of haunting by Amy Robsart is the rectory which stands beside St Mary's church at Syderstone in Norfolk. Prior to her marriage to Robert Dudley she lived at Syderstone Hall, and after her death her phantom returned to her old home. When the hall was pulled down it was believed that her ghost moved across the road and began haunting the rectory, the manifestations there having taken the form of windows opening by themselves after they have been bolted and similar poltergeist activity. Syderstone village is haunted by a highwayman who gallops through on a horse whose hooves make no sound.

Queen Elizabeth's ghost has been seen in the library at Windsor Castle, a well known occasion being in February, 1897, when Lieutenant Carr Glynn saw a lady, "dressed in black and wearing a lace scarf of the same colour over her hair and shoulders", walk across a room in the Queen's Library—he even heard the sound of her shoes on the floor—and disappear into another room. When he followed the figure he found that it had vanished, and there was no exit by which a flesh-and-blood person could have left. He was told by castle attendants that it was the Queen's spectre which had been seen many times before walking across the room as he had described.

Among the other ghosts of Windsor Castle is that of Charles I whose expression is said to resemble his melancholy portraits. He is also supposed to have appeared at Marple Hall, in Cheshire, though there is no explanation as to why he should return there as in his day it belonged to the brother of John Bradshaw who headed the council which passed the death sentence on him.

A ghost from the reign of Charles II was appropriately a royal mistress. Two French ladies, the Duchess of Mazarin and Madame de Beauclair, lived at the Palace of Whitehall when they were on close terms with the King and his brother James. When the palace was destroyed by fire, and the affections of their illustrious lovers had cooled, they were transferred to St James's Palace where they lived in comfortable retirement. Charles was ever a gentleman and always did his best for those who had enjoyed his protection, as his dying words with regard to Nell Gwynne testify.

In their new surroundings the ladies spent most of their time together, doubtless recalling the good old days and denigrating the current favourites. Sometimes their conversation took a serious turn, and they would discuss the possibility of survival after death. In the end they made an agreement that whoever died first would, if there was an after life, attempt to communicate with the one remaining in this vale of tears.

The Duchess of Mazarin was taken ill, and when it was obvious that her hours were numbered Madame de Beauclair tactfully reminded her of the compact. After the duchess died no token came from "the other side" to comfort her friend, with the result that she became highly sceptical and rude to those who had previously shared her beliefs. So heated became her arguments that she lost the friendship of a lady who had once been very close to her.

Some months later Madame de Beauclair's servant came to the lady's house with an urgent message begging her to come to St James's. The seriousness of the request was underlined by a handsome gift of jewellery. The friend, accompanied by a gentleman who later recorded the story, hurried to the palace where she found Madame de Beauclair in good health though rather excited. She immediately began to explain how she had seen the phantom of the late duchess.

"I perceived not how she entered," she told her guest, "but, turning my eyes towards yonder corner of the room, I saw her standing in the same form and habit as in life. Fain would I have spoken, but had not the power of utterance. She took a little circuit round the chamber, seeming rather to swim than walk; then stopped beside that Indian chest, and, looking at me with her usual sweetness, 'Beauclair,' said she, 'between the hours of twelve and one tonight you will be with me.' "

It was nearly midnight when she finished recounting her story, and the lady and gentleman tried to reassure her that it must have been a dream or some such insignificant fancy. Then, as the chimes of midnight echoed over the palace, Madame de Beauclair suddenly cried, "Oh, I feel sick at heart." Within half an hour she was dead.

St James's is also reputed to be haunted by a phantom who appeared with a hideous gash in his throat. This goes back to a royal scandal which occurred on May 31, 1810, when the son of George III, the Duke of Cumberland, sent for Sir Henry Halford urgently. The physician hurried to the Duke's apartments to find him with his shirt stained with blood. He explained that he had been set upon and injured, but the only damage the doctor could find was a cut on his hand. When this was dressed, the Duke sent a retainer for his valet Sellis, but he was found lying on his bed with his throat cut. Some distance from the body—a damning distance away according to some—lay a bloody razor.

A wave of public resentment was directed against the Duke who at the inquest claimed that Sellis had tried to murder him and then rushed off to commit suicide. The popular theory was that the Duke had a liaison with his valet's daughter who was deeply hurt by his conduct. When Sellis remonstrated with his master the Duke killed him with his sword, laid his body on his bed and then cut himself with the valet's razor to give his story weight.

As British royalty became constitutional their supernatural

affinities seemed to fade along with their autocratic power. The last ghost of the Stuart line was that of the Young Pretender, Prince Charles Edward, whose phantom was reputed to appear in the County Hotel in Dumfries. He had stayed there in 1745 in what is now a lounge known as Prince Charlie's room. The last sighting of the ghost took place there about thirty years ago when a guest saw a figure, wearing the dress that the Jacobite leader would have worn, standing deep in thought before he turned and disappeared. Certainly it was not a very exciting incident compared with the drama which surrounded most of the Tudor ghosts.

George II, who was Elector of Hanover as well as King of Great Britain and Ireland, was the final King to return as a ghost. Like his father, George greatly preferred his German territory, and as he lay dying at Kensington Palace in October, 1760, his main preoccupation seemed to be the delay in the arrival of despatches from Hanover. This was because the wind was in the wrong direction, making it impossible for the ship bringing a courier to cross the Channel.

Through the window of his apartment the monarch watched the weather vane (in the shape of a bird atop the clock tower) hoping for a change in the wind, and demanding of his servants in his heavy accent: "Vy don't dey come?"

When the wind changed and the despatches came, it was too late. The King had died on October 25. His phantom has since been reported at Kensington Palace gazing upwards to see if the wind was changing. Perhaps one can see something symbolic in the contrasting manifestations of royal apparitions—the first following a trail of his own blood through the forest and the last gazing anxiously at a weather vane.

OTHER HAUNTED HOUSES

Many of the houses listed here are private homes, and the owners no doubt have enough problems coping with their ghosts without the added burden of uninvited physical visitors. If you plan to make an excursion to a "stately" haunted house check in an up-to-date guidebook that it is open to the public. This will save disappointment, especially as the hours of admission often vary at different times of the year.

ATHELHAMPTON HOUSE, *Dorset* : Haunted by phantom duellists, a Grey Lady, a spectral ape and a priest in a hooded black robe.

THE BLACK HOUSE, *Brixham* : Haunted by the phantom of Squire Hilliard who, four centuries ago, forced his son's sweetheart to marry another man because he did not believe she was good enough for his own boy. Coming across the wedding party, young Hilliard was so distraught he hanged himself. Legend says the squire is searching for his son to beg forgiveness.

BOSWORTH HALL, *Leicestershire* : Haunted by the phantom of a Protestant lady who refused to allow a Roman Catholic priest administer the last sacrament to a dying servant.

BRAMSHILL HOUSE, *Hampshire* : Dating back to the early fourteenth century, the house has a Long Gallery which is haunted by the phantom of a bride who died on the night before her wedding day. (The house is now a police college.)

CHENIES MANOR HOUSE, *Buckinghamshire* : Charles I was once a prisoner here, though whether it is his phantom which has anything to do with the heavy footsteps which make floorboards creak no one knows. They have been heard close to a room where Queen Elizabeth once slept.

CHINGLE HALL, *Lancashire* : A house famous as a secret centre of Catholicism after the Reformation, it is haunted by ghostly footsteps in the upstairs bedrooms.

CLAYDON HOUSE, *Buckinghamshire* : Here has been seen the phantom of Sir Edmund Verney who carried the Royal Standard at Edgehill in 1642. When he was killed the Parliamentarians had to cut his hand off to get the banner away from him. When the standard was recaptured his hand was still grasping the pole and was recognised by a ring. Though his body was never found at the scene of the battle, his hand was buried at Claydon, and it must be this relic which attracts his ghost. (Now in the care of the National Trust.)

———————

COMBE MANOR, *Berkshire* : Originally a religious house, it was one of the retreats where Charles II stayed with Nell Gwynne. Ghosts have been glimpsed in the garden, and the sound of chanting has been heard.

———————

CRESLOW MANOR, *Buckinghamshire* : In one room supernatural phenomena includes the sound of light footsteps and the rustle of silks.

———————

DODDINGTON HALL, *Lincolnshire* : Once this house was said to be haunted by a dramatic re-enactment in which a shrieking girl leapt from the roof to protect her honour from an unwelcome suitor. Good melodrama, but one wonders whether such a sacrifice was worth it.

———————

HALL-i'-th'-WOOD, *Lancashire* : A splendid example of a black and white timbered manor house built at the end of the sixteenth century, it is haunted by the footsteps of an invisible cavalier who races up the main staircase around the Christmas period. (Now a folk museum.)

———————

HAM HOUSE, *Richmond* : A famous stately home haunted by a tapping sound believed to come from the stick used by the Countess of Dysart. She is said to have been Cromwell's mistress and there is a legend that she later murdered her husband to marry the Duke of Lauderdale.

HARVINGTON HALL, *Worcestershire* : The grounds are haunted by the phantom of a witch who was hanged at the nearby crossroads.

HERGEST COURT, *Herefordshire* : The house was once the home of Sir Thomas Vaughan (known as Black Vaughan) who was decapitated in 1483. His spectral head has been seen floating above the surface of the moat.

HIGHLOW HALL, *Derbyshire* : Now a farmhouse, it is haunted by a White Lady who has been glimpsed crossing the courtyard. She was believed to be a murder victim whose body was dragged from her bedroom down a flight of stairs to be hidden in an unknown grave. From time to time nasty bumps have been heard from the vicinity of the stairs.

HINXWORTH PLACE, *Hertfordshire* : Here aural manifestations include shrieks, the wail of a baby, thuds and the noise of splashing water. Tradition says a son of the house tried to frighten a servant girl by putting a sheet over himself. The plan worked too well—the terrified girl struck the "apparition" with a fireiron and with a cry he fell downstairs to his death. The sound of water comes from attempts which were made to revive him by putting his head under a pump.

HOLLAND HOUSE, *London* : According to Aubrey it was here that Lady Diana Rich saw a "fetch"—an apparition of herself. It was a portent of doom because within a few weeks she was dead from smallpox.

IGHTHAM MOTE, *Kent*: Once haunted by Dorothy Selby who was believed to be the anonymous author of the letter sent to her cousin Lord Monteagle in 1605 which led to the discovery of the Gunpowder Plot. Legend says that in revenge some of the conspirators walled her up in this fourteenth century Manor House. There may be something in it as just over a century ago workmen discovered a woman's skeleton sealed in a cupboard there.

LEW TRENCHARD HOUSE, *Devon*: The Reverend Sabine Baring Gould wrote that the house "is haunted by a White Lady, who goes by the name of Madame Gould, and is supposed to be the spirit of a lady who died there—like Queen Elizabeth, seated in her chair—April 10, 1795 ... there is a corridor extending the whole length of the upper storey of the house; along this the lady is supposed to walk at night, and her step has been frequently heard."

LONGLEAT, *Wiltshire*: A stately home famous for its lions, it can also boast the phantom of Lady Louise Carteret who has been seen on the Green Lady's Walk. Her husband, Viscount Weymouth, killed her lover in a duel which may account for her periodic returns to the scene of his death.

MARKYATE CELL, *Hertfordshire*: Haunted by the phantom of a female road agent, the wicked Lady Catharine Ferrers. One night she was wounded on the highway but managed to return to Markyate Cell to die. There are many examples of recent sightings of her, and an intriguing aspect of the story is that a treasure she was reputed to have hidden in the house has never been located.

MINSTER LOVELL HALL, *Oxfordshire*: Once the home of Lord Lovell who supported the imposter Lambert Simnel. Following the Battle of Stoke he went into hiding in a secret room, being looked after by one loyal servant who kept his master locked up for safety. When the man died the trapped Lord starved to death. There is a story that in 1718 a vault was uncovered in which a skeleton was found sprawled across a table.

MOYLES COURT, *Hampshire* : Here Dame Alice Lisle unknowingly harboured a rebel after the Battle of Sedgemoor. For this treason Judge Jeffreys sentenced her to be burned at the stake, but the King mercifully altered the sentence to decapitation. The old lady's ghost has been seen here. It has also been seen at The Eclipse Inn at Winchester where she was held prior to her execution.

PENFOUND MANOR, *Cornwall* : Haunted by Kate Penfound whose family were Royalists during the Civil War. When her father caught her eloping with her Roundhead sweetheart he killed the young man.

PRIOR'S COURT, *Worcestershire* : This black-beamed house boasts three ghosts : the phantom of a girl seen wandering in the direction of the orchard, a woman who became a murder victim while taking shelter from a thunderstorm and a ghostly cavalier.

PUTTENDEN MANOR, *Surrey* : Charmingly haunted by the smell of perfume.

RAINHAM HALL, *Essex* : A very well-known haunting takes place here. Colonel Mulliner, who owned the hall in Edwardian times, returns benignly to the home he loved so much in life. (Now in the care of the National Trust.)

SALISBURY HALL, *Hertfordshire* : It was here that Nell Gwynne threatened to drop her son in the moat because he had no recognition, whereupon Charles II replied suavely: "Spare the Duke of St Albans." The female ghost which has been seen there frequently is thought to be that of Nell.

SAMLESBURY HALL, *Lancashire*: It was here that the ardent Catholic Sir John Southworth refused to let his daughter marry a Protestant. The couple planned to elope, but the girl's brother killed her lover before they could get away. Since then her ghost has been seen coming down the great stairway and gliding through the grounds to the scene of her last tryst.

TESTWOOD HOUSE, *Hampshire*: Haunted by the apparition of a tall man, a female phantom and a ghostly coach which comes smartly up the drive.

19

SPIRITS OF THE OUTDOORS

My interest in the supernatural probably originated when as a child I was given a book of Algernon Blackwood stories. One in particular enthralled me, entitled *The Willows* it told of two young men canoeing on a remote part of the Danube where the river entered the Sümpfe, an area of marshes and islets. Here, marooned on an island, they found themselves at a spot where the barrier between the material world and the realm of the unseen was dangerously thin. In the words of the narrator "we had strayed . . . into some region or some set of conditions where the risks were great, yet unintelligible to us : where the frontiers of some unknown world lay close about us. It was a spot held by the dwellers in some outer space, a sort of peep-hole where they could spy upon the earth, themselves unseen, a point where the veil between had worn a little thin."

Of course it was only fiction, and yet it left me wondering if there could be places where conditions like this might exist. Therefore it was with particular interest that I set about collecting material for this chapter. As with all aspects of the paranormal, outdoor hauntings differ greatly and perhaps the only real bond between them is that these phantoms are not associated with buildings and the other works of man. For the sake of convenience we shall look at sites ranging from south to north.

The dreary mere known as Dozmary Pool is found on Bodmin Moor not far from the famous and also haunted Jamaica Inn. According to legend it is to this sad spot that Sir Bedivere brought the dying King Arthur after his final battle. Here Arthur asked Sir Bedivere to cast Excalibur to the lake. Twice Sir

Bedivere went down to the reed-fringed edge of the water, but could not bring himself to throw the beautiful sword into its depths. Each time he returned to his King who realised from the answers to his questions that the sword had not been returned. On the third occasion, according to Lord Tennyson, King Arthur asked his last faithful knight what he had done and seen.

> "And answer made the bold Sir Bedivere :
> Sir King, I closed mine eyelids, lest the gems
> Should blind my purpose, for I never saw,
> Nor shall see, here or elsewhere, till I die,
> Not tho' I live three lives of mortal men,
> So great a miracle as yonder hilt.
> Then with both hands I flung him, wheeling him;
> But when I look'd again, behold an arm,
> Clothed in white samite, mystic, wonderful,
> That caught him by the hilt, and brandish'd him
> Three times, and drew him under in the mere."

When I visited Dozmary Pool I was definitely conscious of a strange brooding atmosphere hanging over the leaden water, and it was easy to imagine Sir Bedivere in his battered armour hurling the glittering Excalibur to its fairy owner. Yet according to legend the haunter of the lake is an evil spirit known as Tregeagle. Once the steward of Lord Robartes he was known as the "Cornish Bluebeard" and ancient folktale states that because of his infamy his ghost was condemned to empty Dozmary Pool with a limpet shell, a seemingly impossible task as the mere is nearly a mile in circumference.

Although Dartmoor, with its two hundred Tors and cascading streams, is one of the most wildly beautiful parts of Britain it is also one of the eeriest. For centuries its stone circles and remains of prehistoric villages have invested it with superstitious awe, and every village seems to have its share of uncanny legend. These villages, many of them with picturesque thatched cottages, huddle in the sheltered valleys and were populated by people who believed as much in pixies as they did in the Gospel preached in the moor's unique churches. While pixies are now relegated to children's stories, many people on Dartmoor still firmly believe in a mysterious elemental force or spirit which roams through the brooding hills of the great national park. An example of its activity was related to me by Mrs Gwyneth Powell. "A friend of mine was driving in a shooting brake along a road which crosses the moor," she said. "Suddenly she felt what seemed to be a terrific wind resistance against the car. It almost stopped although the engine was running perfectly well but she had to change down the gears and press the accelerator to get the vehicle moving against the unseen force. Her dog in the back nearly went mad. It seemed as though it was trying to attack something that was outside of the car—something that was circling it and trying to find a way in. My friend said she had never been so frightened in her life, she was certain she was under attack from something evil. Her dog was a big labrador and it kept going round the inside of the shooting brake snarling and snapping and trying to keep pace with whatever it was that was prowling about outside. I believe the dog was a nervous wreck afterwards. Gradually the power holding back the shooting brake receded and my friend at last was able to drive hell for leather until she was off the moor. I have heard of such a thing before and I am sure there is *something* evil which roams the area. Round here we don't delve into things on the moor when we are alone."

From Graham Danton, known in the West Country for his *Late Night with Danton* programme which appears on Westward Television, I heard the story of the Hairy Hands.

"In June, 1921, the medical officer of Dartmoor Prison was driving his motorcycle across the wild moorland area, along the road from Two Bridges to Postbridge," he told me. "He had two children in the sidecar. As he drove down the hill to where a little bridge crosses the East Dart, he shouted to the children to jump clear. They managed to scramble out and flung themselves on to the grass verge. The motorcycle swerved off the road and was smashed to pieces. The doctor was killed."

Several months later a man left some friends he had been visiting to ride home by the same road on his motorcycle. An hour later he returned to their house in a dazed condition and with the motorcycle badly damaged. When he was able to speak coherently he said that as he drove down the hill he felt a pair of rough hairy hands close over his on the handlebars, dragging the motorcycle off the road. He remembered nothing else until he regained consciousness on the spot where the doctor had died.

Graham Danton told me that three years later a married couple were camping in a caravan not far from the spot on a cold moonlit night. The wife suddenly awoke and sensed immediate danger. Beside her was a small window partly open. To her horror, clawing their way up the glass was a pair of hairy hands. She managed to make the sign of the cross, prayed hard and the hands slipped from sight. Graham added: "It is a very beautiful spot but even years ago, in the days of horse-drawn carriages, travellers were afraid to travel the road by night."

Stories of the Hairy Hands are still rife and towards the end of 1974 I heard of a motor accident in this spot so inexplicable that the local people were blaming the influence of the mysterious hands. This is similar to a story I heard when I was writing a travel book on the Rhineland. At Adenau I had an opportunity to drive round the Neürburgring, the famous motor-racing circuit which boasts one hundred and seventy curves in seventeen miles and which has a fascinating piece of modern folklore. The southern loop of the ring has been closed since 1935, following protests from racing drivers that along this four miles of track there lurked something evil—they called it the "Mullenbach Phantom"—which swept cars over the edge of the course. When I visited the ring I found that this part of the circuit was still sealed off.

Dartmoor's most famous manifestation is that of the Phantom Dog who is doubtless related to Black Shuck of Anglia or the Barguest of Northern England. It was the legend of this ghostly animal which inspired Sir Arthur Conan Doyle's Sherlock Holmes classic *The Hound of the Baskervilles*. Another traditional Dartmoor manifestation is a black coach pulled by headless horses and followed by an evil pack of hell-hounds whose baying brings death to any normal mortal dogs who hear this.

Wistman's Wood on Dartmoor is a collection of wind-gnarled oaks where the baying of ghostly dogs, known as the Wish Hounds, is sometimes heard. This remote wood, which lies to the north of Dartmoor Prison, is well worth a visit if you relish "other-worldly" atmosphere. Less elemental phantoms have been seen close to the village of Widecombe-in-the-Moor where "Old Uncle Tom Cobbleigh and All" visited before becoming ghosts themselves. About two miles north from the village close to the High Tor Inn there is a grave mound close to the road. It is locally known as Jay's Grave, and is the resting place of a suicide who was buried in unhallowed ground over a century ago. Mary Jay was a poor workhouse apprentice who hanged herself after being deserted by her lover. Now, after a hundred years, her grave is never without flowers and a local guidebook declares "nobody has been able to discover who places them on the mound. The mystery remains in spite of a watch being kept to discover the secret. From time to time a figure has been seen at the grave, people realising that it was no human being when they saw that it was about a foot above the ground and had no feet."

It is easy to imagine a "thin veil" in Severnake Forest in Wiltshire. It was once part of a medieval hunting domain and is reputed to be still heavily haunted, some of the "shapes" which roam through its ancient trees being seen during the daytime. Little is known of these woodland apparitions apart from a persistent legend of a headless woman riding a white horse along avenues between the trees. She was last glimpsed in 1969 by people who had entered the forest for a picnic. One theory is that she was decapitated when her horse bolted through the trees during a royal hunting party.

The village of Aylmerton, just inland from Cromer on the Norfolk coast, has woods which are haunted by terrifying cries echoing from the evocatively named Shrieking Pits. The actual pits are circular holes which are thought to be the remains of prehistoric dwellings which were dug into the ground and roofed with turves.

Hundreds of people have heard the eerie sound which is so bloodcurdling that it has been suggested that they are the cries of pre-Roman sacrificial victims. Sometimes these sounds are accompanied by the appearance of a phantom which haunts the woods, though its connection with the pits of Aylmerton has long been forgotten. One suggestion is that it is a woman, dressed in white, searching for her baby who had been killed and buried in one of the pits by her jealous husband.

The sound of a creaking chain made a sinister obbligato to the wind as it whined over the purple Elsdon moors. Looking up at the gibbet silhouetted against the cold sky, I saw that the chain swinging beneath the gallow's arm supported a wooden replica of a human head. This carving represented the skull of William Winter who, one hundred and eighty-three years ago, had been hanged on this desolate spot for murdering old Margaret Crozier of Elsdon.

His body had been left hanging in irons, close to the ancient Drove Road along which cattle were driven from Scotland into England, as a dreadful warning. A mile farther east a smithy used to stand where cows were shod before being taken on to metalled roads. At the foot of the gallows tree is a stone block which used to be the base of a Saxon cross, known as Steng Cross, and which marked the highest point of the moors rolling eastwards from Elsdon to Harwood Forest.

It would be fitting if this high windswept area was haunted by the spectre of the murderer Winter and indeed could be, but my interest in this vantage point was because of its association with a spirit known as the Brown Man of the Moors. The oldest recorded account of this haunting is to be found in Robert Surtees' *History of Durham*. In 1744 two young men from Newcastle were hunting on the high moors where later the murderer Winter was to kick off into eternity. Around noon they took out their food for lunch and the younger of the two went to drink at a brook. Having quenched his thirst, he raised his eyes and saw "a dwarf very strong and stoutly built, his dress brown like withered bracken, his head covered with frizzled red hair, his countenance ferocious and his eyes glowing like those of a bull".

The apparition began to berate the young hunter for trespassing on his domain and poaching the creatures who he said were his subjects. The youth, awed by the appearance of the small man, apologised for being on his territory and explained that if he had known that he was master here he would never have done so. This seemed to mollify the dwarf who went on to explain that he was the protector of the birds and animals which lived on the moors and that he punished those who hurt them. He added that he was a vegetarian and—perhaps with the idea of spreading his creed—then invited the youth to return to his home and dine with him.

At that moment his companion called out, causing him to turn his head and when he looked back the brown man had vanished. Perhaps thinking he had been the victim of some hallucination, he disregarded the warning of the apparition and continued hunting with his friend, returning to his home that evening with his game bag full. According to the legend this disregard cost him his life for soon afterwards he sickened and died. Since that far off day there have been reports of the strange red-headed apparition being sighted high on the heather-covered fells.

East of Selkirk there is an eerie area known as Murder Swamp which is made up of a pool fringed with bulrushes over which ancient trees spread their branches like clutching hands. Here, if you are at all psychic, you will hear strange whisperings and perhaps see vague figures moving in the mist which rises at twilight. A legend, which sets out to explain the phenomena, goes back to the Jacobite rebellion of '75. During an English raid on the village of Bowden a pair of lovers, who with their friends were enjoying a pre-wedding party, fled into the night with a man known as Geordie of the Mill who was secretly in love with the bride-to-be.

He had led them from the village with a promise of hiding them safely but the following day he returned alone, explaining that he had set them on the road to Leith. Suspicions of their real fate came weeks later when the bride's handkerchief was found by one of the swampy pools close to the village. This was not strong enough evidence to convict Geordie of the Mill although he seemed obsessed by a secret fear, spending more and more time wandering around the miasmic pools until he too disappeared. Later he was found floating amongst the scummy waterweed, a rictus of terror on his features.

Scotland's most mystical area is the two thousand two hundred acre island of Iona in the Inner Hebrides where in 563 St

Colomba founded a monastery which was to become the great centre of Celtic Christianity. In 807 it was destroyed by Vikings and frequently a re-enactment of their long ships can be seen at a spot known as White Sands. The island, which was the burial ground of Scottish, Irish and Norwegian kings, has many ghostly manifestations including strange blue lights, the sound of phantom bells and music and the figures of monks who were massacred by Norse raiders.

In the centre of the island is a spot known as Angel Hill which has something so uncanny about it that local people hesitate to go near at night time.

One of the most unusual aspects of the island's phenomena is that some people, no doubt those who possess psychic powers even if they do not realise it, see the island as it was over a thousand years ago. This is a reverse of the usual ghost theme where something from the past comes to haunt the present—people from the present who seem to be, in their minds at least, transported into the past.

An equally mysterious aspect of Iona is its celebrated "call"— a strange form of enchantment which inspired James M. Barrie to write his famous play *Mary Rose*. According to the traditions of the island the call is a fairy enchantment which lures mortals away from the everyday world. A famous case concerned an Italian girl who stayed on the island studying its folklore. When she decided, on the spur of the moment, that the time had come for her to leave the island, she packed her belongings, but, unfortunately, as it was a Sunday, there was no ferry to take her to the mainland. She returned to her lodging and announced, just as unexpectedly, that she would not be leaving after all. Yet by next morning she had disappeared.

A couple of days later her naked body was found at a spot said to be haunted by the old phantoms of the island. She held a knife in one hand, and the inquest brought in a verdict of death through exposure. The islanders believed she had been a victim to the fatal call.

When I visited Cape Wrath I felt I had reached the *Ultima Thule* of the British mainland. It is a wildly beautiful area on the very north west tip of Scotland; beautiful, that is, if you like utter isolation, the seas roar on desolate beaches and the eerie cries of gulls skimming over grey water. Here, fifty miles away from the nearest railway station at Lairg, it is easy to imagine that one is on the very edge of some other dimension and that the membrane between the reality of this world and some other, which as yet we can only guess at, has for some mysterious reason worn thin.

And so it would seem, for seven miles south from the stark lighthouse which marks Cape Wrath is haunted Sandwood Bay, a sickle of beach and dunes which separates Sandwood Loch from the sea.

The few locals know many strange tales about the bay, and the ruin known as Sandwood Cottage which is situated on high ground behind it. For many years it has been deserted, and those who have been tempted to spend a night there when overtaken by darkness have wished that they had been able to press on to Kinlochbervie. At night it echoes with the sound of phantom footsteps, though they are the least dramatic manifestations which have occurred there. A fisherman who spent a night within its walls reported that he was awakened by being pressed by some black amorphous mass. Needless to say he has given Sandwood Cottage a wide berth since then.

Recently two hikers decided that the cottage would make a good place to bed down for the night, but at midnight they were startled from their deep slumber by a terrible noise above them which they likened to the pawing of a frantic horse. The whole ruin seemed to be vibrating and shaking in sympathy, giving them the sensation that everything was coming apart. This lasted for about five minutes, after which the cottage resumed its normal condition. But there was no sleep for the two who felt that the place resented their trespassing. As soon as dawn began to lighten the sky they fled south to safety.

One supposition for the "earthquake" phenomena and the footsteps is that it is somehow related to a rich Australian visitor who resided there when fishing at the loch. The strange bleak landscape seemed to have captured his imagination, for year after year he came back. He finally died in Australia, but it is thought that his phantom has returned to the spot which he preferred to all others in life.

Sandwood Bay itself is haunted by the figure of a seaman frequently witnessed by crofters and visitors alike. He has been described as wearing a reefer jacket with glinting brass buttons and a peaked seafaring cap. At times his tall figure has been seen stalking the dunes, and he has even been spotted by telescope and mistaken for a poacher. A gamekeeper went after him but found the bay deserted as usual—and with no footprints on the sand. One of the most recent sightings of the old salt was in 1969.

An explanation for his appearance is that he was a member of the crew of a Polish ship which was wrecked in Sandwood Bay, and that he is still looking for his lost companions.

Cape Wrath was the last place I visited in search of material for this book, and it made a perfect setting for a finale. As I stood with the wind keening about me, and the restless sea making an evocative accompaniment to my thoughts, it seemed a very long way from Dozmary Pool in Cornwall where my journey had begun. It was a journey in time as well as distance for though Britain is firmly in the latter part of the twentieth century, with appropriate problems to prove it, I had gained an inkling that behind the highrise façade there is still the unknown waiting to be explored, just as it had been in days immemorial.

Index

à Becket, Thomas, 138
Aberdovey, 99
Aetherius Society, 195
Alexander, Ronald, 121
All Saints (Crondall), 142
All Saints (Faringdon), 143
All Saints (Renwick), 134
Allanbank, 83–5
Alleged Haunting of B—— House, The, 94
Allan, the Reverend J. M., 135
Angel Hill, 246
Animals, 97, 125, 134, 136, 143, 169, 190, 193, 232, 242
Armstrong, Archie, 126
Arthur, King, 239
Ashover Church, 143
Astley Castle, 226
Athelhampton House, 232
Aubrey, John, 182
Aural hauntings, 21, 31, 36, 45, 48, 59, 60, 85, 88, 92, 94, 112, 113, 114, 144, 158, 164, 167, 168, 170, 190, 196, 210, 232, 234, 235, 243, 245
Avenbury Church, 143
Aylmerton, 243

Baker, Derrick H., 150
Balfour, Frances, 66
Ballechin House, 90–5
Barham, R. H. D., 177
Baring-Gould, Sabine, 130, 235
Barlow, Alexander, 34
Barrie, James M., 246
Barritt, Thomas, 34
Battle Abbey, 124
Battlefield House, 59
Bayham Abbey, 124
Bealings Bells, 103
Bell, Archibald, 66

Bell Hotel (Thorpe-le-Soken), 167
Belper Arms (Newton Burgoland), 167
Ben MacDhui, 195–204
Berkeley Arms (Tewkesbury), 166
Berkeley Castle, 217
Berkshire, 143, 233
Bettiscombe House, 31–3
Bickley, Bill, 164
Big Grey Man, 195–204
Biggs, Mrs Connie, 154
Bisham Abbey, 125
Black Abbot, 111
Black Horse, The, 112
Black House, The, 232
Black Prince, 217
Black Shuck, 242
Black Vaughan, 234
Blackwood, Algernon, 239
Blanchland Churchyard, 141
Blickling Hall (Norfolk), 224
Blinking Owl Restaurant, 165
Blisworth Tunnel, 79
Blomberg, Captain Edward, 177
Bloody fountain, 124
Bloody Mary, 226
Bluebell Inn (Belmesthorpe), 167
Blue face, 156
Blue Lion (Cwm), 168
Boleyn, Anne, 220, 223
Bollin Hall, 224
Bomere, 99
Bonnie Prince Charlie, 61
Borley Church, 213
Borley Rectory, 205–13
Bosworth Hall, 232
Bovington Tank Museum, 15
Boynton, Mrs Wickham, 37

249